Brooklyn Dreams

My Life in Public Education

SONIA NIETO

HARVARD EDUCATION PRESS

CAMBRIDGE, MASSACHUSETTS

Library of Congress Control Number 2015937067

Paperback ISBN 978-1-61250-856-6
Library Edition ISBN 978-1-61250-857-3

Published by Harvard Education Press,
an imprint of the Harvard Education Publishing Group

Harvard Education Press
8 Story Street
Cambridge, MA 02138

Cover design: Wilcox Design
Cover image: Courtesy of the author;
background image: ©iStock.com/Huchen Lu
The typefaces used in this book are Adobe Garamond Pro, Scala Pro, and Futura

Contents

Mi Fortuna

[handwritten annotation: - Author grew up in Brooklyn - left when 31 to pursue doctorate in education in Massachuttes and vowed never to return]

I'VE HEARD IT SAID that one in eight people in the United States can trace their heritage to Brooklyn. This doesn't surprise me. The largest of the five boroughs of New York City, Brooklyn has been, and still is, home to millions of residents, mostly immigrants, first-, second-, and third-generation folks from Europe, the US South, the Caribbean, and, later, South America, Africa, Asia, and every other region of the world. All these people have arrived with their own dreams. From Brooklyn, they have dispersed to other big cities, small cities, suburbs, and rural areas throughout the country. But Brooklyn claims its inhabitants, gives them its stamp of approval—or not—and then sends them on their way to propagate Brooklyn dreams elsewhere.

I am one of those one in eight who trace their heritage to Brooklyn. I was born in 1943 in Beth-El Hospital (in 1963, the hospital, now expanded, changed its name to the Brookdale University Hospital and Medical Center) on Yom Kippur, the Day of Atonement, a high holy day in the Jewish calendar. My mother told me she didn't get lunch that day, no doubt because the staff thought she was Jewish, like most of the other women giving birth that day. I spent my formative years in several Brooklyn neighborhoods, an experience that indelibly stamped me as a Brooklynite. Though I have spent more than half my life in Massachusetts, leaving Brooklyn at the age of thirty-one to pursue a doctoral degree in education and vowing never to return, Brooklyn has left its mark on me. There's clearly something to the saying "You can take the girl out of Brooklyn, but you can't take Brooklyn out of the girl." Ironically, two of the three neighborhoods where I grew up—Williamsburg and Fort Greene—have become so trendy and costly that nowadays, young professionals hope against hope to find an affordable place to live in these now-hip neighborhoods. In my youth, people wanted to escape Williamsburg and Fort Greene for greener pastures, figuratively and literally. The third neighborhood, East Flatbush, was then a more desirable community, where unpretentious one- and two-family houses seemed grand in comparison to the poor working-class communities of Williamsburg and Fort Greene. Ironic, too, that East Flatbush is now mostly home to immigrants from the Caribbean and many of the homes there have lost their luster.

Despite the tough life endured by many Brooklynites in those days, the city instilled in me three lasting desires: to be a writer, a teacher, and an educated person.

⸻

I WROTE MY FIRST BOOK AT TEN. Not surprisingly, it concerned a girl of about my age, a girl who, like me, lived in Brooklyn with a family similar to mine. Sitting cross-legged on the bed in the room I shared with my sister Lydia, I documented my life as a novel. I wrote every day for months, relentlessly and consistently. When the book grew to more than a hundred pages, I threw it in the garbage.

I don't know why I threw it away. Even though I wanted to see myself as an adult—highly educated, successful, an accomplished writer—I probably thought it absurd that I should even attempt to write a book. At the same time, the incident also says something about the aspirations and identity I saw for myself in the future. For years, I've regretted having thrown the manuscript away, wondering what it would reveal about me as a child.

Besides writing a book, another great desire was to become a teacher. Around the same time I was writing a book, I fantasized about teaching. I saw myself standing at a blackboard with pointer in hand, teaching a lesson in grammar or math or talking with my young charges about the wonders of science. My overarching desire, really, was to become highly educated. Teaching appealed to me because I wanted to be a professional even before I knew the meaning of that word. Teachers were the only professionals I knew close-up. To me, they were powerful, in charge, and smart. As I got older, my desire to be a teacher intensified so that by the time I got to college, it was the only career I envisioned for myself. I loved the idea of working with young people, of seeing that light in their eyes when they understand or get excited by an idea or learn a new skill. That image of wonder stayed with me throughout my career, whether it was teaching reading to fourth-graders, preparing young adults for a life of teaching, or tackling challenging but exhilarating ideas about diversity and multicultural education, my future areas of endeavor.

My parents did not share my fantasy, at least not directly. Though they wanted the best for their children and sacrificed in every way they could, they had limited formal schooling. It was probably hard for them to imagine a college education for us. They knew little about middle-class pressure-cooker dreams for the Ivy League, about hiring tutors, or about SAT prep courses. They had come from Puerto Rico by ship, my father in 1929 at the age of twenty-eight, and my mother in 1934 at twenty-six, not knowing one another and each seeking the fortune, or at least the relative security, they had been told existed in New York City, the landing place for most Puerto Ricans at the time.

Mother & Father both came to NYC from Puerto Rico by ship

My life, on the other hand, has been defined by education. From the day in 1949 when I started first grade at PS 55—the once rather regal-looking urban school had been built in the late nineteenth century but had since lost its sheen—to the day I was awarded a doctoral degree from the University of Massachusetts in 1979 and beyond, I knew that education was the only way out of poverty and a life of unfulfilled hopes and dreams. How did I know this? While my parents certainly told us how important it was to be "good" (that is, to behave and be respectful) at school, to pay attention to our teachers, to get good grades, and to complete high school, college was not part of the equation. My parents probably knew better than anyone else that a good education was the only chance their children would have for a better life than they had, but a good education for them meant high school graduation. Unable to help with homework, disconnected from our school lives, and working long hours to give their children everything they could, my parents neither expected nor demanded a higher education. My sister Lydia, fourteen months my senior and my constant companion and best friend, and I surpassed our parents' wildest dreams. And though they didn't always understand why we pursued higher education so doggedly, they were immensely proud of us.

There was a huge chasm between our experiences and theirs. One incident, years after I had graduated from college, epitomizes this difference.

In 1979, just as I was ready to defend my dissertation, Robert Sinclair, my doctoral adviser, said, "Sonia, I want you to make three copies of the dissertation: one for yourself, one for me, and one for your mother" (my father had died a few years earlier). While I appreciated the thought immensely and did make a copy for my mother, I ended up giving it to my sister instead, knowing Lydia would get a lot more out of it than my mother. The irony is that my dissertation study concerned Puerto Rican families, particularly mothers, in curriculum decision-making. And yet I knew that for *my* Puerto Rican mother—given her limited education and unfamiliarity with the abstract ideas and fancy language in the dissertation—the document would make as much sense to her as a dissertation written in Chinese. One of the penalties higher education extracts is that in becoming highly educated and crossing over to the middle class, a greater gulf is often created between generations.

———⋅◆⋅———

THE IDEA OF WRITING this memoir began to form when I realized that— besides my great good fortune to have parents who, despite poverty and lack of opportunity, made certain their children would have better options—my life has been a story of the redeeming social and emotional value of public education. Education has been my defining moment, my mission, my goal, and my odyssey.

Yet, though it has been so significant in my life, public education has failed the Puerto Rican community in general. Those of us fortunate enough to get through the eye of the needle that is higher education often realize that success has as much to do with luck and opportunity as with intelligence and merit. I am tired of hearing that it is individual effort alone that makes the difference between failing and succeeding in life. Yes, resilience and determination have something to do with it, as do other personality traits and the choices we make along the way. But I am not so naive as to believe humans completely control their destiny; there are too many conditions beyond our power to believe this. Poverty, limited opportunities, and other conditions play equally important roles in our lives. But poverty or limited opportunities are not necessarily destiny. Although people may have little power over many things in life, they can make choices that can help define their future.

I cannot claim to have experienced the crippling poverty of Frank McCourt, whose life was so powerfully documented in *Angela's Ashes,* or the heartbreak of living with an alcoholic father as Sonia Sotomayor described in her memoir *My Beloved World.* But as the daughter of working-class and poorly educated immigrant parents living in relative poverty, I have a story to tell about the potential of public education to change the course of a person's life. Yet my experience does not reflect the experience of most second-generation immigrant Puerto Ricans or of other young people with limited opportunities. Although I believe passionately in the value of public education, it has failed too many young people, particularly the children of immigrants, the poor, and the dispossessed.

That public education has not worked for everyone is an indictment of the system. This failure is amply documented in government statistics, research studies, commission reports, and policy documents. I certainly don't want my readers to conclude that because I have been successful, there must be something wrong with all the others who have not been successful in similar situations. I've heard this argument all my life, and rather than making me proud or grateful—as surely it has been meant to do—it annoys and angers me. Following this line of reasoning, the only conclusion you can reach is that failure is an entirely individual choice caused by laziness, lack of effort or personal resolve, or what is deemed an undesirable cultural background. These are, in fact, the arguments made by many educators and policy makers. Yet through my personal experience and research and the benefits of an excellent education, I know that individual effort explains only a small part of success. Many institutional barriers, including inadequate health care and nutrition, poor housing, parental unemployment, limited work opportunities, a paucity of educational and cultural opportunities, and racism and bigotry, are at the heart of the failure to learn. My life's work has been fueled by this reality. In fifty years as a teacher, researcher, lecturer, and writer, I hope I have influenced others, from students to community members to educators, to fight to change these institutional barriers so that all public school students can reap the benefits of a good education.

What made the difference for me? I wish I had an easy answer, one that might satisfy pundits who wish to claim that the answer lies in acquiring the right attitudes, in having the will to learn English and assimilate,

education can change the course of a person's life

Failure to learn is a result of many barriers

Her life work fueled by this reality

in parents who learn the ways of the middle class, or in other panaceas. In my case, it was most likely a variety of factors, primary among which is my family's move to a middle-class neighborhood when I was thirteen—a move that gave me the opportunity to attend excellent public schools. I was not born a genius; nor am I one now. But I was always a serious and hardworking student with more resilience than brainpower and with more determination and grit than brilliance, and somehow I knew from an early age that I wanted more out of life than what I saw around me. Whether in first grade or graduate school, I was the classic overachiever, doing more than was asked of me, wanting to please, to be teacher's pet, to learn and compensate for what I couldn't claim by birth or privilege. But this alone doesn't explain how I got to where I am. My stable family life, a wide supportive network, a few great teachers and mentors throughout my life, a social and political environment that made it possible for my father—with a meager education—to be gainfully employed throughout his life, and serendipitous opportunities all helped, although others in similar circumstances have not been as fortunate.

My nuclear family (my father, Federico Cortés; mother, Esther Mercado; older sister, Lydia; and younger brother, Freddy) are as critical to my story as I am. The many cousins who grew up with us in Brooklyn, all within blocks of one another, also played a role. And the relatives who lived in other neighborhoods in Brooklyn and the Bronx, and even my many cousins in Puerto Rico, along with their parents, also shaped who I am today. The extended family in our community, our neighbors, and those we called *como familia* (who I was convinced were cousins, aunts, and uncles until I found out years later that they were actually only very loosely related to us) formed part of that stable network and gave my siblings and me a safety net not available to many young people today. This family network is a major theme in my story.

IMMIGRATION IS NEVER EASY, and although it often holds the promise of a better life, the immigrant experience is also fraught with pain, loss, and desperation. In a recent interview, the Haitian American author Edwidge Danticat was asked to select a literary passage that had particular meaning for her. She selected a passage from Patricia Engel's memoir, *It's Not Love,*

It's Just Paris (2013), in which the author's father tells her, "All immigrants are artists because they create a life, a future, from nothing but a dream. The immigrant's life is art in its purest form."

I found this quote moving and enormously insightful. It made me rethink my parents' pilgrimage to New York. I saw them in a new light, as creative explorers rather than as victims of colonialism, poverty, and helplessness. When my parents arrived in the States in the first decades of the twentieth century, there were just several thousand Puerto Ricans in New York City, compared with five million in the United States today. As part of the group referred to by historians as *pioneros* (the first large-scale group to arrive after Puerto Ricans were made US citizens in 1917), my parents found a small network of compatriots but little else save the hard life of poor working-class immigrants. My mother and father led difficult lives and yet were remarkably successful, not in monetary or even educational terms but in making a good life for themselves and for us, their children, and inspiring us to follow their example of hard work, family devotion, and drive.

Many of the Puerto Ricans I went to school with were as smart as, and often smarter than, me. They had hopes and dreams just as I did. Yet many ended up dropping out of school and, like their parents, remaining part of the unemployed or poor working class; most were never able to attend college. Even today, Puerto Ricans still have one of the highest high school dropout rates of any ethnic group in the United States, just as they did when I was a child. The rates range from 40 to 60 percent or more, depending on the city or town and the year in question. Employment is often precarious, and unemployment remains stubbornly high even in good economic times, while the college completion rate of Puerto Ricans continues to lag behind that of Whites, Asians, and African Americans.

The issue of identity also looms large in my memory and in this book. How I constructed my identities and how they shifted—what it meant to be Puerto Rican in Williamsburg, then a largely Puerto Rican community in Brooklyn; in East Flatbush, a largely Jewish and middle-class community; and, later, in my university, where I was one of the few Puerto Ricans—are also part of the story. That I managed to retain my native language—moving from a monolingual Spanish speaker to practically abandoning the language and, later, to claim it again in young adulthood—is an equally significant issue in my identity. I am grateful to my parents for their tenacity in speaking and encouraging us to speak Spanish. No less significant is that we were a light-skinned Puerto Rican family, something that surely helped my sister and me because teachers and other authority figures in our lives (most of whom were White) then saw us as more like them, thus more acceptable or, at most, as different from other Puerto Ricans.

Mentors have also been a significant reason for my success, though some of them may not even know how they changed my life. These include some family members, especially my parents and Lydia; my husband, Angel; and teachers, professors, colleagues, and supervisors in a variety of positions. I describe them here in ways that I hope honor their influence.

I also decided to write this memoir so that I myself might make some sense of my life and the trajectory it has taken. As I write this, I am about to turn seventy-two. Thinking about my story has helped me understand more deeply what I have attempted to do with my life. I hope that what I have learned will help others on a similar journey. At this age, I am still a work in progress, as my career has not taken a rest. I write extensively; speak often at schools, colleges, universities, and conferences; and consult with school systems and other educational organizations a good deal. I feel blessed to have such an active and fulfilled life.

Thinking back on my childhood in Brooklyn, I am amazed at my good fortune, *mi fortuna*, to take a page from my father's life (whose first bodega was called La Fortuna, named after the farm on which he worked in Puerto Rico as a boy). Although my Brooklyn dreams have been more than realized, those of many other young people, from Brooklyn to Detroit, Orlando to Los Angeles, and everywhere in between, have not. I hope that this memoir will shed some light on how our society can make these young people's dreams come true as well.

At the same time, writing a memoir is a tricky business. What to include and what to leave out are momentous questions. A person's memory—fading at this age—is also a challenge. I never had a very good memory to begin with, so it's ironic that I took up the challenge of writing a memoir, something that relies so heavily on memory. In writing, however, I have found that long-lost memories have been recovered—something for which I am grateful. Some memories have come back slowly; others have catapulted into my mind. This book is based on real events, although, of course, I've had to reconstruct the dialogue and some of the sequence of events. Occasionally, I've changed people's names and descriptions to protect their privacy.

This book describes my journey from a declining urban elementary school in the Williamsburg section of Brooklyn in the 1950s to my doctoral work in bucolic Amherst, Massachusetts, in the 1970s and beyond. My story, however, is not just one of individual achievement or a Puerto Rican version of the Horatio Alger story. I refuse to be cast as "the Puerto Rican exception," as if I was so different from other Puerto Ricans. Rather than just my story, the book is about the potential promise and, ultimately, the disappointing outcome of public education as it was first envisioned at the dawn of public schooling in mid-nineteenth-century United States. Granted, initial pronouncements of the benefits of a free, tax-supported, universal public education were steeped in paternalism, not to mention racial and ethnic exclusivity in that they included only children of European descent. Recently freed slaves, Indigenous Americans, Mexicans, and other non-Europeans were conspicuously missing from such noble pronouncements and are—not coincidentally—those most neglected by public education even today.

Nevertheless, the ideal of a universally available and common school experience for rich and poor and for those of all ethnic and racial backgrounds remains a lofty, though perhaps never-to-be-realized, goal. It is, however, one worth fighting for. Whether or not the promise of public education will ever be achieved, those who have benefited the least have been the ones to struggle the most fervently for this goal. In fact, the educational history of the United States is replete with the stories of such struggles, from desegregation to multicultural education, from gender-fair to special education, and others, a history documented in a 2005 article I wrote for the seventy-fifth anniversary of the *Harvard Educational Review*.

The book covers many of the events, values, and inspiring ideas that have defined and enriched my life. I describe how I came to understand and develop my ideas about education; the emergence of my political consciousness through my firsthand experiences in the contentious movements of community control, bilingual education, ethnic studies, and multicultural education; my own growth as a scholar and researcher; and the impact my ideas may have had on the field. I share my thoughts on how education has changed in the fifty years that I have been an educator. I also describe my own personal coming of age, how I fell in love and started and raised a family, and how the themes of family, education, community, and justice have intertwined to help me become who I am.

Sadly, today the forces of privatization and marketization, the scapegoating of teachers, the high-stakes testing frenzy, and continuing racism and bigotry are making the goal of an equal and high-quality education more unreachable than ever. As a result, the gulf between the haves and the have-nots is not only reflected in our public schools, but also exacerbated and perpetuated by them. If this situation continues, the grand vision of public education imagined by its proponents over a century ago is certain to disappear. Yet what brings all the themes of my life together is precisely public education: mine as well as that of my sister and brother, my children and grandchildren, the children I taught directly, and the children I have never met but who have nonetheless been my professional concern throughout my life. In writing this book, I have understood, perhaps more clearly than ever, that without public education, my life would be vastly different and immeasurably poorer, not necessarily in economic terms but in meaning and purpose. Given current defeatist ideas about the purpose and meaning of education, I hope that this memoir offers instead a story of the redeeming value of public education, if it is ever given a chance.

PART I

Growing Up

CHAPTER 1

From *La Isla del Encanto* to the Streets of Brooklyn

WHAT COMPELS PUERTO RICANS to leave their homeland, *la isla del encanto*, a land memorialized in countless songs and poetry about its natural beauty, distinctive culture, and warm and loving people? Motives have changed over the years, but the dream of many of the Puerto Ricans who migrated to the United States during the years of early migration, from the beginning of the twentieth century to the 1960s or so, was to return wealthier than they arrived, to buy a small farm in the mountains, and to live out their lives in quiet peace, serenaded by the ubiquitous song of the *coquí*.* It was an unfulfilled dream for most—a dream sadly chronicled by Pedro Pietri, the best known among the Nuyorican poets, in his epic poem "Puerto Rican Obituary" (Pietri, 1971). The poem describes Puerto Ricans' migration experience, including their submissiveness and hard work ("They worked ten days a week and were only paid for five"), as well as their resilience and determination.

This obituary, a wake-up call to Puerto Ricans to discover their dignity and self-worth, describes in sad detail what the migration experience has been for many. To get an idea of the immense exodus from the island to the United States, we need only look at the numbers: in 1910, there were only 2,000 Puerto Ricans living in the States, but by the late 1950s, that

* Puerto Ricans are, strictly speaking, neither migrants (a term generally reserved for those who move within the borders of a country) nor immigrants (those who cross national borders). The scholar Roberto Márquez has instead suggested the term *(im)migration* as best describing the experience of Puerto Ricans who, although they are crossing national borders, are US citizens. In this book, I use both *migrants* and *immigrants* interchangeably, depending on the context.

number had jumped to 550,000 (Mastropasqua, 2013; Rand, 1958). My parents, as well as my uncles and aunts, were some of those who "worked ten days and were only paid for five." Jobs for unskilled workers were more plentiful than they were after the 1960s and 1970s, when many industries moved or closed. This situation made it possible for migrants, including my parents and other relatives, to take on many hours, something not true anymore. And although it was a hard life, it was also a decent one, where people experienced the dignity—if not necessarily the respect—of hard work. By the time of the so-called Great Migration (1945–1960), when hundreds of thousands of Puerto Ricans arrived, the situation had changed. Fewer jobs, as well as opportunities, were available for the newer migrants. Years later, in 1989, Pietri, at my sister's request, read the poem in its entirety at our mother's wake. (Pietri's brother Joe was my sister's partner at the time.)

The answer to why Puerto Ricans leave *la perla del Caribe*, another nickname for Puerto Rico, is, of course, desperation and opportunity, the traditional push-pull of migration. Abject poverty on the island caused primarily by four hundred years of exploitation by Spain, followed by over one hundred years at the hands of the United States, left Puerto Rico at the mercy of imperial powers. Its original inhabitants, the Taíno people, were largely eradicated after the island was accidentally "discovered" by Christopher Columbus on his second expedition to the so-called New World in 1493. This time, with seventeen ships, far greater resources than on his first trip, and the gratitude and blessings of the king and queen of Spain, Columbus came upon Puerto Rico on November 19, the only part of what is now the United States ever touched by the explorer. This date became the island's equivalent to Columbus Day and was known on the island as Día del Descubrimiento. The so-called discovery was followed by campaigns to populate the island. Spanish explorers and settlers were lured with the prospect of gold and fabulous wealth, neither of which materialized on the island to any significant degree. Enslaved Africans were brought to the region beginning in 1508. The dependence on slave labor, finally abolished in 1873, especially in the production of sugar, characterized the island's economy. The result was a society based on chattel slavery and a serf-like existence among most inhabitants, many of whom were subsistence farmers.

The United States had had its eye on Cuba and Puerto Rico for decades, and in 1898, the explosion of the USS *Maine* in Havana Harbor gave US leaders the justification they needed to invade Cuba and Puerto Rico. The Spanish-American War was brief, lasting only ten weeks and famously called "that splendid little war" by Teddy Roosevelt. When Puerto Rico was handed over to the United States as spoils of war by Spain—obviously without the involvement or consent of the Puerto Rican people—some improvements in education and infrastructure began. Still, the island remained a colony, first under military rule and two years later as a "protectorate" of the United States. In 1917, again without consent or consultation, Puerto Ricans were made US citizens by an act of the US Congress, just in time for an estimated eighteen thousand Puerto Rican men to don US Army uniforms and go off to fight for the United States in World War I.

Because of the unique relationship Puerto Rico has with the United States, the issue of status is always paramount on the island. Some observers, especially those who favor independence, say Puerto Rico is nothing more than a colony with a fancier name. Officially, it is a commonwealth. In Spanish, it is called Estado Libre Asociado de Puerto Rico, or "Free associated state of Puerto Rico," although it is neither free nor a state. Island-based Puerto Ricans are US citizens, but they neither vote in presidential elections nor pay federal taxes; mainland-based Puerto Ricans, of course, do both. Although the island is headed by a popularly elected governor and two legislative chambers, many of Puerto Rico's laws are nevertheless subject to federal, that is, US, approval. Puerto Rico's currency, trade policies, communication, and most other significant issues are under the control of the United States. Yet few Americans know very much about Puerto Rico, even though it has been associated with the United States since before 1898, when many in the government already thought of the Caribbean as an outpost of US imperialism. I still marvel that many Americans, when contemplating a trip to the island, will ask what the currency is or if anybody speaks English there. Puerto Rico and Puerto Ricans are barely mentioned in US history curricula, though the presence of nearly five million of us in the States should make other Americans curious to find out more about us.

Even before 1917, there were small settlements of Puerto Ricans in New York City and in Tampa, Florida. These immigrants were mostly skilled tobacco workers and small groups of intellectuals planning a revolution for independence from Spain. Becoming US citizens made the trek to the United States possible for hundreds of thousands of Puerto Ricans. Beginning shortly after the US takeover, US-based absentee landowners bought huge tracts of land, mostly to grow sugar, in the process displacing many Puerto Rican farmers with small tracts of land. Given the short growing and harvesting season, workers employed by the sugar plantations worked for only brief periods, followed by long periods of *tiempo muerto*, or dead time, with widespread unemployment. Poverty bred more poverty, and disease and joblessness were rampant. The movement of Puerto Ricans from farm to town to city and then to the United States has been well documented in history, novels, plays, and family lore. Most Puerto Rican migrants made their way from San Juan to New York City, the final destination, on ships that brought immigrants with big dreams but little else.

MY FATHER, FEDERICO CORTÉS (Tito to family and friends, Tío Tito to his many nieces and nephews, and Don Tito to neighbors, acquaintances, and the people with whom he did business), was among those early pioneers to New York's Spanish Harlem. He left Puerto Rico in 1929 by boat, which was the only means of transportation at the time, arriving in New York with two good friends—*tres zánganos*, or a motley crew of three, as he called his little group—all seeking their fortune and an escape from dire poverty and a difficult life.

Papi's pilgrimage to New York City was understandable. The second of eight surviving children, he became in effect the head of his household after his father died and his older brother married at an early age. Papi's father, Francisco Cortés, born in 1831, was sixty-three when he married his second wife, Herminia Matos (known affectionately as Mita), who was somewhere between sixteen and eighteen years of age when she and my grandfather got together, although they did not marry until 1894. Between 1894 and 1915, they had eleven children. Juan De Dios (Juanito) was the oldest; followed by Aurelia and Vicente, both of whom died at birth or shortly thereafter; then my father; his brother Cruz de Dios (Crucito); Alfredo; Justo; María Ysabel, who also died as an infant; Amparo; Jesús, who died as a teenager; and Juan Providencio (Chencho), the youngest. In 1916, when Chencho was just a year old, Francisco died, leaving his large family not just fatherless but also penniless. Family lore has it that my grandfather had many more children, some say as many as fifty, if you count his first and second wives and his many *chillas,* or concubines. By the time Francisco died, his oldest son, Tío Juanito, older than Papi by seven years, had married and started his own family. This left Papi, at fourteen or so, the oldest child at home.

Devoted to his mother and siblings, Papi had no choice but to take over the family reins. He quit school in fourth grade, found work on a farm called La Fortuna (the name he would resurrect for his bodega in Brooklyn years later), leading a life similar to the lives of the majority of poverty-stricken Puerto Ricans on the island. Life must have been grim, enough so that he decided to seek his fortune, *su fortuna,* elsewhere. His trip, however, was not one of escaping a difficult personal situation, as was the case with Mami several years later, or of seeking individual fortune, but rather one of continued obligation to family: he dutifully sent most of his earnings to Mita until she died in the early 1930s.

Poorly educated and with little English, my father quickly found a job sweeping the floors of a Jewish delicatessen on Delancey Street in Lower Manhattan, the destination of countless immigrants from many nations around the world. He arrived a month before the market crashed, the event that signaled the beginning of the Depression. By the time he left the deli twenty years later, he was a chef and had brought three of his siblings, Titi Amparo, Tío Chencho, and, years later, Tío Justo, to work with him at the deli. Papi made good friends there too, among them Willie Sacconino, an immigrant from Italy, and a woman we knew only as "Mama Kulka," from Poland. She would often send Papi home with gifts for us. Willie became a lifelong friend and went to Papi's wake almost fifty years after they began working together. How they all managed to communicate remains a mystery. Each spoke a language unintelligible to the others. Only the immigrant experience could create a bond stronger than language.

My father's other brothers remained in Puerto Rico, marrying, raising children, and living out their lives on the island. Ours, then, is the typical Puerto Rican story of a family split and splintered, the result of colonialism and immigration.

My mother, Esther Mercado, came to New York several years later, in 1934, possibly on the same boat that my father took. Her reasons for leaving Puerto Rico are less clear. We do know that she was orphaned at thirteen and sent to live with her maternal grandparents, known to her as Papa Beto and Mama Beta (Purcell). Her father, Rafael Mercado, and her seven-year-old brother had died in 1918, victims of the devastating Spanish influenza that decimated the population not only of Puerto Rico but also of much of the rest of the world. An infant brother had died before his first birthday, an occurrence so common in the first decades of the twentieth century that families are often described according to the number of children who survived and those who did not. A woman, for example, might be described as "having nine children, three of whom survived."

Mami's mother, Felícita Gutiérrez, died when Mami was thirteen. This left my mother and her younger sister by two years, Sarah, the only remaining siblings, a small family for the time. Titi Sarah was sent to live in a poor neighborhood in Ponce, the family's hometown, with an aunt named Diosdada (no doubt cherished by her parents, as her name means "God-given"), who lived in impoverished circumstances. My mother was sent to live with her grandparents who, although lacking in formal education and wealth, had what was recognized as "class." Ponce, often referred to as La Ciudad Señorial, or "The Stately City," has a reputation as a place that is correct and, at its worst, veers on pretentious. I imagine my grandparents' home as poor but proper: no scandals allowed, and manners as de rigueur as they were for Ponce's upper-class families.

It was only years later, when I was an adult, that my mother told me the full story of how she came to live with her grandparents. Although she had indeed been orphaned, the generally given chronology was not quite accurate: her father died when she was eight, her mother when she was thirteen, but her grandparents took her to live with them at the age of ten or so, removing her from her mother's home because her mother had remarried, this time to a Black man, an unforgivable sin for her mother's class- and race-conscious family. Mami didn't offer this information willingly; it simply came out one day as she was telling me how, when I was a kid, she had run into her mother's second husband on the street in Brooklyn.

"What?" I asked. "Why didn't you ever tell us your mother had remarried?"

"My mother married a *moreno*," she explained quietly, looking down in shame, an admission she clearly wished to keep to herself.

This was one of several times that prevailing Puerto Rican attitudes toward race, especially about people of African descent, became apparent to me. Although she would claim she harbored no prejudice, my mother nevertheless made comments that gave the lie to this claim. She would, for instance, say, "Our Blacks are nicer-looking than *morenos*," referring to Blacks in the United States. Other stories revealed the bigotry among Puerto Ricans, despite protestations of many to the contrary. For example, as a child, Mami was told by her very proper (and light-skinned) grandmother to put a clothespin on her nose to help make it thinner. She also described hair as *pelo malo* (nappy hair) or *pelo bueno* (straight hair), feeling fortunate that we all had the latter. My sister, Lydia, describes being very conscious of her wavy hair as a child. She particularly worried about the hair near her temples, as it was dangerously close to *pelo malo*. By the time she was in high school, Lydia was having her hair straightened professionally, afraid her curls would confirm that Puerto Ricans are a mixed-race people. Although almost all Puerto Ricans are racially mixed— a combination of Europeans (primarily but not exclusively from Spain), Africans brought as slaves to the island by Spaniards beginning in the early sixteenth century, and traces of the Indigenous Taínos—there has been a stubborn resistance to embrace our African heritage, which is, in some ways, even more prevalent than our Spanish heritage.

But attitudes about race among Puerto Ricans are complicated, not so easily categorized as, excuse the pun, black or white. As far as I remember, my parents never said anything outwardly racist about Blacks, whether the Black people were African American or Puerto Rican, but their attitudes sometimes emerged. While Mami initially disapproved of the fact that my husband and I adopted our second daughter, Marisa, I think it was partly because Mami considered it unnatural to raise the children of strangers. I'm sure her disapproval also had to do with Marisa's skin color, which was noticeably darker than the rest of ours. Had Marisa been a blond, light-skinned baby, Mami's discomfort doubtless would have disappeared.

Nonetheless, she quickly grew to love Marisa, although her love was tempered with a clear distinction between our two girls: whenever she introduced them, it was as "Alicia, their daughter, and Marisa, their adopted daughter." How much race had to do with this distinction is unclear, but it certainly had something to do with her attitude.

Race is both more and less consequential in Puerto Rico than it is in the United States. Rather than define themselves according to race, most Puerto Ricans define themselves ethnically. This doesn't mean there's no racism; it's just a different kind of racism. As a result, race is also more consequential. There are all sorts of sayings about race, and most of them inevitably refer to dark-skinned Puerto Ricans more negatively than light-skinned Puerto Ricans. For example, there's a saying that if you marry someone lighter skinned, you are *mejorando la raza*, improving the race. Many Puerto Ricans also express almost a reverence for children with blond hair and blue eyes, as if these children were inherently more beautiful.

Every family has its myths, and a popular one in many Puerto Rican families is that at least one grandfather (for some reason, never a grandmother) had come directly from Spain. I always thought this particular myth strange, since I had never met a Spaniard in any of the Puerto Rican families I knew. My family was no exception to the myth: I often heard it said that my father's father, Francisco, traveled in the 1800s directly from Spain to Peñuelas, the small mountain town where the family is from. My cousin Jaime, after doing extensive research on my father's family lineage, put a damper on this fairy tale. Not only did my grandfather Francisco not come from Spain, but neither did his father, his father's father, his father's grandfather, or his father's great-grandfather, all the way back to 1799. On the other hand, although many in my family are happy to claim a grandfather from Spain, I've never heard anyone in my family or in most other Puerto Rican families proudly declare that they could trace their heritage directly to Africa in spite of Africa's significant role in our history and our cultural legacy.

———◆◆◆———

MAMI HAD BEEN ADOPTED informally and raised by her grandparents. Her adoptive family reflected the convoluted lineages common among

Puerto Ricans. While married to Mama Beta, Mami's grandfather apparently had an affair, the result of which was Mami's mother, Felícita, my grandmother. Thus, his daughter with Mama Beta, Petrita, was Mami's aunt although they were raised as sisters. Five years older than Mami, and the only surviving child of thirteen, most of whom had died at birth or shortly thereafter, Petrita was placed on a very high pedestal by her doting parents. In that situation, my mother became a kind of Cinderella in the household. While her grandparents were never intentionally cruel or abusive, their devotion to Petrita resulted in their seeing my mother as more of a stepchild than a daughter. While Petrita had piano lessons and nice dresses, my mother had neither. I imagine life was hard for Mami, losing her parents as a young child and then being treated as less than a welcome addition to the family.

Her early life helps explain my mother's lack of outward affection to us, her children, at least when we were young, although her affection increased as she grew old and less responsible for our upbringing and the household. Her childhood also helps explain her depression. Lydia recognized my mother's condition as such even when we were children. She remembers Mami, a blank look on her face, sitting in the apartment on Stockton Street in Brooklyn, looking out the window into a brick wall while mindlessly eating one slice of Wonder Bread with butter after another. Her life, already difficult, was made immeasurably sadder when it became clear that my brother, their adored Freddy, was, in the language of the time, "not normal."

Freddy had been diagnosed as mentally retarded and, later, as also having autism and OCD (obsessive-compulsive disorder), the latter conditions being unknown diagnoses earlier in his life. My parents, however, did not recognize his condition as an actual illness, claiming he had gotten this way because a dog had scared him when he was two years old. His failure to speak and his other developmental delays were conditions they refused to acknowledge. As a result, when they sent him off to kindergarten in 1951 at the age of five, his teacher immediately recognized that something was very wrong. Freddy cried incessantly, and the staff had to call Lydia down from her fourth-grade classroom every day to console him. Nor did he play with the other children or take part in class activities. By the end of the first week, the teachers sent a note home with Lydia, asking my parents to come into school to meet with the principal. I imagine the meeting went something like this:

Principal: Mr. and Mrs. Cortés, I'm afraid I have bad news for you. (Pause.)
Mami: What bad news?
Principal: Freddy has been in class all week, but he hasn't participated in any activities. He can't speak, he can't play with the other children, and all he does is cry.
Mami: He doesn't speak English.
Principal: Does he speak Spanish?
Mami: (Pause.) A little.
Principal: The problem, Mrs. Cortés, is that Freddy is *not normal* [those words must have stung]. There's no place in this school for him. I'm sorry, but he can't come back to school.

And that was the end of that, no school for Freddy. After this meeting, he would stay at home all day, every day—a child with numerous needs, to be taken care of by my mother.

Brother Freddy stayed home - mom had to take care of him

———— ✦ ————

AFTER TITI PETRITA MARRIED her husband, Carlos Costas (a kind man we called Tío Carlos), my mother, by then a young woman, lived with them for the first years of their marriage. The arrangement was undoubtedly a stifling experience for my aunt and uncle and an uncomfortable one for Mami. She left Puerto Rico for New York City in 1934 at the age of twenty-six to live with her aunt Paquita. Only when I became an adult did I realize what it must have meant in those years for a young woman with scant education and a fair-to-middling knowledge of the English language to leave family and homeland and strike out on her own. At that point, I became acutely aware that the passive and easily intimidated woman I was familiar with had mettle, a determination strong as steel. After all, most immigrants, though they may leave their home countries in difficult circumstances, at least have the comfort of facing the turmoil of immigration with other family members. Hers must have been a lonely journey

Sonita's mom lived with her aunt Paquita

Sonita's mom came to NYC at 26 years old

Mettle - a determination strong as steel

and sojourn in Brooklyn, New York, where she settled. Like most Puerto Ricans in New York at the time, she took her place as a member of the unskilled and low-paid working class. In her case, it was at a factory, one that made Dixie Cups.

My mother and father met in New York City through her aunt Paquita several years later. Theirs was an uncommon courtship: by the time they married in 1941, Papi was forty and Mami thirty-two, unusually late in those years for Puerto Ricans, especially those of the working class, to marry and start a family. Scant evidence remains of their courtship. There are a few photos of them on a date at Coney Island Beach: Mami, a shy smile on her face, Papi, his arm around Mami, looking handsome and pleased. She never told us much about their courtship. If it had been anything like courtships in Puerto Rico, it would have been conducted under the strictest supervision. But being in New York City away from the prying eyes of fathers and mothers, and being adults, they no doubt felt a lessened grip of Puerto Rican propriety that insisted that young women never date without a chaperone.

My parents were married at Queen of All Saints Church in Brooklyn on September 27, 1941. Their wedding picture reflects both the era and their social class. An evocative portrait, it was taken in a studio in Williamsburg, the neighborhood in which they were to settle. With shades of sepia and blue, the photo has an ethereal feel to it. In the background is a fancy cathedral, and in the foreground are Mami and Papi, trompe l'oeil: the photo is heavily retouched, and the background is, of course, fake. Mami is wearing a lovely dress, rented, as they could not afford to buy one, and Papi a formal suit, probably also rented, as he had little occasion to wear suits in his job at the deli. Mami's hair is dark, another fiction since by that age, her hair was almost completely gray, a trait I inherited. The final invention: since Papi was only five feet three and she about five feet six (very tall for a Puerto Rican woman then), the photographer stood him on a step, using her gown to cover this little deception.

The apartment building where they lived for the first twelve years of their marriage, a fifth-floor walk-up at 229 Stockton Street, no longer exists; the entire block is gone, having made way for projects, what we all considered a step up from the old tenement buildings that had been around for nearly a hundred years. We were happy to have missed the projects.

[handwritten margin notes: "mom worked @ Dixie cup factory lived in Brooklyn"; "parents married late dad 40 mom 32"; "Parents lived in Williamsburg"]

Moved to Fort Greene in Brooklyn

After our building was demolished in 1953, we moved to another tenement building in the Fort Greene neighborhood of Brooklyn; the building would also be scheduled for demolition shortly after we moved in.

Stockton Street itself, like all those around it, was gray; so was the sky, a gunmetal gray that never seemed to allow the sun in. Storefronts, housing bodegas as well as "American" grocery stores, cleaners, bakery shops, meat markets, and others, most of which were owned by first- and second-generation Jewish immigrants, were on other streets, not ours, and those streets were bustling with life. Ours was fairly deserted by comparison. One exception was the venetian blind store owned by Sol in the basement of our building. A kind man, Sol often invited us into his shop to see the newest colors and versions of blinds; he also looked out for us when we played outside.

These tenement buildings, dull and gray on the outside, throbbed with immigrant life within. They had seen many waves of newcomers, first Europeans and, later, Puerto Ricans, who came with stories of streets lined with gold. African Americans from the South also arrived and moved in with their own dreams. The block had several tenement buildings, most with stoops where mothers sat watching their children play hopscotch or other games until it was time to go upstairs to dinner. The supers of these tenements tended to live in the basement apartment, rent-free in exchange for taking care of repairs and the upkeep of the building. The flooring in the halls and landings of our building, small black and white hexagonal tiles, had probably been handsome at one point in the distant past. There were four apartments to a floor. Ours was the first door on the right as you reached the fifth and top floor.

The door opened to our kitchen. A small window on the right provided a good view of the factories and other tenement buildings in the neighborhood. Catty-corner to the kitchen was our bathroom, a small room with just the basics: a tub, toilet, and small sink. Beyond the kitchen was the living room, the heart of the apartment. We had no art to speak of, just the perennial porcelain knickknacks, including swans and elephants, always with trunks up for good luck. Instead of art, our heritage stared down at us: huge photos, elaborately framed, of a stern grandfather (Francisco Cortés, Papi's father), white-haired with a handlebar mustache; a striking portrait of a young and handsome Papi shortly after his arrival in New York; and Mami and Papi's wedding picture. Our furniture was spare: a couch, two armchairs, a coffee table, and a lamp. To the right of the living room was a very small bedroom where Freddy slept. Beyond the living room were two more bedrooms, the first, my parents', and to the left of that, the one I shared with Lydia. The fire escape, ubiquitous in those tenement apartments, stood outside our bedroom window. We spent many afternoons sitting on those metal steps, looking out at Brooklyn, wondering what lay beyond. Little did we know that the same year my parents wed, in 1941, the Brooklyn Dodgers had won the pennant for the first time in twenty-one years or that very much of anything else was going on outside the perimeter of our street.

As children we didn't have pets. Our resident creatures, not dogs or cats but cockroaches and mice, usually stayed indoors. I would see mice scurrying from one hole in the wall to another, or from under the couch to under the armchair, and it seemed normal to me then. Lydia once tried to catch a mouse so that we could have a pet, but the creatures were much too clever to let themselves get caught.

Our neighbors spoke a cacophony of languages and dialects. Though there had been a vibrant mixture of Jewish, Polish, Italian, Irish, Ukrainian, and other immigrant languages and accents in the past, by the time we moved in, the building was becoming home mostly to Puerto Ricans, the newest pilgrims to our Williamsburg neighborhood. Our next-door neighbor, a Jewish widower, was single-handedly raising a son and daughter. Near the entrance to the family's apartment was a mezuzah, which the family members touched every time they entered the apartment, a tradition I always thought was like greeting the apartment and asking for its blessing. Loretta, the daughter, was my sister's and my best friend. Her family was among the first ones in the building to get a television set. One of my fondest memories is of all of us—Mami, Papi, Lydia, Freddy, and me—going over on Monday nights at 8 p.m. to watch *I Love Lucy*. We got to know Lucy, Ricky, Ethel, and Fred, who also lived in apartments—although the TV dwellings were clearly better than ours—as if the characters were our own neighbors. It never occurred to us at the time to be offended by jokes at the expense of Desi Arnaz's accent or humorous use of English when he played Ricky. We laughed along with everyone else, happy at least to see a Latino on such a public venue.

———◆·◆———

MOVING INTO THEIR FIRST APARTMENT, Esther and Tito settled into the life of working-class first-generation immigrants, with a robust network of family members within three or four blocks. Lydia was born on July 19, 1942, four days before my mother's thirty-third birthday and just ten months after their marriage, a fact that was a source of great embarrassment for my mother. I followed just fourteen months later, on September 25, 1943, and my brother Freddy—the long-awaited prodigal son—arrived on August 9, 1946, when Mami was already thirty-seven.

My birth was a disappointment for my father, who by now, at forty-two years old, was desperate for a son. My mother used to tell the story of how Papi, so disillusioned when I came along (two girls in a row was not something to celebrate), didn't even show up at the hospital on the day I was born. My aunt Carrie, the wife of my father's youngest brother, Chencho, was horrified at my father's behavior, although she generally had nothing but enormous affection and respect for him. Feeling sorry for the future that might await me, Carrie bought a gold *jorobaíto* (a charm in the shape of a hunchback, symbol of luck among Puerto Ricans) for me to wear on a gold chain, hoping this would bring me the good fortune I would need later in life.

Despite Papi's initial disappointment at my birth, he quickly took to my presence. Like any toddler, Lydia was by then a handful, and my mother couldn't keep up with both of us and all the work of a 1940s housewife. Just climbing the stairs to our apartment several times a day must have been tiresome, not to mention all the cleaning, cooking, laundering by hand, ironing, and numerous errands she attended to while my father labored six days a week at the deli. By this time, my father's only sister, Amparo, the youngest after Chencho, was living in our apartment. Amparo, who insisted we call her Titi without the addition of her name to make sure she had primacy among all the aunts, was attractive, conniving, and vindictive, making life impossible for Mami. Titi doted on Lydia, a favoritism that lasted until Titi's death in the 1980s. Her devotion to Lydia made me feel invisible and superfluous, feelings I couldn't then name but that were nonetheless sharply hurtful. "You be quiet!" my aunt reportedly said when I cried after Mami brought me home from the hospital as a newborn. "Shhh! There was someone else here before you!"

Still, I loved Titi. Strikingly beautiful and fastidious about her appearance, she was also affectionate and generous. After she moved out of our apartment when I was still a preschooler and until our adolescence, she would visit every Sunday, loaded down with candy, cookies, potato chips, and other goodies, though she couldn't help always bringing a little something extra for Lydia. (Did she think I wouldn't notice?) Those Sundays were wonderful not only because she brought gifts. Her very presence was thrilling. Her harsh treatment of my mother, however, was evident to Lydia and me even as young children.

When years later I found out more about my aunt, I began to understand why Titi was the way she was. The next-to-youngest of eight surviving siblings, the only girl, and gorgeous to boot, she was well protected by her brothers, who were jealous of the many suitors who showed an interest in her. As a result, she never married and she spent a lifetime loving other people's children rather than any of her own—and in each family, she always chose a favorite.

Even when I was an infant, my father recognized the psychological cost to my mother because of Titi's toxic presence in our household. To lessen her burden, he took on my upbringing as his responsibility, at least when he was home. He was a quiet man but affectionate and nurturing, and I always seemed to be starved for that affection. He often took us three children to Marcy Playground, the neighborhood park, pushing us on swings and supervising while we attempted the seesaw and monkey bars. When he was home, I made sure to sit on his lap or, when I was older, next to him, always to his left. As a teenager, I decided that my nickname should be Tita, after his nickname Tito, because I wanted so much to be like him, but the nickname never took. Meanwhile, he called me Sonita. In Spanish, adding *-ita* (for a girl) or *-ito* (for a boy) is the proverbial way to add a note of affection to a name. Only my husband and my friend Gloria Ladson-Billings, once she learned of this name, continue to use it.

Although Papi worked many hours at the deli and, in later years, many more hours at his bodega, he always had time for us. I remember in particular sitting on his lap at the kitchen table on many nights, even when

Her dad gave nickname Sonita, "ita" is affection, her name is Sonia

he walked in at 10 p.m. or later, as he ate his supper. In spite of the fero-
cious love I had for him, I was also afraid of Papi, as was Lydia. This fear
was common among Puerto Ricans. Fearing your father, and sometimes
your mother, was a sure sign of respect and obedience. Not that he gave us
reason to be afraid: Papi never raised his voice. But we knew he could, and
that knowledge alone kept us in check.

Living on the fifth floor of a tenement building with no elevator, not
having a washing machine, dishwasher, telephone, car, or any of the other
conveniences we now take for granted, made for a challenging existence.
Mami, never the best housekeeper, seemed overwhelmed by so many
chores. How could she not be? Though larger items such as towels and bed-
clothes were sent to the block-long Cascade Laundromat a couple of streets
away, she washed everything else by hand, hanging the clothes on the outside clothesline hung between our living room and the living room of a
neighbor across the way. Once the clothes were clean, however, they often
languished in bags waiting to be ironed, probably her least favorite chore.
One of my earliest memories is of a closetful of bags of clean laundry.

On the other hand, Mami was a superb cook, making the best *carne
mechada* and *rellenos de papa* I've ever eaten, as well as tasty rice, beans,
yucca, plantains, and other typical Puerto Rican foods. She outdid herself
at Christmas and other holidays, making every special food of the season.
The production of *pasteles*, meat-filled patties made of plantains and yucca,
was an all-girl affair, taking an entire day to prepare. Lydia and I helped,
grinding the plantains by hand on aluminum graters. We often grated
some skin right along with the plantains. A running joke was that a little
blood made the pasteles even tastier, but we washed our hands often and
made sure to not let any blood get into the mix. The project continued
with the making of the *masa*, the dough, and then the *sofrito*, the base for
most Puerto Rican food. We would cut up the pork for the filling and fry
it, rolling out the dough on special parchment paper and, when we could
get them, plantain leaves, filling the center with the pork mixture. Finally,
we would fold the paper into rectangles and tie it with twine before dropping each pastel into boiling water for an hour or so. Eating the pasteles
on Christmas, surrounded by whatever cousins and other family members
living in New York or others who happened to be visiting from the island,
is a cherished memory.

As a young bride years later, I tried to keep the tradition going with pastel-making parties with other Puerto Rican young women. For this activity, women's liberation stayed outside the kitchen. Even though we challenged tradition in all sorts of other ways—our husbands changed diapers, cleaned the house, joined us at baby showers, and even stayed home with the kids while we worked—making pasteles was our private domain. Grating, chopping, sautéing, rolling out the dough and filling it with meat, while talking, joking, and laughing, we made sure to have plenty of rum and Coke to help ease the burden (not our mothers' way of making pasteles). But with a busy career and children, many women let the practice of making pasteles fall by the wayside. It has unfortunately become a lost art in many Puerto Rican households, with lots of us now relying on strangers, either individuals or bodegas, that make large batches to sell to other Puerto Ricans who want to keep up the tradition without all the hassle.

Not only Christmas but other holidays too were special when I was a child. Because Papi was considered the elder of the New York–based Cortés clan, our apartment was the center of most of the festivities, with family, extended family, almost family, and those we defined as *como familia* in attendance. These included all our stateside aunts, uncles, and cousins, other cousins who happened to be visiting from Puerto Rico, and far-flung family members. When we were teenagers, our friends also joined the festivities. By then we were living in a more middle-class neighborhood with no Puerto Ricans to be found, and our friends were Jewish, Irish, and Italian Americans. They adapted fairly quickly to our food, our music, and our family, learning to dance salsa and even to say a few words in Spanish, becoming what we affectionately called "honorary Puerto Ricans." They also learned to love Mami and Papi, probably becoming the first in their families to have close ties with Puerto Ricans.

There was always music and food—was there ever food!—all made by my mother. I still cannot imagine how she did it all. She made pasteles, *pernil* (pork roast), *arroz con gandules* (rice with pigeon peas), *arroz con dulce* (a kind of rice pudding that took many hours to make, with fresh coconut that was grated and put through a strainer), and *coquito* (a kind of Puerto Rican eggnog but much better, with coconut, rum, egg, and spices), all staples for the holidays. There were other traditions as well. On

[handwritten margin note:] Family festivities always @ Senia's household because dad was considered the elder of NY & used as Cortés clan

New Year's Eve, Mami made sure we all wore something yellow for good luck, even if it was just our underwear. At midnight there was a kissing marathon: having to kiss everyone in attendance took a good fifteen minutes. Some of our older cousins, those who had been raised in Puerto Rico and had since moved to New York, closed the bedroom doors and, right at midnight, cried their eyes out, homesick for warmer weather, siblings, and parents. Just young children at the time, Lydia and I couldn't understand what all the fuss was about.

These memories of holiday food and family gatherings were so powerful that in 1965, when I graduated from college and was ready to venture to Spain to study for my master's degree, I asked Mami if we could have Thanksgiving in August, knowing the holiday wasn't celebrated in Spain and afraid I wouldn't by then be able to stand the homesickness. Mami promptly consented and prepared everything with her usual good humor. Thanksgiving had by then become, and still is, my favorite holiday, not for any patriotic reason but because it isn't about material things the way Christmas has become, but rather because it means being with the people I most love and eating delicious food.

I've always marveled at how immigrants make US holidays their own. This is true especially of Thanksgiving. No matter what a person's ethnicity or national origin is, and knowing little of the actual history of the holiday, almost every group adds a little taste of home, as well as a taste of other cultures, to the menu. Imagine us sitting around the table in the August heat with a big turkey, stuffing, cranberry sauce, rice and beans, *tostones*, and, the pièce de résistance, Manischewitz wine, which had mysteriously become part of the Thanksgiving ritual of many Puerto Rican families in New York.

In spite of how good a cook she was, it was never my goal to cook like my mother. She always seemed to be in the kitchen—standing over the stove, chopping, stirring, cooking, serving, and washing dishes. Although there is nothing quite as irresistible as the smell of sofrito—a sauté of olive oil, chopped onions and peppers, garlic, cilantro, *ajíes dulces*, cumin, and other spices—even that smell didn't entice me to the kitchen until after I married. I thought cooking dinner was an all-day affair, and already as a young girl, I knew I would have better things to do with my life. Mami never seemed very happy, even when the house was filled with people. I

[handwritten margin note: Junio pts out that immigrants have made US holidays their own. Especially Thanksgiving]

understand it now, thinking about how tedious it must have been to cook for what seemed like a busload of people. Yet she did it, as she did everything, with quiet resignation.

———◦•◦———

QUESTIONS OF IDENTITY AND belonging have been with me my entire life, whether I was a child trying to decipher why people like me were unwelcome in some places, an adolescent attempting to craft my own character in a place where you were assigned a rigid identity, a young adult negotiating my way through college, or an educator with a growing awareness of the benefits—largely unrecognized in the general population—of bilingualism and biculturalism. All these questions are part of who I was and who I have become.

Assimilation pressures began very early for me, to be precise, at fourteen months old. That was when my parents brought me to Queen of All Saints, an imposing Gothic Revival–style church in Brooklyn where they had been married, to arrange for my baptism. With striking stained-glass windows, the church catered to its immigrant parishioners with a clear mandate to "Americanize" them. No concessions such as Spanish-language Mass existed at the time. Because the name Sonia is not found in the Bible, the parish priest insisted my parents choose a middle name from the Bible if I was to be baptized. Most of the priests were Irish and, true to his own experience, the priest who spoke with my parents suggested they give me the middle name Mary rather than María, the one my parents had preferred. "After all, you're in America now," he said, "so you should prepare her to be an American." Never one to question a priest, they quickly acquiesced.

Our lives were far from the typical middle-class existence, but this is not to say we didn't have what educators now call enrichment activities, though our teachers might not have recognized them as such. Although there were no books in the apartment, Papi, who even after forty-five years in New York never really mastered speaking the English language (I often joke that he knew more Yiddish than English, although that's not really true), read the newspaper religiously every morning—not *El Diario*, the Spanish-language paper, but the *Daily News*, the conservative English-language one. Our parents told us stories from back home, children's tales of Juan Bobo

Spent time w/ family

and other folk heroes as well as stories about the comical exploits of *jíbaros*, country folk or greenhorns only recently arrived from Puerto Rico. Having by this time been in the States for over a decade, my parents felt they were veterans, with the right to laugh affectionately at their newest compatriots in New York. We spent lots of time in the company of family members celebrating birthdays and holidays or just getting together for any reason whatsoever. If they came to our apartment, as they inevitably did, we often went up to the roof, our version of other people's backyards, decks, or neighborhood parks. There, with the sticky tar surface underneath, we would see Brooklyn beneath and before us: tenement buildings, factories, the stores on Broadway and Graham Avenues, the Brooklyn Dime Bank, and of course, the Williamsburg Bridge, gateway to Manhattan.

Would stop @ 'vivero' (meaning life) for chickens ironically it was their place of death

On Saturday mornings, Lydia, Freddy, and I accompanied Mami to the local businesses on Broadway or Graham Avenue, stopping at the bank, the butcher shop, the bakery, and the local bodega. The most impressive place we stopped was the *vivero*, a term suggesting a place of life. This was where we bought our fresh chickens. Ironically, it was also their place of death. The vivero was owned by Orthodox Jews, and being a kosher vivero, it was the best place to get fresh chickens in the entire neighborhood. There, Mami would select the plumpest and healthiest-looking chicken. The bird would then be brought promptly to the back, where it was killed, plucked, and cut up for her tasty arroz con pollo. When we finished shopping, we would stop for ice cream or for a five-cent candy bar at the local candy store, our treat for good behavior and for helping Mami on the weekly excursion.

Time @ beach

We also went to the beach, generally Orchard Beach in the Bronx, but the trip was a long slog, one we could make only after Papi bought our first car in 1953, the year he turned fifty-two and learned to drive. For a ride of over an hour, we would go in a caravan of four, five, or six cars of family and friends, with enough food for an army. The day before we went, Mami would stay up half the night cooking and preparing, organizing and packing hot food, cold sandwich food, tons of fruit, and drinks, especially the ever-present Kool-Aid. Orchard Beach was not the best beach in the world and probably not even the nicest one in New York, but to us, it was a little piece of paradise. Despite the rocks, seaweed, and crowds, it was a welcome escape from the steamy urban streets.

With few exceptions, we did little in the way of family vacations. We went to Puerto Rico when I was five, staying with Titi Petrita and Tío Carlos, Mami's sister/aunt and her husband, and then with Tío Crucito and Tía Ana, Papi's brother and his wife. All I remember of that trip is being in my father's arms, looking up at the starlit night sky. Because there were millions of stars—unlike in Brooklyn—I remember seeing fireworks too, or is that just my imagination running wild? On that trip, we must have joined in the month-long Christmas festivities, eating pernil and arroz con gandules, savoring the sweet flavors of *turrón* and arroz con dulce, and visiting neighbors. Unlike the more solemn New England–inspired Christmas tradition, the holiday in Puerto Rico is a more raucous affair, with jubilant music and instruments, dancing, food, and parties that move from house to house and end in the early morning hours.

We also had one stateside vacation around 1949 at Las Villas, also known as the Puerto Rican Catskills, about a hundred miles north of New York City. Established by Spanish immigrants in the 1930s, these rural hotels, run by Spaniards, became the largest Latino resort in the East in the 1950s and 1960s. The Jewish Catskills are better known, of course, as the breeding ground for comedians such as Milton Berle and musical performers like Eydie Gormé and Steve Lawrence. But for Puerto Ricans, Las Villas represented an oasis from the harsh realities of the city. Every Puerto Rican in the 1950s knew about the resort and, when they were able, vacationed there. We were no exception. Like everything else we did, we didn't venture on vacation alone: family photos suggest that several cousins and family friends came with us. The photos depict scenes of such bucolic peace that, for Mami and Papi, the scenes were probably reminiscent of Puerto Rico. In the photos, I am a grinning five- or six-year-old, Lydia a more serious six- or seven-year-old, and Freddy a beautiful, smiling, curly-haired cherub of two or three. There is also a humorous photo of Mami holding a scythe over Papi's head, a photo probably taken by one of the numerous friends and family members on the trip with us.

———◆◆◆———

LATER IN OUR CHILDHOOD, when I was almost twelve and Lydia nearly thirteen, our parents sent us by ourselves to spend the entire summer in Puerto Rico. That trip is imprinted indelibly in my mind. It was the first

time we had traveled alone, a scary proposition, but knowing that traveling with Freddy would be difficult, our parents still wanted us to have a
connection with their homeland and our relatives. It was a memorable trip
for many reasons. For one, it was the first time I became aware that not all
Puerto Ricans were poor. Although we had a hint of Puerto Rican social
class diversity when Titi Petrita had visited us in New York, the existence
of other middle-class or even wealthy Puerto Ricans was a revelation. In
New York City, every Puerto Rican I had ever met lived in circumstances
similar to, or worse than, our own. But in Puerto Rico, there was a huge
range: in the rural areas, desperate poverty, much worse than we had either
experienced or seen in Brooklyn, and in some parts of cities and towns,
more or less middle-class life and even luxurious wealth.

At the time, flights from New York to San Juan, strictly on propel-
ler planes, lasted about five hours, almost double what they take now. I
threw up on the plane; Lydia, always by my side, helped me deal with the
embarrassment. As was the custom then and sometimes still is today, entire
families went to the airport to pick up the native sons and daughters or
their offspring. In our case, it was Titi Petrita and Tío Carlos who came to
get us. The trip from San Juan to Ponce, before the cross-island highway
was built, was a perilous five-hour affair, with hairpin curves along La
Cordillera Central, the west-to-east mountain chain that cuts the interior
of Puerto Rico in half.

Although they were not wealthy, Titi Petrita and Tío Carlos were at
least very respectable. They lived in a proper wooden house on a major
street in Ponce and had a piano that, to me, was a sign of wealth. (On one
of my trips to Puerto Rico as an adult, long after my aunt and uncle had
died, I asked my husband to drive by the house. I was astounded at how
small and worn it looked. But when we visited that summer of 1955, it
looked grand.)

After staying at Titi Petrita and Tío Carlos's house, Lydia and I went
to a much fancier place, also in Ponce. It was the home of María Luisa, my
mother's distant cousin, and her husband, Pedro, who owned a pharmacy
in the center of town. They were truly wealthy, at least compared with
what we were accustomed to. María Luisa, Pedro, and their two teenage
daughters, María José and María Josefina, lived in a beautiful two-story
house next to Ponce High School. It was the finest home I had ever set eyes

on, with several bedrooms and a bathroom with a bidet, something I had never seen. I remember puzzling over it with Lydia: Was it for washing our feet? Rinsing out our underwear? Bathing a baby? (Even though they didn't have a baby, this latter purpose seemed most reasonable to me.) Later in the month, we went with them to their country home for a few days, surrounded by nature and the ever-present sounds of the *coquí*. Despite the beauty and peace of the place, we also got to see abject poverty while there. There were a number of *arrendandos*, tenant farmers who lived in shacks on the extensive property. This poverty, unlike any we had seen before, was sobering. The contrast between tenant farmers' lives and the grand country home in which my mother's relatives lived made me uncomfortable, although I couldn't yet explain why.

We spent most of the summer in my mother's hometown of Ponce. Part of the time, we stayed at Tío Crucito's house. His five children— Milagros, Amparito, Marianita, Toñín (their only son), and Crucita, who at eighteen would become a nun—were welcoming and fun to be with. They laughed at our American accents (our Spanish improved a lot that summer) and were patient with us as we learned what it was like to live in a very different environment than the one we knew. Their house was quite small, but to us, it was grand and beautiful. Rather than climb several flights of stairs in a dark tenement building, all we had to do to get to their house was climb a few stairs. We could sit or stand on their front porch and watch the passersby, something we did quite often that summer. Although the home was located on Calle Mayor (Main Street), one of the major thoroughfares of the city, there were nevertheless chickens in the backyard. A favorite pastime was walking to the local *colmado*, the neighborhood grocery store down the street, to buy *gofio*, a starchy, sugary grain that melts in your mouth. Our cousins also brought us to El Vigía, the hills on the outskirts of Ponce, where we could see striking views of the town as we climbed higher than we ever had before. Our cousins taught us how to wash our clothes by hand, how to live with chickens in the backyard, and how to keep our brains from shutting down while speaking only Spanish all day.

Summer was cotillion time at the Club Deportivo, Ponce's country club, where María Luis and Pedro were members. Titi Petrita, although she was not wealthy, was a master seamstress and sewed for many of the

Ponce elite. This is why she was invited to the event. As a result, Lydia and
I got to attend as well. She brought Lydia and me shopping to buy fabric
for the dresses she would make for us and for several of the young women
to be presented at the cotillion, another term unfamiliar to us. Her son
Juan Luis, sixteen at the time, was to accompany María Josefina to the
ball. Titi Petrita made us beautiful dresses for the occasion, giving us strict
instructions on how to behave when we got there. On the big night, we
got dressed in our finery and felt very special as we entered the kind of
place we had never thought we'd see in real life. The young women were
stunning in their floor-length gowns, with their escorts decked out in tux-
edoes. My cousin Juan Luis, an exceptionally handsome young man who
I had a crush on for years, was a fitting escort. But what happened in the
ladies room that night made it clear to me that we did not belong, either
in the country club or in Puerto Rico. As I was in the stall, I heard one
young girl say to another, "Has visto las americuchis?" ("Have you seen the
americuchis?") I had never heard the term, but I knew immediately that
it was a disparaging one. How ironic that in New York, we were Puerto
Ricans, unwanted foreigners, and here, in our supposed homeland, we
were equally unwanted and foreign. It was the first time I understood what
it meant to not really belong anywhere. This duality is something I carried
with me for many years, as do many Puerto Ricans still.

In spite of how eye-opening and enriching these trips were, our teachers never seemed to consider them educational, or at least they never mentioned the trips as such. I doubt that Lydia and I ever considered them
educational, either. We had already learned that what happened at school
was *real* learning; what happened at home was just about family. For our
teachers, it was likely that our trip to Puerto Rico and the trips down
South that our African American classmates took in the summer to stay
with grandparents or cousins were just inconsequential visits by the poor
migrants or immigrants in the teachers' charge. On the other hand, when
our daughter Alicia began teaching French in an elite private school in
New York City, she told us about how her students would jet off for weekend trips to island getaways in the French-speaking Caribbean or longer
jaunts in France or Switzerland. The teachers of these students, in contrast,
probably viewed the trips as culturally enriching. This different perspective is one of the major differences between the education of the poor and

that of the wealthy: children's life experiences are either acknowledged or discounted according to their social class.

<u>CULTURE</u>, <u>SOCIAL CLASS,</u> and <u>education</u> are the <u>triumvirate</u> forces that largely shaped my identity. But at home, I was surrounded by family, good food, music, and a great deal of love as a young child. It was a sheltered childhood, with few material distractions. No bikes, few toys, no television or family car until I had reached double digits. On birthdays, we received one gift, and that was about it; Christmas might bring two or three gifts, and we were usually content with that. What we didn't have were books, bedtime stories, piano lessons, or ballet classes. We didn't even know that most of these existed. Nor did Lydia and I have sleepovers or play dates; we simply played with the children who lived on our block. Mine was the typical childhood of second-generation immigrant children, but we didn't know that anything was missing. My parents hadn't heard about the benefits of having a book-rich environment at home (who ever heard of such things back then?) or reading us bedtime stories, taking us to museums, or speaking to us in English (I'm always grateful they kept on speaking only Spanish to us).

Nor did we ever attend overnight camp. It was unseemly for Puerto Rican girls at the time to do so. I'm sure my parents would have been mortified to think we would be sleeping in the woods with strangers. My only camp experience, years later when I was ten and we had moved to Fort Greene, another Brooklyn neighborhood, was a free PAL (Police Athletic League) day camp around the corner from our apartment in a vacant lot I could see from the bedroom window I shared with Lydia. It provided us with our only leisure activities during those steamy summer days. On unbearably hot days, the counselors would open up the fire hydrant on the street (known to us as *la pompa*) so we could get some relief from the heat. When it rained, we stayed home.

These early years provided me with love, nurturing, and a sense of self and place, but not necessarily with what schools deemed an appropriate preparation for school. When Lydia and I started school, we were probably as underprepared as were most of our peers in the immigrant school we attended. Mami and Papi knew little about what was expected of parents as partners in the education of their children. Little could my parents know that we were not "ready" to start school according to the expectations of our teachers. I cannot imagine my parents speaking to us in the ways of middle-class parents, asking us questions whose answers were as clear to them as to us ("What color is this doll's dress, Sonia?" or "Lydia, which is bigger, this blue car or the red one?") or teaching us colors, numbers, and the alphabet. As far as they were concerned, they were doing their job: raising us with strong values, good manners, dreams for our future, and a safe, secure environment. It was up to the school to do the rest.

We were not, however, culturally deprived, to use a term popularized by the sociologist Oscar Lewis in the 1960s. I've always marveled at the paternalism of this term, the audacity of claiming culture for one select group and denying it to everyone else. Although we started school with no English and without the benefit of the middle-class opportunities enjoyed by children in other communities, we were far from deprived. We were being raised with rich cultural values that would sustain us for the rest of our lives: close family relations, the Spanish language, and mutual responsibility and obligation. Expectations on the part of our teachers, however, were quite different. Starting school, for Lydia and me, opened up a whole new world, one at once exciting, alienating, and sometimes even downright frightening, that would either prepare us for a consequential future or not.

Sonia felt lucky to have been raised w/ rich cultural values, close family relations, Spanish language, mutual responsibility & obligation.

CHAPTER 2

PS 55

Learning English, Learning School

Horace Mann—credited as the father of public education that began first in Massachusetts and later spread throughout the United States—envisioned the common school as "the great equalizer." In some ways, he was right: the privilege of an education was heretofore unknown to the children of immigrants, the working class, and the poor. Gaining the stature of myth, legions of stories have attested to the power of public education to lift individuals and families out of poverty and into the middle class, in some cases even to great wealth and social prominence. But in other ways, my experience and that of countless others, especially Latinos, African Americans, American Indians, other immigrants of color, and poor White children, challenge Mann's claim. Because education is one of the ways through which power and privilege are maintained, Mann hadn't anticipated the tenacious resilience of the rich and powerful to hold on to their power by any means at their disposal, including keeping the best education for their own children. Educational historians such as David Tyack, Michael Katz, Larry Cuban, and Joel Spring and economists such as Samuel Bowles and Herbert Gintis, among others, have long investigated the role of US education in equalizing—or not—opportunities for the poor. These scholars have uniformly concluded that rather than erase social class and other differences, public schooling has largely duplicated and even exacerbated them.

39

At the dawn of public education, the children of immigrants and the poor for the most part attended overcrowded urban schools that focused their lessons on hygiene, cleanliness, obedience, and basic literacy; children of the well-to-do attended schools that promoted critical thinking, the appreciation of the finer things in life, and leadership skills. Many things have changed in the intervening century and a half since Mann promoted his noble vision of schools as the great equalizer, but one constant has been this: the greater the wealth of the parents and the lighter their skin, the better their children's education.

Public schools have always expected children to enter school with some basic skills: kids should know their numbers, letters, sizes, shapes, and colors and know how to hold a pencil—in a word, know how to "do school." But immigrants and others living in poverty—particularly those whose heritage or experiences have not included high levels of literacy—are often at a loss as to how to meet such expectations. This was true of my parents. Like many immigrants of the time, both were from poor families with little literacy experience.

By today's standards, my parents might have been considered uninvolved, even oblivious to education. This attitude, though, was far from the case. They were always quick to stress how important education was, insisting that we study and do our homework. But they were unable to help us with it. My father never stepped foot inside our schools. My mother did so rarely, reserving this trip for our yearly Open School Night, when I would beg her to go. Nonetheless, they were good, caring parents and, like all parents, wanted a better life for their children than they themselves had known. They were proud of us when we did well in school, pushed us when they thought we could do better, and were happy with everything we were able to accomplish.

US schooling was foreign to many of our classmates' parents. The traditions and rituals of US education were a puzzle: Open School Nights, PTAs, class plays, and others were unknown to most immigrant parents. On the other hand, my parents were, if not comfortable with US schooling, at least not entirely unfamiliar with it. As a colony of the United States in all but name, Puerto Rico had schools that were firmly Americanized. Consequently, my parents had experienced firsthand some of the rituals and curricula of US schools. They grew up saying the Pledge of Allegiance

[handwritten margin note: The greater the wealth and the whiter the skin, the better the education.]

[handwritten margin note: Parents were encouraging however had little experience and heritage did not include high levels of literacy]

every morning; they had read the same Dick-and-Jane-type readers Lydia and I read many years later in our Brooklyn schools; they had Girl Scouts and Boy Scouts, Future Homemakers of America, and other such US organizations. They had also celebrated US holidays, particularly patriotic ones such as Columbus Day, Washington's and Lincoln's Birthdays, Memorial Day, Arbor Day, and the Fourth of July. It didn't occur to me until I was an adult that it was a cruel irony for people on an island that had been a colony for five hundred years to be celebrating US independence. If in the States our schools were "100 percent American," in Puerto Rico they were often "150 percent American," outdoing mainland schools in such celebrations. No Puerto Rican heroes were celebrated, and the curriculum included US but not Puerto Rican history, as well as mandatory daily English classes.

In spite of the growing visibility of Puerto Ricans in New York City—about half a million by the late 1950s, with almost a quarter million of us in the New York City public schools—there were few concessions to our presence. Classes in English as a second language (ESL) were rare, and special training for teachers was virtually nonexistent. There was, until then, a quiet policy of sink or swim, that is, children who spoke no English would either learn the language and advance academically or would not learn English and would be likely to fail. Under this policy, too many ended up drowning. Lydia and I were two of the fortunate ones who learned English quickly, although not without some cost to our self-esteem. But few people spoke about these things at the time.

I don't remember much about learning English, but I know I had to learn it *de golpe*, fast and furiously, if I was to get ahead. By second grade, I was a reader and doing well in school. At the same time, my teachers made it clear to me, through their actions and words, that continuing to speak Spanish would hinder my progress. Upon hearing me speak Spanish to one of my classmates, my second-grade teacher said, "Sonia, here we speak only English. It's rude to speak Spanish." *How could that be?* I thought. It's not rude to speak Spanish at home. That admonition was a line in the sand for me: I quickly learned that English is for serious learning at school, while Spanish is reserved for the family, a private affair. It was a lesson that would take me years to unlearn. Sadly, it is still a message that many immigrant children hear today, explicitly or in less direct ways.

There were, however, inconsistencies in that message. Though I was admonished not to speak Spanish in the classroom, by the time I was in the upper elementary classes, I was called more than once to the principal's office to translate when a teacher or an administrator had to communicate with a Spanish-speaking parent. To me, this situation exemplifies our nation's love-hate relationship with languages other than English, something reinforced over my many years as a student, teacher, and researcher. I've seen many examples of children being exhorted to drop their native language—and even punished for speaking it—while, in the same school, monolingual English speakers are encouraged, often even required starting in middle school, to learn a foreign language, one that few students will ever master or even use later in their lives.

For all my parents' familiarity with the rituals and traditions of US schooling, parental participation was still uncomfortable for them. Mami made sure to attend not only the Open School Nights, but also the plays and pageants when Lydia and I were involved. In fifth grade, I was the narrator for a play to be given one evening at the school. Preparing for the big night, I had studied my lines again and again at home, with Mami and Lydia helping me. But when I got up, all I could remember was the first word: "Tonight . . . tonight . . . tonight . . . " After several awkward moments, Miss Berman, my teacher, moved to the side of the auditorium and, in a stage whisper, said, "Tonight, Class 5-3 presents . . . ," and to my great relief, the flood of words finally came out of my mouth.

Many years later, after my mother's death, I found report cards in her basement from most of my elementary, junior high, and high school years—further proof, if I ever needed it, that our education was so significant for my parents. I was stunned to see Papi's uneven signature on my fifth-grade report card in 1953; Mami's neat handwriting was on all the others, something I would have expected.

LYDIA STARTED KINDERGARTEN in 1947. She was five years old, I was four, and Freddy had just turned one. Mami would bring her down five flights of stairs and two blocks away to PS 55, our local elementary school, while she left me to care for Freddy. When half-day kindergarten was over at noon, she trudged back down the five flights of stairs and those two blocks to pick my sister up, again leaving me with Freddy for the few minutes it took her to return. Although kindergarten was not mandatory, Mami considered it important enough to complicate her already-busy life.

PS 55, on Stockton and Floyd Streets near Tompkins Avenue in Brooklyn, had been an elegant building when it was built in the 1880s. By the time Lydia started school, it was showing its age. My third-grade teacher, Mrs. Goldwater, told us that when she was first assigned to the school as a new teacher, she walked right by it, thinking it was an abandoned building. Constructed of dark red bricks, it was a massive structure, a foreboding building with a concrete yard for a playground and a dark basement that served as our lunchroom.

Because we had been exposed to only Spanish at home, Lydia spoke no English and remembers being terrified of school. Tío Chencho and his wife Carrie lived across the street from the school and just a couple of blocks away from us. One day, from her apartment window, Carrie saw Lydia returning home in tears from kindergarten. Not knowing English, Lydia hadn't brought in the supplies the teacher had requested for a class art project. After this, Carrie became determined to speak only English to her own children, as she didn't want them to suffer the same fate that Lydia and, later, I faced. Unlike Tío Chencho, who grew up in Puerto Rico and favored Spanish, Carrie was brought up in the States and, although she was bilingual, preferred English. In their family, only Millie, their daughter, learned any Spanish, not unusual for a girl who had to stay indoors most of the time while her brothers were allowed more freedom to play outside.

In our home, however, everything was in Spanish, as was most of our life outside. With no television and only the radio—also mostly in Spanish—and with family and friends speaking only Spanish, we knew very little English when we started school. Lydia's most important job in kindergarten was to learn English. By first grade, things got better for her: she was fortunate to meet Miss Powell, an ESL teacher. ESL services were almost unheard-of at the time. Lydia still remembers this time and documented it in "I Remember," a poignant poem about her K–12 schooling (Cortés, 2000). Here is how the poem begins:

I remember kindergarten
I remember having to say good-bye to Mami
I remember crying
I remember not understanding the teacher
I remember the English lessons with pretty Miss Powell
who made the boxy words fit just right in my mouth without pain.

I was not as fortunate as Lydia: I never made it to kindergarten. For Mami, the trek to school and back four times a day, with no one to take care of Freddy, made it impossible. I had to wait to start school until first grade in 1949. By then, I was ready, anxious to get out into the world and determined that I would love it. And, for the most part, I did.

By the time I got to school, the ESL program at PS 55 had ended, so there was no Miss Powell to soften the blow of traveling from one language and one world to another. Lydia was my first tutor, preparing me for school by teaching me the words and phrases she was learning. Because of her, I had a few words for the basics I needed to communicate when I began school. Not that learning English was without its burdens. In spite of her tutoring, Lydia could not have prepared me for all the contingencies of first grade, including how to ask Miss Ashkenazi, my teacher, for help in tying my hat, a skill I had not yet mastered. I don't remember much about learning English, though I do recall the sheer panic of not knowing how to ask for her help; all that came out were grunts and gestures.

Life at school was typical of most New York City public schools in immigrant neighborhoods. All the teachers were White, most were young and inexperienced, and they knew very little about the children in their charge. The student body, on the other hand, was quite diverse, a mix of first- and second-generation European immigrants, a few African Americans, and a growing Puerto Rican population that would soon outnumber all other ethnic groups. What we all had in common was poverty, not the down-and-out poverty that I later saw when I began my own teaching career, but the kind of poverty experienced by immigrants and the working class between the post-Depression era of the 1930s and 1940s and the drug era that was to begin later.

Nevertheless, by the end of first grade, I spoke English and I was a reader, falling in love with literacy from the start. I was one of the lucky ones. Though I couldn't know it when I started school, education, reading, and writing eventually became my life. My love for social justice and equity took root later, and more slowly. The seeds of awareness flourished further when I became a teacher, and even more so when I became a faculty member at Brooklyn College and, later, a doctoral student at the University of Massachusetts. That awareness, though, was still years away.

I quickly became a good student, usually also the teacher's pet, probably because I completed all assignments and was well behaved. In fact, what stands out in my report cards are the inevitable "Excellent behavior!" comments, as well as the high marks in "conduct," "appearance," and "good health habits"—categories that no longer appear on most report cards but say a lot about what was valued in New York City's immigrant schools at the time. But in addition to being an obedient child, I was also an enthusiastic learner who couldn't get enough of books and reading and homework. For my hard work, I garnered good grades and the approval and appreciation of my teachers. Even during recess, I would sometimes sit on the concrete steps of the schoolyard, workbook in hand, rushing through all the exercises so I could be way ahead of my peers as they played hopscotch, tag, and other games.

One day in third grade, Mrs. Goldwater said, "Sonia, put down your workbook and come over here and jump rope with me." This was a skill I had never learned before, because Lydia and I didn't play outside very much. It was exhilarating to leap into the air, balancing precariously before finding the ground again. I became a good rope jumper and was forever grateful to Mrs. Goldwater. Even many decades later in my aerobics classes, when almost everyone else groaned when we had to jump rope, I loved it. Even though I've lived in a small Massachusetts town for so many years, my urban roots are still evident.

———◆———

IN MANY WAYS, THE TRADITIONS and rituals of urban schooling have remained remarkably constant and not so different from my own experiences. In most of my classes from grades 1 through 6, we had weekly spelling tests, basal readers, and three reading groups. Even as young children, all of us were able to figure out pretty quickly who was in the "smart," "middle," and "dumb" groups. Our readers were the traditional Dick-and-Jane-type books with lives so different from ours as to be unrecognizable. In those books, Dick and Jane, brother and sister, lived with their parents and their dog Spot in neat and charming homes in the countryside or the suburbs. Father had a clean office job, while the stay-at-home mother was the quintessential housewife. Dad was always sitting in his easy chair reading the newspaper, Mom, wearing an apron, was either preparing food or cleaning. In these books, there were bubbling brooks (I probably didn't see a brook until I moved to Massachusetts at the age of thirty-one) with scenes reminiscent more of fairy tales than of real life. Our lives could not have been more different; our schooling experience as immigrants was especially in bold contrast.

For one, the sink-or-swim approach used before the advent of bilingual education in the late 1960s was both harsh and heartless. Our teachers may have believed they had the best interests of children like me in mind. We may have entered school without the English language, but we were not without our own talents and experiences, including fluency in another language. Besides, the reasoning behind sink-or-swim was patently faulty. Another wrong-headed policy was automatically to place newly arrived Puerto Rican students one grade behind their age-mates when they arrived in the States, a practice that made no pedagogical or common sense. Lydia and I were fortunate not to suffer this fate. Since we started school in the States rather than in Puerto Rico, there was nowhere to "put us back" to.

Handwritten margin note: Bilingual education 1960s was 1) Sink or swim 2) P.R. students were placed a grade behind

A FEW OTHER INCIDENTS IN my early schooling stand out as well. One happened in third grade. I don't know what Mrs. Goldwater was then discussing in class, but it must have been related to education because she abruptly stopped to ask, "Who here wants to go to college?" I proudly raised my hand way up in the air, but when I looked around, I was surprised to see that my hand was the only one up. Mrs. Goldwater also noticed. Without skipping a beat, she calmly said, "Well, we always need people to clean toilets." The comment left me at a loss for words, uncertain whether I should feel insulted or, on the other hand, pleased that I was exempted from that fate. I liked Mrs. Goldwater a lot and considered her a good teacher, but looking back, it was one of the first times I had an inkling that even good teachers can harbor biases—some more visible than

Sonia was turned off by assumptions other teachers had about immigrant students — this stayed with her

others—and that these can make a tremendous difference in the quality of education their students receive. This incident stayed with me for many years and haunts me still. It was a defining moment that taught me never to make assumptions about the children in our classrooms.

I never quite knew what had compelled me to raise my hand. College certainly wasn't a topic of conversation in my family. I didn't grow up like so many middle-class children whose parents raise them with the mantra "*when* you go to college" or even "*if* you go to college." Lydia and I heard no such statements in our home. But a recent event helped me realize why I so confidently raised my hand that day over sixty years ago. In 2013, Lydia and I traveled to Florida to attend the surprise birthday party for our cousin Tito (real name, Herminio), who was then turning eighty. Tito had a great time at his party and especially loved hanging out with his daughters, grandkids, siblings, and cousins, some of whom, like Lydia and me, had come from as far away as New York, Massachusetts, Ohio, and Puerto Rico to join him in celebrating this auspicious occasion.

When it was time for family members to share their memories, Lydia was one of the first to speak. She talked about when Tito first came to New York by himself at the age of fourteen to keep his older sister Virginia (as yet unmarried) company and to finish high school. I was about four years old at the time, but what truly made an indelible impact on me was when Tito started his studies at City College a few years later. Listening to Lydia at Tito's party, I suddenly realized that he was the first person I recalled in our family to mention college, much less to actually attend, at least as far as I knew.

———————

Although college was certainly not on my parents' radar in those early years, they nevertheless sensed the importance of our public education. Late August every year meant a trip to Delancey Street in Lower Manhattan to be outfitted for school. Delancey and the surrounding side streets had been home to many immigrants since the turn of the twentieth century, when waves of Jews, Italians, and others lived in the area's teeming tenement buildings, sold their wares on the street, and, later, started storefront businesses. Though by the 1950s many of these immigrants had moved on to more spacious apartments and even houses in various other neighborhoods and the suburbs, their businesses remained. By this time, most of the merchants were Jewish, and because the majority of their customers by now were Puerto Ricans and other Latinos, many sellers spoke Spanish. The trip to Delancey Street was always a big thrill, almost like a precursor to Christmas. We'd return home with bags of pencils, notebooks, erasers, rulers, and crayons. We'd also get new dresses for the first day of school and usually new shoes, socks, and underwear as well. Lydia and I—and Freddy and our parents—had just two or three outfits each (only dresses or skirts and blouses, no pants), but wearing something new for the first day of school was practically mandatory for all children, regardless of social class or family income.

Though lacking not only a college education but even a full elementary school education, Papi was fortunate to land a job almost immediately upon arriving in the United States in August 1929. He might have worked at the deli forever, but the shop came on hard times and closed its doors in 1949, making way for a bank. He had worked since he was fourteen years old; not working was anathema to him. Years later, my aunt Carrie told me that Papi had refused to accept public assistance when he became suddenly unemployed. As Carrie was our most Americanized and upwardly-mobile-thinking relative, she didn't trust the ways of *jíbaros*, country folks from Puerto Rico who, for example, sometimes hid their money under mattresses, and she had urged Papi years earlier to start a savings account for just such an emergency. Thanks to this wise advice, he was able to use these modest savings to buy his first bodega, a tiny hole-in-the-wall Latin American grocery store he promptly named La Fortuna. Despite his low literacy skills and absolute lack of business experience, he had always had to fend for himself and his family, and he was adventurous by nature. Most evident was his drive—something I believe I inherited from him—so that, in spite of his lack of formal education or business experience, he took a chance on the bodega.

As a college student years later, I was astonished to come across an old photo in our basement. Rolled up, yellowed, and frayed at the edges, it was a formal photo of a fancy banquet. Taken from a balcony, the photo shows several hundred people dressed in all their finery at the St. George, then the only hotel of consequence in Brooklyn, celebrating some occasion or another. My mother was right in front, but I couldn't see my father until I looked at the elevated dais on the right.

"Why is Papi sitting up there, while you're down here by yourself?" I asked my mother.

"Oh, that's when he was elected president of the Puerto Rican Merchants' Association," she said.

"President of the Puerto Rican Merchants' Association?" I asked, dumbfounded. How could that be? He could barely write, and his English was never very good. Not only were my assumptions about what it took to be a leader challenged that day, but the photo also made me realize that I had a lot to learn about both Papi and the resilience and inventiveness of the Puerto Rican community. All we ever heard were stories of deprivation and crime, but here was Papi, an inspiring example of perseverance and grit.

———◆———

LA FORTUNA, LIKE OUR APARTMENT building, was also on Stockton Street, number 199, just a block away. This made it convenient for us to be there often, helping to stock shelves and tend to customers. Mami was there for several hours each day, with Freddy in tow, leaving only to return home to cook our evening meal. Lydia and I took liberal advantage of the penny candy Papi sold in the front counter, and we played with the kittens he kept to deal with the mice. I was the steadier worker, learning how to pack groceries so that the heavy products were on the bottom and the lighter and more delicate ones on top. I loved to weigh the produce, attempting to hit the exact weight. One day, very proud of myself, I packed ten pounds of potatoes on the nose. Even Papi, generally reserved and not given to blatant demonstrations of pride, beamed. But especially impressive was to watch Papi, with his meager education, take a pencil to a paper bag, write down the total for the *plátanos*, potatoes, tomatoes, cans of beans, bags of rice, and other provisions and add them up with lightning speed. I never inherited his natural talent for math; literacy was always more my forte.

At La Fortuna, we catered to the tastes of our Puerto Rican neighbors, selling everything from beans, rice, plantains, yucca, spices, chicken and other meat, tropical fruits, and even, when Mami could make it, *budín*, a Puerto Rican bread pudding. When I was eleven and had learned to crochet, I would make outfits for eight-inch dolls, with extravagant gowns and fancy hats replete with beads, pearls, and sequins, and Papi would place them in the window and sell them for three dollars each.

Given the clientele and because Papi had a trusting nature, when people didn't have the cash on hand to pay for their groceries, he let them buy *fiao*, on credit. Near the cash register, he kept a notebook with a running tab of what the customers owed him. Some never did pay up, but many were grateful for the trust he had in them. To make up for the lost revenue, he also sold tickets to *la bolita*, the numbers game. Illegal as it was, it was too lucrative to pass up, so to keep himself out of trouble, he paid off the local cops. Papi was arrested once, however, because it seems the cop on duty hadn't gotten the memo. But my father was quickly released, and the situation reverted to business as usual.

Nineteen fifty-three, when I turned ten, was a banner year for another reason. We got our first car and Papi, at fifty-two, had just learned to drive. He never became very good at it, but the automobile gave us a freedom we had never before experienced. No more freezing walks to our apartment from the Myrtle Avenue elevated subway station, where one frigid night, I remember he carried me all the way home. We were also able to drive to other neighborhoods in Brooklyn or the Bronx to visit family or friends.

Living so close to Papi's bodega made me feel as if we lived in a little village. We knew many of our neighbors on the block, and by now, Williamsburg, though not yet completely Puerto Rican, was mostly so. The sounds of Spanish were everywhere, and we began to see more signs in Spanish and more businesses, including *botánicas*—stores selling all manner of spiritual and homeopathic remedies, often with a resident fortune teller—and a funeral parlor, with Spanish names. At the same time, we shared our tenement buildings and storefronts with our remaining Jewish, Ukrainian, and Italian neighbors. Our more or less comfortable existence on Stockton Street, however, was soon to come to an end.

WHEN I WAS TEN, we learned that our entire block of tenement buildings was to be torn down to make way for the "projects." By the time we left Williamsburg, the community had become almost entirely Puerto Rican;

most of the European immigrants had moved on to greener pastures—middle-class neighborhoods in Brooklyn and Queens or the suburbs on Long Island. We moved from Williamsburg to Fort Greene, another Brooklyn neighborhood, one that was even poorer. On the day we moved into our apartment at 292 Ryerson Street, a notice was tacked onto the outside of the building informing residents that the structure was scheduled for demolition in two years. So from the day we moved in, we knew we'd have to move again in a couple of years.

On Ryerson Street, we lived in a second-floor apartment that was somewhat smaller than our apartment on Stockton Street, but with the saving grace that we no longer had to climb five flights of stairs. A bit older now, Lydia and I also had the freedom to play outside more often and to wander beyond our street. One of our favorite places was the local branch of the Brooklyn Public Library. Little did I know then that my first job, at sixteen, would be at the East Flatbush Branch of the Brooklyn Public Library. It was, naturally, a perfect job for me. When we had lived in Williamsburg, Mami used to walk us to the local library—a beautiful old brick building with warm wood paneling in the center of a little park—but now that we were living in Fort Greene, Lydia and I could walk by ourselves to the local branch there. Adelphi Academy, a private elementary school, was on the corner of our street. The school later moved to Bay Ridge, a quieter neighborhood then considered more desirable. When the kids streamed out of Adelphi at the end of the day, it was one of the few places we'd see White faces. Pratt Institute, a premier art college a few blocks away, was the only other place where Whites were visible in large numbers.

Rather than the close-knit Puerto Rican community of Williamsburg, Fort Greene included a variety of people of different ethnic backgrounds, all somewhat uneasy with one another. Besides the growing number of Puerto Ricans and Caribbean people from other islands, there were African Americans, many of whose families had moved up from the South during the Great Migration of the 1940s and 1950s. My best friend while we lived in Fort Greene was Belinda, a girl from Bermuda, whose family lived in one of the brownstones in the neighborhood. These elegant buildings had been built in the late nineteenth century as homes for the middle class and the upwardly mobile. By the time Belinda and her family moved in, the structures had been converted into multiple apartments, some even into SROs (single room occupancies), where residents shared bathrooms and, sometimes, kitchens.

When we moved to Fort Greene in November 1953, we also changed schools. I started fifth grade at my old school, PS 55, with Miss Berman, and when we moved, I continued fifth grade at PS 45, my new school, with Mrs. Hauser. My good conduct and grades followed me there, but I encountered a noticeable difference at PS 45: here, the other kids had no use for someone who was teacher's pet and did well in school. Here, the promise of an education didn't resonate as much as it had with the first-generation immigrants of our previous neighborhood, where people clung tightly to the American Dream of meritocracy and upward mobility. For older, established communities, the promise had too often proven both futile and shallow.

I also found the kids to be tougher, more streetwise. One vivid example comes to mind. Lydia and I were playing with some other kids on the street in front of our apartment building one day when all of a sudden, I saw that she and Phillipa, an African American girl bigger and tougher than either my sister or me, were exchanging angry words and menacing gestures. When I walked over, Phillipa was saying to Lydia, "Oh, yeah? You wanna fight?" Not knowing what to do and seeing me approach, Lydia answered angrily, "No, but my sister will fight you!" as she shoved me toward Phillipa. What?! I stood there, paralyzed. Somehow, I used my developing rhetorical skills, and we never did get into a fight. In fact, after this incident, Phillipa became one of our best friends and we often hung out, skating together and playing street games.

Miss Phillips, my sixth-grade teacher and the only African American teacher I had until many years later, when I was a doctoral student, was without question my favorite teacher in elementary school. I loved Miss Phillips so it was doubly shameful for me that she was the only teacher in whose class I ever cheated. Usually a straight A student, I was also a good speller, always earning 100s on the weekly spelling test. But one week, feeling a little shaky about my ability to get all the words right, or perhaps not having studied with my usual diligence the previous night, I had written some of the words on my arm. I was hoping that with a long-sleeved shirt, I'd be able to conceal my little ruse. Miss Phillips was, of course, too smart for that. She caught me, giving me a look of such intense disappointment that the zero she subsequently put on my test paper paled in comparison to the shame I felt in trying to deceive her. I went home and sobbed.

As sixth grade was coming to an end, I dreaded not seeing Miss Phillips on a daily basis. On the last day of school, I stayed around to help her clean up the classroom. Shortly before we parted, she handed me a gift, a dictionary I still own. Now tattered, missing its front cover, and with no copyright page, I assume it was published shortly after World War I, as it has a section titled "World War Names." The page is described as "Pronunciation of many names of towns, provinces, rivers, etc., mentioned in connection with the great European War, together with important facts about them." The book is coming apart now, of course, but as my only memento of the year with Miss Phillips, I cherish it. At the end of that final day, carrying boxes of her supplies, we walked to her car. "You can kiss me goodbye if you'd like," she said. I think we had probably both self-consciously wondered how we'd part. It was the only time I'd kissed a teacher, and it made me realize how much I loved her. It was also the end of elementary school and the start of a new adventure, junior high school.

In September 1955, I started seventh grade at Francis Scott Key Junior High School, also known as JHS 117. A spanking new building, JHS 117 reportedly cost over one million dollars to build, an enormous sum for a school in the 1950s, particularly one in a ghetto that served primarily African American and Puerto Rican youngsters. Although the building was brand-new, the problems inside were not. Most teachers were White and uninvolved, unaccustomed to teaching their Puerto Rican and African American students. Discipline at JHS 117 was a big problem, with children running wild in the halls and cafeteria. I remember teachers screaming a lot. I was afraid for much of the time I attended that school because there was also a good deal of bullying, with older kids stealing the lunch money from younger ones; numerous fights in the hallways, cafeteria, and yard; and the growing presence of gangs. Walking home was sometimes frightening for these same reasons. Once on my own street, I felt safer.

I liked most of my classes at JHS 117, and I did very well there. As in my previous schools, the curriculum was monocultural, with hardly a mention of Puerto Ricans and African Americans, who made up the vast majority of the student body. The only time I saw anything related to Puerto Ricans was in a civics class in seventh grade. It was a reference to Operation Bootstrap, the 1950s push by the Puerto Rican government, assisted by the US federal government, to industrialize the island by establishing a number of homegrown industries and luring US companies to the island with tax-free incentives. The metaphor was intended to encourage Puerto Ricans to pull themselves up by their bootstraps, with the erroneous assumption that Puerto Ricans had boots to begin with. The economic situation on the island at the time was disastrous, with extreme poverty and high unemployment—a situation that explains the massive emigration of people from Puerto Rico between 1945 and 1960. It also explains why classrooms from Williamsburg to Fort Greene and from El Barrio (Spanish Harlem) to the South Bronx were becoming more and more Puertoricanized. The textbook gave Operation Bootstrap a very positive slant, omitting any mention of US colonization, the depletion of the island's resources, and the exploitation that has continued to this day. Not until I was a graduate student did I learn anything else about Puerto Rico or begin to question the received knowledge from my first sixteen years of schooling. But as a child, I swallowed wholesale the policy of Manifest Destiny and regurgitated without question the many glories of the United States.

There were some good teachers, however. One day, a teacher stepped from her classroom into the hallway and pulled me over. I recognized her immediately. "Miss Ursula!" I screamed, happy to see her. She quickly shushed me, saying, "No, here I'm Miss Wilson." She had been one of our PAL camp counselors the previous summer in the empty lot around the corner. I had never heard the name Ursula before and hadn't realized it was a given name rather than a surname. She pulled me closer to her, whispering, "I'm hearing great things about you!" What?! Teachers talk about their students? What a novel idea.

My dream of becoming a teacher was first nurtured on Ryerson Street. Across the street from our tenement building was a row of brownstones where I would gather the three-, four-, and five-year-old children from the street and seat them on the stoop of one of the homes to conduct "school." I would bring school supplies downstairs with me and teach them their letters and numbers, having them first repeat and then copy the material onto their sheets of paper. Once they tired of the lessons, we'd play hop-scotch, Mother, May I?, or other street games.

It was also on Ryerson Street that, at the age of eleven, I became a babysitter. One of our neighbors, Mrs. Goldschmidt, an immigrant from Germany, entrusted me with her children, Larry, who was four, and her brand-new baby son, Ari. Besides inviting our family down to her apartment from time to time to eat tongue and other delicacies she cooked, she also taught me how to crochet. One day, I noticed some writing on her arm and asked what it meant. She told me she had been in something called a concentration camp, which meant nothing to me at the time. Because these things were not taught in school, I didn't learn what it was until I was in college.

One of my favorite classes was home economics, where we focused on cooking. We learned to follow simple recipes: cinnamon toast, poached eggs, and others. My interest was piqued when we got to more tantalizing foods such as cakes and cookies and, right before Christmas, lollipops. The thought of making lollipops at home intrigued me. The recipe was simple enough, so I asked my mother to buy the ingredients. It was Christmas Eve, 1955, and I thought I'd make lollipops as gifts. Mami, Lydia, Freddy, and Titi were sitting in the living room after dinner, Papi no doubt still at the bodega. I was in our small kitchen, stirring a pot of the ingredients: sugar, corn syrup, water, and food coloring. Just as I added the peppermint extract, the pot went up in flames. My entire left hand was on fire, with flames shooting out of each of my fingers. Before the first scream came out of my mouth, Mami and Titi were there putting out the flames with a kitchen towel. They had me put my hand under water, and then Mami put some butter on the hanging flesh. Titi cut up a potato and rubbed it carefully on the delicate skin before binding up my hand in a homemade bandage.

We didn't do anything more about the burn for several days, but when it hadn't improved, Mami took me to the emergency room of Brooklyn Hospital, close to home. There, the doctor questioned me about the incident. I told him about the lollipops, the fire, the water, the butter, and the potato. With a look of utter disdain, he said, "I'm surprised you people didn't think to put spaghetti sauce on it." At the time, it didn't occur to me that he was confusing Puerto Ricans with Italians; all I knew was that

"You people" made her embarrassed for her family... later she realized she should have been embarrassed for him. —

his comment about "you people" was supposed to make me feel ashamed, and it stung. Years later, I realized that rather than making me embarrassed for my family, his comment should have made me embarrassed for *him*, a person of advanced education with a show of such ignorance and so little common decency and respect for his patient, not to mention for an entire group of people. That comment stayed with me for many years. On top of that, I still have the scar from that burn on my left index finger.

fact that a person of advanced education should show such ignorance respect common decency stuck with her/caused mental scar and physical scar

———— • ◦ • ————

OUR FINAL MONTHS ON Ryerson Street were difficult. Because our building was scheduled for demolition, we knew we'd have to move out sometime that winter of 1956. Since we didn't have another apartment to move into, and with Papi working so many hours of the day and seven days a week, finding a place was not easy. This is how we ended up being the last family in our building that winter. The landlord was anxious to get us out so that demolition could begin. To speed up the process, he turned off the heat in the dead of winter. Mami piled all our blankets and covers on the beds and, during the day, on the sofa and armchairs, so we could feel some semblance of warmth. She even kept the oven, powered by gas, on all the time. But to no avail: I had never, and have not since, felt such bone-chilling cold. Finally, Mami decided that we'd had enough and it was time to get some help. The next morning, Mami sent Lydia to school as she, Freddy, and I bundled up and went in search of the appropriate agency for relief. She called the agency "Borofels." When we got to the designated stop on the subway, we emerged, looking for the street name.

Board of Health

Some forty years later, I was recounting this incident to some friends: Roberto (Bob) and Maddie Márquez, and Catherine and Martín Espada. I had long since gotten over the shame I had felt that day in 1956 and now had a deep respect for my mother, who, despite all the obstacles she and Papi faced, made her way with dignity through the morass of red tape that is the fate of first-generation immigrants. As soon as I finished my story, Martín and Bob, both poets in addition to their renown as, respectively, a lawyer-advocate and a public intellectual, looked at one another and in unison said, "There's a poem in that story!" Within a few days, Martín had penned this testament to our ordeal and, to my delight, dedicated it to me.

The poem, later published in his book *City of Coughing and Dead Radiators* (Espada, 1993), is reprinted here with his gracious permission:

Borofels

FOR SONIA NIETO

In Brooklyn, the mice were crazy
with courage, bony gray pickpockets
snatching crumbs from plates
at the table. The roaches
panicked in spirals on the floor,
or weaved down walls
for the sanctuary of cracked paint.
No heat, so the oven door drooped open
like an immigrant's surprise.
Sonia's mother was mute in English,
mouth chapped and coughing
without words to yell for heat.
But the neighbors spoke of *Borofels*:
Tell *Borofels*, and mice shrivel in traps,
roaches kick in poisoned heaps,
steam pipes bang so loud
that windows open in winter.
Sonia and her mother sailed
on a subway train rocking like a ship
desperate for light, then rose
in an untranslated territory
of Brooklyn. So Sonia translated:
"Where is Borofels?"
No one knew; the girl pinballed
by strangers in a hurry, hooded against frost
as mouths puffed quick clouds of denial.
Sonia saw the uniform then,
bluecoated trooper of the U.S. Mail,
and pleaded for *Borofels*.
His face, drowsing in bewilderment,

awoke with the gust
of what he suddenly understood,
and he pointed down the street:
"You want
the Board of Health."
They could yell now
like banned poets
back from exile.

CHAPTER 3

JHS 246

Ascent to the Middle Class

My family's slow ascent into the middle class began in early 1957, when we moved to East Flatbush, a neighborhood far different from those we had known before. But the change started years earlier in baby steps through experiences that helped me understand that there was more to life than what we knew as children. For example, we had a cousin, Virginia, about twenty years our senior, who moved to New York in her early twenties. She and her husband, Luis, had met in New York and lived in a large, rambling apartment in Washington Heights on the Upper West Side of Manhattan, a neighborhood that was then almost entirely White and Jewish. Theirs was a steep street leading to Riverside Park. Their apartment building even had an elevator, for me a sign of wealth and prestige, though I now realize that this was hardly the case. Both Virginia and Luis worked, she as a secretary and he as a postal worker, a plum job and one of the best positions any working person could have because it included benefits and a secure future. Virginia loved us and, not yet having children of her own, would sometimes take me, Lydia, or both of us, to spend a weekend with them. We looked forward with great anticipation to these visits since we got to do things we never did at home. Once in a while, they'd take us to a restaurant for dinner; we'd also go to Riverside Park, a couple of blocks away.

Titi Petrita, Mami's sister/aunt from Puerto Rico, also gave us a different sense of the wider world. Not wealthy by any means, she nevertheless had a sense of class that elevated her from the seamstress she was. She had

[handwritten margin note: Sonia & Lydia would go to cousins on Upper West side of Manhattan building had a hotel-sign on the wealth]

Also would go shopping w/ weird sister

graduated from Ponce High School, a very respectable education for a girl of the early twentieth century, and she spoke good English and had an air of confidence and even sophistication about her that my mother lacked. When we lived in Williamsburg, Titi Petrita visited us a couple of times to buy fabric and other provisions for her home sewing business. Lydia and I accompanied her to stores in Brooklyn and Manhattan as she searched for the things she couldn't find at home in Ponce. We traveled by subway to Midtown Manhattan, something we seldom got to do except when we went to Delancey Street for our school supplies or made our yearly optometrist visit for a new pair of glasses. When we went to Manhattan with Titi Petrita, we saw unbelievable sights: stores that sold only buttons, others that sold the finest silks.

Titi Petrita showed them diff. sense of world also she had "feeling of power"

We once went with her to Tiffany's to buy a watch for Tío Carlos. I had no idea what Tiffany's was. Years later, I marveled at the image of this petite brown Puerto Rican woman going into one of the fanciest stores on Fifth Avenue with a sense of what my husband, Angel, calls *sensación de poderío*, or a feeling of power. This is a term he used when we had been married for just a few years and I was telling him how intimidated I felt about something or other, probably related to my first experiences as an academic in higher education. "Tienes que entrar," he said, "con sensación de poderío," which can be loosely translated as "Go in as if you owned the place." That's how Titi Petrita seemed to me. It's ironic that Angel, humble as he is, was the one to tell me this. He has never walked in anywhere as if he owned the place!

She gave them "edicate lessons" here & there informally

A memory of one of Titi Petrita's visits is especially strong: coming back from one of our excursions, she took us to a little Italian restaurant in a basement. The place was adorned with fake carnations and red and white checkered tablecloths, with olive oil, vinegar, and grated cheese on each table. It seemed one of the fanciest places I had ever seen. We ordered spaghetti for lunch. Before it arrived, she explained how to eat it. We should wind the spaghetti on our forks as we held it in a spoon in our other hand and make sure to put on a bib to guard against spills. She gave us similar lessons when we visited her in Puerto Rico a few years later. There, she talked to us about how to greet people properly on the street (never, *ever*, shout from across the street as I had done, to her great embarrassment), how to hold a fork, how to sit correctly at the table, how to stay still in the movie theater. Very correct herself and one of our first sociocultural mentors, she taught us the ways of the proper middle class.

It would take me many years to feel solidly middle class; doing so would involve almost a complete change of social and cultural knowledge, tastes, traditions, and even language. It would mean dropping the "ain't" for "isn't" or "aren't," the "mines" for "mine," the "youse" for "you," and countless other words we had grown up with. It would take even longer until I could claim to be middle class *and* Puerto Rican *and* American at the same time.

After the fiasco on Ryerson Street (yes, the Board of Health did respond, and yes, the heat was eventually turned on again), we realized it was time to move on. We were looking for another apartment when Papi, with his newfound success as a small business owner, decided it was time for us to buy our own house. With the growing crime in Fort Greene and the poor reputation of the neighborhood schools, he wanted to move us to a better neighborhood. Owning a car now made it possible for us to explore Brooklyn, searching for a house we could afford. Seeing how other people lived was an eye-opener. For the first time in my life, I realized there were communities in Brooklyn with tree-lined streets, large lots with what we called "private houses," some even with garages. I remember staring wide-eyed at what I considered mansions with neatly manicured lawns, porches, and balconies that later I would realize were fairly typical one-family homes with small lots. I ached to live in one of these.

The day I first set my eyes on the house on 217 East 37th Street is one I will never forget. On a quiet residential street, the house stood between Church Avenue, a bustling street of shops and other businesses, and Linden Boulevard, a tree-lined street with large, handsome homes. The house had been described to us as an unattached two-family house. It had a postage-stamp-sized yard in front, planters on each side of the front door, and a chest-high row of hedges surrounding the front of the house. Lydia and I got to know these hedges very well: it became our job to trim them every few weeks in the growing season. On the right side of the house was a long, narrow concrete driveway leading to a small one-car garage and a tiny garden in back.

With the whole family in tow, we parked on the street and followed the real estate broker up the four steps to the front door. The house was quite modest, but when the door opened to a small vestibule between the front door and a door with glass inserts leading to a hall, I caught my breath. It was the most beautiful sight I had ever seen: a hanging stained-glass lamp (that as a young adult, I realized was made of plastic, not glass) hung in the center of the vestibule. Beyond the next door to the right were stairs that led to the upstairs apartment, and a door to the left led to the first-floor apartment.

I took Papi's hand and whispered, "Papi, *please* buy us this house!"

"No te preocupes, Sonita; pronto estaremos aquí," he answered ("Don't worry, Sonita; we'll be here soon").

True to his promise, within a few days, Papi bought the house with a small down payment, taking out a thirty-year mortgage for the remainder of the $8,000 cost of the house. Because he hated buying anything on time, he paid off the mortgage eight years later. We moved into our new home on February 11, 1957, choosing to live in the upstairs apartment, which was more spacious and sunny than the one downstairs. Besides, there was already an elderly couple occupying the downstairs apartment. In one fell swoop, we went from being apartment dwellers to owning our own home and being landlords as well.

There is something about home ownership that transforms people. Our lives changed considerably: from being subject to the whim of others, as we had been on Ryerson Street, we were now in charge of some of the major decisions about our lives. They might seem inconsequential to others, but to us these decisions were both huge and daunting: deciding what colors to paint the rooms in our apartment (we opted for yellow in the kitchen, a light blue for the bedrooms, cream for the living room); whether we should put in carpeting (a year later, we did install in the living room royal blue carpeting that cost, at the time, an astonishing $700); whether the kitchen should be renovated (we went for it: Mr. Bergstein, our next-door neighbor, was a contractor and did a beautiful job putting in a modern kitchen for us a couple of years after we moved in); and what to do with our tiny backyard (remembering his days on the farm in Peñuelas, Papi promptly planted tomatoes, peppers, and okra).

We were thrilled to live in a real house and to be out of the ghetto. Though still in Brooklyn, the neat, small one- and two-family homes felt like worlds away from the packed communities of Williamsburg and Fort Greene. Our neighbors on East 37th Street were mostly second-, third-, and fourth-generation immigrants, almost all of them Jewish. I had known Jews before, but they were the immigrant variety, not the assimilated Jews who were our new neighbors, soon to become our friends. To my mind, this was a completely different thing: unlike most of the Jewish people we had known before, our new classmates and neighbors spoke without a Russian or German or Polish accent, although they couldn't always hide their Brooklyn accents. They lived in far grander homes than the apartments we had known, frequented restaurants, and had other middle-class ways about them.

There was also one Italian family across the street (I dated one of the sons in high school) and a Chinese family down the block, and we were told that the actor Jeff Chandler (aka Ira Grossel) as a child had lived on our street. We were the first Puerto Ricans to integrate the street, and we passed muster fairly quickly, no doubt because we were light-skinned, and at least in that way, we were more acceptable to our new neighbors and fit right in. In fact, a few months after we had been living there, our next-door neighbor Mrs. Bergstein, in what must have seemed to her a kind and generous remark, told us she preferred us as neighbors to "some of our own kind," who might not be as quiet and courteous as we were. We shattered their expectations, to be sure, but with no other Puerto Ricans around, you have to wonder where they had picked up their stereotypes of Puerto Ricans in the first place.

———◆———

THE MOVE TO EAST FLATBUSH, where we were no longer in the cocoon of a Puerto Rican community, immeasurably changed our lives. We still connected mostly with family, of course, though our cousins were now dispersed around other neighborhoods in Brooklyn, the Bronx, and even further. But walking down the street, we no longer heard the familiar sounds of Spanish; nor did we run into family members as we had in Williamsburg. Except for home, our world became mainly White and English-speaking.

Not surprisingly, my identity began to shift as well. Having once been only Spanish speakers, and then for a time still speaking mostly Spanish while learning English, Lydia and I gradually switched to English as our preferred language. By the time we were teenagers, when our parents spoke with us in Spanish, we inevitably responded in English. To this day, Lydia and I converse almost exclusively in English, even though we both speak Spanish fluently. Our cultural identities also began to shift as we took on more of our classmates' and neighbors' mores, which were not only middle class but also White. We still loved our arroz con pollo and tostones, but our tastes now also included hot dogs and hamburgers and, with a nod to our Jewish and Italian neighbors, bagels, knishes, pizza, and spaghetti.

The people who lived on our street differed a great deal from our previous neighbors. Here, albeit in an urban setting and with mostly Jewish surnames, were the Dick and Jane characters we had been reading about since our early grades. Gone were the accents and the immigration stories. Replacing them were the two-parent, two-children families with a pet dog, families that had cars and took vacations and sent their kids to camp and piano and ballet lessons. Here were the stay-at-home moms wearing aprons, and here were the dads with office jobs. Here were the families who went out to dinner once a week at local restaurants. Most of these things had been almost unknown to us.

One of our neighbors across the street was Jackie, a girl my own age and a classmate of mine at JHS 246, my new school. In my mind, Jackie led a charmed life. She and her family lived in a private house, not one with two apartments like ours. The house had an upstairs and a downstairs, the kind of layout that would for many years epitomize for me what it meant to live in a home of your own. This was the American Dream personified. Jackie's parents were everything my parents were not: they were young and educated and spoke without an accent. Jackie's father was in the military and had the look—sturdy, strong, and athletic—to go with the profession. Her mother was thin, blond, and beautiful. They had a son younger than Jackie by a few years. They were, in a word, the quintessentially American family. They were kind to my family, and her dad drove Jackie and me to school on many days so that we wouldn't have to take the bus. In a 1958 diary that I found recently, I had written, "Jackie has so much poise," obviously something I felt I lacked, adding, "I wish I did!"

My family, in contrast, represented the past: my parents were older than our new friends' parents by a decade or more. By this time, my father was in his midfifties; my mother, in her late forties, had hair that had turned completely white (as I would in my late thirties). Compared with our new friends' parents, they were foreign and uneducated; at least, that's how I saw it at the time. They were unaccustomed to the ways of the middle class and uncertain of themselves in new situations. In another diary entry about a year after we moved to East 37th Street when I was fourteen, I wrote, "Papi just told me I'm never to stay out on the stoop alone with a boy! It's 11:30. What can happen? They're living in the Middle Ages!"

Almost as soon as we moved into the neighborhood, I longed for our family to be like the middle-class families we saw around us. For the first time, I was uncomfortable with my immigrant parents. I remember one day as Mami was fumbling with her keys while trying to open the front door. I stood beside her, looking at her white hair, stocky built, and old-fashioned dress. Feeling supremely embarrassed about her looks and demeanor, I wanted her to go into the house quickly so others wouldn't notice. As I got older and became more comfortable with my identity, I began to realize just how impressive my parents were, how courageous, how resilient, how admirable. But this was something I could not yet understand as a thirteen-year-old.

WITHIN MONTHS OF LIVING ON East 37th Street, we moved from the upstairs to the downstairs apartment because of a terrible incident with Freddy.

I was in the bedroom I shared with Lydia when I heard "Freddy! Freddy!" They were my mother's shrieks, a terrible sound, coming seemingly from somewhere far away. I ran to where I thought the sound was coming from and found my mother screaming in anguish and horror. "Freddy," she screamed, pointing to the kitchen window. I rushed over and looked down. There he was, my ten-year-old brother, his body limp and spread out on the cement driveway, two floors below.

It all seemed to be happening in slow motion. I recall trying to calm my hysterical mother (did I slap her? I think I did), and then my next instinct, although I was terrified to do so, was to run downstairs and see

[handwritten margin note: Freddie fully from window]

Freddy. He was moaning softly, obviously in terrible pain. It was only then that it occurred to me to phone for an ambulance. Phones were not yet natural to us, and it took some thinking for me to get on the phone and call the police. I spoke in a calm voice, surprising even myself, explaining what had happened and where we lived. I ran out again, this time with a wet towel, applying it to Freddy's bloody face.

Freddy broke several bones, as well as his nose, and he was hospitalized for a number of weeks. Because his intellectual and psychological challenges limited his ability to communicate (he spoke only a few words, and those only to family), Freddy's fall wreaked havoc on my parents, who knew that his condition would not allow him to express how he felt or what was hurting. This was also a time before parents were allowed to stay in the hospital with their sick children, so I can only imagine the distress they must have felt.

After that terrible fall, my parents asked the elderly couple living downstairs to move out so that we could move in, away from the danger of second-floor windows. From then on, we always rented out the second floor. It was then, too, that I began to understand the overwhelming responsibility that awaited me: that as Freddy got older, it would be my role to be his caretaker. This was a decisive moment for me, one that also marked my coming of age.

It was not the first time that, as a child, I mustered the courage and will to deal with a difficult situation; nor would it be the last. I had what the adults around me called *capacidad*, a term used by Puerto Ricans to describe a child with a high degree of maturity, a capacity for stepping up in times of need, and a clear sense of responsibility. Even though I was the second and middle child, my parents turned to me when something needed doing. It wasn't that they didn't see Lydia as competent. But I was always a serious child, and they saw my demeanor as the first requirement of *capacidad*. That's why my mother felt comfortable leaving me alone when she took Lydia to kindergarten, a four-year-old taking care of a one-year-old. I was the one my mother kept out of school to accompany her to the Board of Health so that we could lodge a complaint against our landlord on Ryerson Street; that's also why I was the one who went with her to other important and official appointments. Though she spoke English well, Mami never really felt secure about her English in such situations, so I became the official translator for the family, a role many children of immigrants have to take on. Later as an adult, I was the one my parents turned to when they made a will, making me the executor.

She became the "official" translator for the family

———◆◆◆———

Life on East 37th Street differed a great deal from either Stockton or Ryerson Streets. We had been used to seeing lots of people on the street, running errands, paying bills in person (nobody among our family or friends had checkbooks yet), going from one shop to another, or simply stopping to talk with acquaintances and family members. When not on the street, people hung out on stoops or leaned out of windows, speaking in various languages with neighbors or calling out to children to come in for dinner or do homework. Children were everywhere, playing on sidewalks, skating and biking in the street, or sitting on stoops or fire escapes. Here in East Flatbush, fire escapes were nowhere to be seen; even the big stoops we were accustomed to were not in evidence. Here there were little stoops such as the one on our house, with only three or four steps, discouraging the game of stoopball we had played on more expansive stoops. Here, houses had front porches and backyards. But few people used them, preferring instead to stay indoors, probably to watch the by-now ubiquitous television sets that graced most living rooms. I always thought it strange that the poor, who had no place of their own outside, were always on the street, while the more well-to-do, with porches, balconies, terraces, and ample backyards, were nowhere to be seen out of doors.

Because we had moved in February, I had to leave my previous school, JHS 117, midyear to attend my new neighborhood school, JHS 246. For the first time, I was entitled to a bus pass, and I learned to ride the city buses on my own. All the students at the school were White; most were Jewish. This was a new experience for me.

At JHS 246, I was assigned to Class 8-4. My homeroom teacher was Mr. Costello. On my first day there, to my utter disbelief and mortification, he announced to the class as he held up my report card from JHS 117, "Look, folks, *this* is what an ideal report card should look like. Look and learn!" He then passed around my report card for everyone to see. Hadn't

New teacher sent around her report card for class to view

She Realized Different academic and curriculum expectations in different settings

anyone told him that this was not the way to win friends and influence people? Despite this buildup, my academic performance at first proved disappointing: the first grade I received on a math test was 18.

Talk about differences in curriculum and expectations! My previous school and the present one epitomized these differences. By the end of eighth grade, I had recuperated fairly well, but I would not earn the grades I had gotten at JHS 117 for quite a long time. Still, the experience taught me a lot about expectations and opportunities and made me realize that I had received a less-than-stellar education in my previous schools. It's not that I had changed; rather, my surroundings, and the expectations that went along with those surroundings, had changed dramatically, all because of moving to a new neighborhood.

I noticed too that in my new school, being a good student was not the disadvantage that I had started to feel it was at JHS 117. Almost everyone here strove to get good grades. Students were already talking about college as an inevitability. The school even had an accelerated track called SP (I think it meant Social Progress, but other students referred derisively to students in that track as Special People). The SP track offered classes for students who would go directly from seventh to ninth grade, skipping the eighth, and from there to Erasmus Hall, our local high school. With two grades crammed into one, the classes included high-level and demanding work in all subject areas. There had been no such program at my former school, but I am certain that, given my performance and grades in elementary school, I would have been placed in an SP class had I lived in East Flatbush.

There were different accelerated tracks (combining 2 years into one)

Lydia, meanwhile, already a student at Girls High School in our previous neighborhood, remained there for the remainder of the first academic year that we lived on East 37th Street. Our experiences differed greatly that first year: while her high school could best be described as one with few opportunities and low expectations for its students, my junior high school was a demanding and competitive school with high expectations for most. Entering JHS 246 made very clear the tremendous gaps in my previous education. Lydia's poem "I Remember," cited earlier (Cortés, 2000), illustrates this point beautifully as she describes her move from one high school to another a year after we moved to East 37th Street:

Lydia attended 1 school Sonia attended other this highlighted differences in academic opportunities

I remember going from Girls' High to Erasmus Hall
I remember going from smart to borderline in one day

And that's exactly how I felt: I had been an excellent student at
JHS 117, but at JHS 246, until I got my footing, I tumbled pretty low
for a while. By the time I graduated at the end of ninth grade, my grades
had mostly rebounded. Still, I would never be able to make up some of the
academic gulfs between my classmates and me.

JHS 246 was not without its problems. Whenever you put hundreds
of adolescents under the same roof, considering the hormones and other
changes taking place in their bodies and minds, there are bound to be
issues. The boys had only sex on their minds, and the girls spoke mostly
about boys, getting "nose jobs," and subscribing to *Seventeen*, a magazine I
had never heard of before.

But we had some excellent teachers. The one I remember most is
Mr. Slotkin, my ninth-grade science teacher. He helped me make the transition to JHS 246. Kind and patient, he was also a gifted teacher. Although
science was not generally my forte, I looked forward every day to going
to his class. It was hard not to recognize good teaching when you saw it.
Even then, it was clear to me that Mr. Slotkin took great care in preparing his classes, making them captivating to hard-to-please adolescents. He
was interested in all his students, often speaking to us after class. Even
after school, Mr. Slotkin had an open-door policy, welcoming any student
for special help. It wasn't special help that I wanted; it was just to be in a
comfortable and welcoming place. He was neither young nor particularly
handsome, and I certainly didn't have a crush on him (though one of my
friends was madly in love with him). It was just that he pushed us to excel,
at the same time making us feel competent and relaxed. He clearly felt
close to us as well. Mr. Slotkin came to our ninth-grade prom and danced
with most of the girls, including, to my great joy, me.

Attending JHS 246 was my first dawning recognition—one I could
not yet put into words—that where you lived and went to school could
dramatically affect the quality of your education. I would return to this
observation many times over the years as a teacher and, later, as an academic and a researcher. At the time, it didn't fully occur to me that I had

been in substandard schools; rather, I thought I had attended schools with children who were not as smart or motivated as my new classmates. Today, I recognize that my former classmates did not have anything like the same opportunities that the students in JHS 246 enjoyed and that some of these opportunities had become available to me when I transferred. A student's chances are often dictated by where the child lives and goes to school, not simply by the child's attitude, aptitude, or merit. This connection between students' environment and their success is real, despite the stronghold of the meritocracy myth in our culture. One thing is certain: if my family had not moved to East Flatbush, I am certain I would not be where I am today.

MAKING NEW FRIENDS AT JHS 246 was not easy. By the time I arrived at the school, most of the students had been together since at least seventh grade—some even since kindergarten. Moreover, the students probably saw me as very different from themselves. Being a newcomer in junior high is never easy to begin with, but on top of that, I didn't share my classmates' experiences or background. Nevertheless, and to my astonishment, by the end of eighth grade, I received the Character Award, an award voted on by students in each class to be given to the person they considered to have the most character, whatever that meant to thirteen-year-olds.

But there was one person, Joanne Ansell, who welcomed me and, in fact, actively recruited me as a friend from my very first day at school. Joanne was a vibrant and vivacious girl. In spite of our differences, we hit it off immediately. She seemed to take in the strays, those of us who didn't quite fit in. I remember clearly when one of our teachers approached me to whisper that the teachers were "concerned" I was hanging out with her, because Joanne wasn't someone they thought I should befriend. I was a good girl, my teacher said, whispering something about Joanne having stolen something from the girl's locker room, a charge that I never believed and that was later disproved. Years later, I couldn't believe a teacher had said this to me.

Joanne lived in an apartment, not a house like most of our classmates. Her parents were an unorthodox pair. Her father, a reserved businessman, was quite a bit older than her mother. He was short, paunchy, quiet, and kind. Because he had an office in the Empire State Building, I had the opportunity to visit that hallowed building for the first time in my life, with Joanne. Joanne's mother was young, pretty, tall, and spirited. Seeing her, I understood immediately how her husband had been smitten with her when they first met. When Joanne and I reconnected more than fifty years later, she told me that her father used to say about me, "That girl is going to make a name for herself someday." I like to think he would be pleased with how I ended up.

Joanne and I spent all our time together, going to the school's Friday night dances, sharing our secrets and our hopes and dreams as young girls do. Her mother was the one who prepared me for my first period, which, luckily, began on one of the many times I slept over at Joanne's house after the school's Friday night dance. Though my mother had briefly mentioned menstruation to me, emphasizing how scared she had been when she had first gotten her period and what a curse it was, she hadn't really told me much more about it. Being old school, my mother would have been mortified telling me more, even if she had known the clinical explanation. As soon as I told Joanne I had woken up with stains on my panties, her mother rushed downstairs to buy me my first sanitary napkins and belt (what women wore at the time). She explained what menstruation meant and reassured me that it was a normal part of growing up and being a young woman.

I thought of Joanne and her mother as thoroughly modern and American, everything we were not. I went to a Chinese restaurant for the first time with them, something I thought was both exciting and *muy americano*. I also learned how to use the subway with her, going to Manhattan to visit her father's office, a trip my mother might not have allowed me to take if it weren't with Joanne, whom she trusted implicitly. We went to the movies often, and even to Radio City Music Hall. At the same time that she was instructing me in the ways of becoming American, Joanne was becoming a bit Puerto Rican, a regular part of our everyday lives and one of those "honorary Puerto Ricans" we Puerto Ricans like to induct into our families. She often came over on Sundays to spend the day. She also spent many holidays with us, dancing salsa with Papi and learning to eat, and love, all our food. She brought Papi out of his usual timidity, and he loved her like another daughter. Comfortable coming into the house and making herself at home, Joanne got along with the entire family, becoming almost as close to Lydia as she was to me. In fact, Joanne and Lydia's best friend Jeannie were the only friends through high school who became como familia, treasured friends we could trust with all the details of our lives and with whom we never felt ashamed or embarrassed of who we were.

We drifted apart after junior high; perhaps it was the sheer size of our high school or because we were in different classes there. In spite of our growing separation, Joanne figured prominently in all my journals from junior high and high school. In revisiting them, I saw how much a part of my life she had been, how sad it was when we grew apart. At graduation, I went off to St. John's University, she to New York University, each of us carving out her separate life and future. We continued to see each other even after we went to college, but it wasn't the same. I think we both felt an incalculable loss after we drifted apart.

Even though she might never have guessed it, Joanne played a big part in my crossing over to the middle class. She was not just my friend, but also my teacher and patient adviser, helping me adjust to life in East Flatbush.

Joanne and I lost touch for many years. Seven years ago, at the age of sixty-five, I received a message on my Facebook page from her. Searching for Lydia and me, she had found both our Facebook pages. I welled up with tears when I received that message and immediately asked for her phone number. We spent almost two hours on the phone catching up. Many years had passed, but there was an instant connection. Joanne, now living in Florida, had retired as a middle school science teacher. It didn't surprise me that she had chosen this age to teach, probably still looking for the strays among the kids, those who didn't quite fit in but who deserved a chance. From what I saw on her Facebook page, she was especially close to some of her Latino/a students, something that made me grateful my family had been the first to teach her about our community. It also didn't surprise me that she had chosen to teach science, having been even more influenced by Mr. Slotkin, our ninth-grade science teacher, than I had been.

WITHIN MONTHS OF LIVING IN East Flatbush, I resolved to become more like our new neighbors and classmates. I can see this clearly in my writing. After my failed effort to write a novel, as an adolescent I had turned to keeping a journal. Like diaries of most young girls, my early diaries are often self-centered, self-conscious, and self-recriminating, but they are also a touching reminder of what I was like as an adolescent. They are full of details about the Friday night dances, my various crushes, wishing someone would invite me to the ninth-grade prom, rumors about my classmates, my first kiss while playing spin the bottle, and going to Brooklyn's Mayfair Theater to hear the singer Tommy Sands, with whom both Lydia and I were infatuated at the time. My diaries also show me as a fourteen-, fifteen-, and sixteen-year-old becoming more distant from my parents, impatient with their ways, and at times argumentative and disrespectful. I had remembered little of this, preferring instead to think I had been the near-perfect daughter, as well behaved at home as at school. But I was no different from most other teenagers as they try to figure out who they'll be for the rest of their lives. My search was complicated by my new surroundings and my growing awareness of the class and ethnic divides I was trying to cross.

I recall one particular incident that clearly illustrates this stage of my life. Tío Justo, the last uncle to move from Puerto Rico to Brooklyn with his family, died very young, at fifty-four. A handsome man with a sweet and reserved personality, he was the sibling who most resembled Papi in both looks and temperament. Because Tío Justo and his family had lived only a brief time in Brooklyn, Lydia and I hadn't really gotten to know him or his three children very well. Neither of us felt a tremendous sense of loss or grief at his passing. There was to be a wake for Tío Justo at a Latino funeral parlor in Brooklyn (there were by then funeral parlors catering to the Latino community). Not only would our Brooklyn- and Manhattan-based uncles, aunts, and cousins go, but also the brothers who had made the trip from Puerto Rico for this somber occasion would be there. Lydia and I, preferring to hang out with Joanne and Lydia's best friend, Jeannie Stumpf, announced we didn't want to go. Papi, who never raised his voice or lost his temper, gave us a look of such disappointment that it shut us down immediately. He simply said, "Tienen que ir" ("You have to go"), putting a quick end to our momentary rebellion. Of course he was right. Even though we hadn't yet developed for Tío Justo the same affection we felt for our other aunts, uncles, and cousins, we cried and grieved as much as everyone else at the wake, learning that family is always family, no matter what.

Over time, my diaries begin to reveal a more generous side: making cakes for my parents', Lydia's, and Freddy's birthdays; buying presents for the family; doing a bit of housework; cooking the evening meal every once in a while; and even sewing a dress for Lydia. Nor did I complain as much when my mother was sick or had errands to run and I had to stay home to take care of Freddy. In a March 1962 diary entry when I was still a practicing Catholic, I wrote, "I've made a resolution for Lent: to be more charitable."

My journal entries also clearly illustrate how I was trying out all sorts of new identities that would inevitably separate me from my working-class roots. For one, my tastes in clothing began to change. Mami had always taken Lydia and me to shop at May's, a Brooklyn-based discount department store known for its bargain-price clothes. I don't think Lydia and I had ever really thought too much about our clothes before. But when we became teenagers and were now living in a middle-class neighborhood with fashion-conscious classmates, clothes took on an immense importance. In my diaries, I mention everything from the color and cut of bathing suits to the sweater sets that were all the rage at the time. Once we moved to East Flatbush, Lydia and I began shopping with Jeannie. We started to favor the clothes at Abraham & Strauss (A&S to those in the know), a much more upscale store with prices to match. Our daily activities also changed: not only did Lydia and I begin to frequent the skating rink with our new friends, but we also went bowling, swimming, and, on a couple of occasions, even horseback riding at Brooklyn's one existing stable. In 1959, Lydia and I went to our very first barbecue at Jeannie's house and also to our first Broadway play. I visited places I never had before except in the context of school trips, for example, a museum with Jeannie. We also had some never-before-dreamed-of experiences, for example, accompanying Jeannie and her family on their cabin cruiser and to "the country" for vacations.

In addition to wanting to obscure my working-class roots, I was trying to hide my Puerto Rican roots as well. Throughout my diaries, I find references to "Mommy" and "Daddy," at first thinking, "Who on earth can I be referring to?" Then it dawned on me that these were the names Lydia and I had started calling our parents, abandoning "Mami" and "Papi" for these more American names. In spite of our efforts, though, the names "Mami" and "Papi" escaped our lips; old habits die hard, thank goodness, and by the time we were in college, my parents had regained their original titles. In East Flatbush, we also started speaking to them almost exclusively in English, but I'm glad to say that they kept right on speaking Spanish to us. Because of their stubbornness in this one nonnegotiable area, Lydia and I, fortunately, maintained our Spanish.

Our slow ascent to the middle class was full of challenges, both beneficial and perilous, demonstrating that crossing class and ethnic lines is not without both its perils and rewards. Lydia and I had entered a new world, one populated with people who were different from us not only in ethnicity and social class but also often in history, experience, tastes, expectations, and values. How I learned to navigate these differences has been the subject of the rest of my life. How I learned to regain a sense of my own cultural identity and be confident and happy with myself is also part of my story.

The girls maintained Spanish because parents continued to talk to them in Spanish

✱ She had to learn to regain a sense of her own cultural identity & be confident & happy w/ herself

CHAPTER 4

Erasmus Hall

Navigating Adolescence and Identity

THE NEXT STEP ON MY journey was Erasmus Hall High School. Even more than JHS 246, Erasmus Hall gave me the high-quality education that served as a springboard for my future education and professional life. Attending Erasmus Hall was one of the most difficult, alienating, and ultimately valuable experiences of my life. It opened up future prospects for which I would always be grateful, while also making me feel like an outcast, as if I could never really belong anywhere.

◆──◆──◆

ERASMUS HALL HIGH SCHOOL is the oldest New York City public school chartered by the New York State Regents. Unlike most schools in New York, Erasmus has what you might even call a campus, with a quadrangle and the small original two-story Georgian-style building in the middle, surrounded by four large structures, one on each side facing Flatbush and Bedford Avenues, with Church and Snyder Avenues close by. There are elaborate carvings on the buildings, and striking stained-glass windows in their halls. The original building, now included in the National Register of Historic Places, is called the Academy Building. When I was a student, it served as the main administrative offices of the school. Right in front of the Academy Building is a copper statue of Desiderius Erasmus, the Dutch Renaissance humanist and scholar whom the school was named after. The statue is thought to bring good fortune to those who rub its foot, something that all of us students made sure to do before taking an exam, for instance.

When you meet a stranger who is also from Brooklyn, often the first question asked is, "Where did you go to high school?" Your high school education can mark you for life: it says something about where you lived, who your people are, what they had in store for you, and your own values and ambitions. It also says a lot about your privilege or lack thereof. After I graduated from high school, people were often impressed that I had attended such a prestigious high school, asking if I had known any of its notable graduates. "Were you a student when Bobby Fisher, the great chess champion, was there?" or "Did you know Barbra Streisand?" I'd reluctantly answer that I had never met either of them, although Barbra Streisand had graduated only a year before me, in Lydia's year, and Bobby Fisher was in my own graduating class of 1961 but dropped out in 1960. Considering the huge student body of fifty-six hundred, I wouldn't even have recognized them. In fact, given the school's size and impersonal nature, it was hard to get to know very many people at Erasmus Hall.

The school, when I attended, was one of the most highly respected in the city, distinguished by its faculty and many successful alumni. Its reputation was surpassed only by Stuyvesant High and Bronx High School of Science, both of which were and continue to be examination schools, that is, schools where only those who receive a high score on an entrance test are admitted. Erasmus Hall had an enviable number of Merit Scholarship winners, as well as graduates who were accepted to some of the most prestigious universities in the nation, although the dream of most of my classmates was to attend Brooklyn College, just a mile away. Graduates of Erasmus Hall number among the most successful of those who attended New York City public schools, and they include illustrious scientists, researchers, physicians, lawyers, and, of course, many teachers. After the 1970s, the school lost much of its luster. In 1994, it closed because of, by then, a poor academic record. The campus reopened soon thereafter as Erasmus Hall Educational Campus, with five separate small schools.

How the slow deterioration of Erasmus Hall came about is not just the tale of one high school. Rather, it is the story of the decline of public education in the United States, a decline too often blamed exclusively on poor teachers, lazy students, overly aggressive teacher unions, and a changing racial and ethnic landscape that has allegedly led to lowered standards. And while the cultural landscape has changed, other circumstances have clearly had a greater impact: the wholesale neglect of public institutions, including schools; the loss of respect for the teaching profession; skyrocketing poverty; and old-fashioned racism and bigotry.

I DO NOT HAVE fond memories of high school. When I entered Erasmus Hall High School in September 1958, I was one of three Puerto Ricans. Lydia was another, and a boy named Bobby Rodriguez was the third. There may have been one or two more, but in such a huge student body (my 1961 graduating class was over eighteen hundred students), it was hard to know. There was also a handful of African American students. The vast majority of our classmates, though, were Jewish, with some Irish, Italian, and other ethnic Whites in the mix.

As in elementary and junior high school, there was barely a mention of Puerto Rico or Puerto Ricans in the curriculum. I learned US and European history, American and English literature, French language and literature, art history (of course, primarily European). We learned nothing about Jews, even though Erasmus Hall's student body was overwhelmingly Jewish, or the other White ethnics who were then the majority of the population in Brooklyn. We heard nothing about African Americans and little about immigration. At Erasmus Hall, I never learned that Puerto Ricans wrote books, created art, or did anything else of public significance. That knowledge took many years for me to discover. No surprise, then, that I felt invisible. I learned that identity was something you didn't talk about. If you were not completely assimilated, your culture remained behind closed doors; at best, it was a source of embarrassment and, at worst, a source of shame. This cultural invisibility surely had something to do with my sense of alienation. On the bright side, the invisibility of my culture in those years, and my ultimate acceptance and embrace of it, also had a lot to do with the focus of my chosen profession.

I remember clearly when I saw the words *Puerto Rican* in print for the very first time while in high school. It happened between my junior and senior years, when I was sixteen and working at the Brooklyn Public Library. I loved my job at the library, especially when I could work at the front desk helping to check out books. At the time, computers were non-existent, so we did everything by hand, but meeting the clients was interesting and working in the Children's Room was fun. The job was at times tedious, particularly when I had to shelve books. It was while I was shelving books one day that I had one of my major aha! moments. I was in the psychology section when the words *Puerto Rican* jumped out at me. *Puerto Rican* in a title? To me, this was both remarkable and inspiring because I saw myself as a future writer and because it was the only time until then that I thought anybody wrote anything about us.

Unfortunately, as I looked closer, I saw the title, which was something like *Mental Illness Among Puerto Ricans.* In spite of the title, I immediately checked out the book and took it home to read, though I should have realized from the title that, given the esoteric vocabulary and the tables and charts, it was not an appropriate book for a sixteen-year-old. But I was so excited, it didn't matter. Someone had actually written about Puerto Ricans! And if they had, this meant we had some level of significance. But it also made me think that the only way Puerto Ricans could be written about was through the lens of pathology.

Few people in the school, either students or teachers, knew I was Puerto Rican; my heritage rarely came up, and because of my light skin, most people wouldn't have guessed it. But in early 1959, shortly after we had returned to school from our holiday break, Puerto Ricans were mentioned, not by a teacher but by a student. We were discussing the Cuban Revolution in my social studies class one day when a student bemoaned how disastrous this turn of events was for our country, how it would bring legions of Cubans to our shores, and—the statement that provoked my ire—that it would mean we'd have more hoodlums like Puerto Ricans in our midst. I was stunned; I felt shamefaced. Turning red, I couldn't find my voice. I was usually quite reserved in high school, rarely speaking up, particularly about controversial issues, but I knew I had to say something to this boy. It was probably the first time in my life I did something that made me feel courageous, though in hindsight, it was probably silly and undoubtedly ineffective. As class finished, I walked over to him.

"I'm Puerto Rican, you know," I said to him.

"Really? Oh, I didn't mean you. You're just like us," he said (the typical response in the few instances when I publicly identified myself as Puerto

Rican). He stepped back a little as we had this conversation, for the first time becoming wary of me. I was angry, and he could see it.

"Well, I'm in a girl gang, you know," I said with false bravado, "and I know where you live. We're going to find you and beat you up!" I walked away, wondering what on earth had compelled me to say such a thing. I never said another word to this boy, and after that day, he never approached me either.

JUST AS AT JHS 246, making friends at Erasmus was hard. I always felt like an outsider, never quite fitting in, even though I was a good student with definite plans for a professional future and, in this way, like most of my classmates. I made few friends at Erasmus and often felt on guard, as if needing to protect myself. Besides Joanne, I remember only a couple of other classmates. One incident typifies this sense of alienation. The kids at Erasmus ate either in the school cafeteria or, for those with the money to do so, at Garfield's, a local automat on Church Avenue, or at Charcoal Chef, a burger place on Flatbush Avenue. These two places were where the popular kids usually ate. I, on the other hand, ate in the cafeteria almost every day. Eating at a restaurant was usually beyond my means. One day, I believe it was in my junior year, I had forgotten to bring in lunch money for the cafeteria. Rather than ask a friend or even a teacher or someone in the office to lend me money for lunch, I circled around the huge block, all sides of Erasmus Hall, for an entire hour. Thinking back on this incident years later, and knowing my friendly personality and open disposition, I'm surprised I then felt so lonely. Perhaps it was because I had been raised not to ask people outside the family for anything, but it still makes me sad.

In spite of these things, I am grateful to have attended Erasmus. It took me many years to realize I had been fortunate to receive the education I did while there. I have ever since thought about the powerful difference just one school can make. Erasmus gave me a different sense of what was possible. Because of this sense of possibility, I was ultimately fortunate enough to benefit from the ideal of an equal and high-quality education that should be the birthright of every American regardless of station. My advantage, though, happened only because my family happened to move to

a community where an excellent education was both available and insisted
on by the community. Erasmus Hall epitomized these values.

Despite the alienation I felt, the 1961 *Erasmian* yearbook notes that
I was involved in several extracurricular activities. Most surprising of all,
I was a class officer during my junior year, something I do not remember
at all. I also was a good student, graduating with nearly an 87 grade point
average in this most demanding of high schools, but the social scene I
desperately needed was missing. Erasmus Hall was an impersonal place,
and I had no sense of community life there. Interesting that the issue of
community became so pertinent for me later on, in college, in teaching,
and, later, as a professor and scholar.

———◆◆———

ERASMUS HALL WAS AN isolating place, but it was there that I learned more
of the ways of middle-class life, particularly as they concerned education.
The school gave me some of the cultural capital, the smarts I would need
to navigate my way through college and early adulthood. The best thing
about Erasmus was the quality of teaching, and I soaked it up. The expectations for students were considerably higher than those at the high school
to which I would have been assigned had we not moved to Flatbush.
Everyone I knew at Erasmus planned to attend college, most wanting to
get into Brooklyn College, which was free then and a first-rate institution.
There were three distinct tracks at Erasmus—academic, secretarial, and
general—but it was clear that everything was geared to those going on to
college. Because of my previous grades, I was in the academic track and in
some honors classes.

One of the most useful classes I took at Erasmus was typing and steno,
but rather than in the secretarial track, where the classes spanned two years,
those of us in the academic track could condense them into one year. Were
we better at typing and steno, I wondered, simply because we were in the
academic track? There was obviously a bias in favor of us, one that I didn't
question at the time. I became a fast typist, and that class, at least the typing section, prepared me for the manual and electric typewriters and, later,
the computers that have since been my constant companions.

My best subjects in high school were English—not surprising since I
had always loved to read and write—and French, a language I found easy

[handwritten margin note: She found Erasmus alienating + isolating but knew academics were top & it prepared her for college]

since it was fairly close to Spanish. I was placed in honors classes in both French and English throughout my years at Erasmus Hall, and I had excellent teachers not only in those subjects but also in most of the rest of my classes. I had a terrible crush on Mr. Occhiogrosso (it made me laugh that his name meant "fat eyes" in Italian), my tenth-grade English teacher. A new teacher, he was young and handsome, and it broke my heart when he married another English teacher that year. He was also a good teacher, one who kept me on my toes and interested in English and in writing.

Despite how well I did in Mr. Occhiogrosso's class, however, the sense that I was different from my classmates, and even that I didn't belong at Erasmus Hall, was clear. One morning my homeroom teacher, Mr. Saiz, looking directly at me, loudly asked, "Did anyone here learn English as their second language?" With all the others' eyes on me, I raised my hand timidly. In a voice louder than warranted, he then asked, "Are you in a special English class?" meaning, I guessed, an ESL class. I suppose this meant there were a few immigrant kids at the school by this time, though I must admit I had never been aware of them. In a strong voice, surprising even myself, I responded, "Yes, I'm in Honors English." He seemed surprised and embarrassed by my answer. I, on the other hand, felt vindicated. It's not that I felt superior because I wasn't in an ESL class; it was just that I resented the assumption that, given my name, I needed ESL. This incident also taught me that when I became a teacher, I should ask such questions more discreetly.

I fell in love with the French language in high school, even fancying myself living in Paris at some point in my life. My favorite French teachers were Mr. and Mrs. Fried, a middle-aged married couple. I had one of the Frieds during my sophomore year and the other as a senior. On Jewish holidays (which in those days were not yet official holidays in the public schools of New York, as they are now), Erasmus Hall emptied out, with only a handful of students in each class. On those days, Mr. and Mrs. Fried, although they were Jewish, didn't take off. Instead, they'd come in and speak with those few of us who had shown up, in both English and French. Getting to know teachers more personally was unusual when I went to school. Yet these were some of the few times I felt comfortable at Erasmus. I didn't continue with French in college but switched to Spanish, by then recognizing that I wanted to recover some of the Spanish I had abandoned during my adolescence, when I had wanted little to do with the language.

Dr. Carlin, my English teacher for senior year, was also an inspiration, although I didn't realize it then. A white-haired woman in her fifties or early sixties, with an old-fashioned air about her, Dr. Carlin was a wise and good teacher. The only person I ever knew who had a doctorate, at least until I got to college, she made sure we called her Dr. Carlin. Perhaps she did this to show us, before the women's movement of a decade or more later, that a woman could do anything a man could do, and more. One day, she asked how many of us had been to see *My Fair Lady* on Broadway. Rocking back and forth on her heels—her usual posture when she was excited to share something—she said, "Oh, you *must* go! It is part of your cultural legacy!" Years later, in my more culturally critical era, I would question exactly *whose* legacy she was referring to, but I now know and appreciate what she meant. As a lover of the English language and literature, she wanted us to expand our horizons beyond our parochial Brooklyn neighborhood and experiences. Seeing Broadway plays was a surefire way to begin. She also wanted us to know something other than television and magazines.

On another occasion, again rocking back and forth on her heels, Dr. Carlin asked how many of us had not yet read *Gone with the Wind*. When most of us raised our hands, she exclaimed, "How I *envy* you!" At first, this statement surprised me, but then I realized she meant we had a great treat in store. And when a few months later I did read the novel, I agreed with her. But again, years later, when I became aware of the racism of the novel, I rejected her response, although not her enthusiasm or the care she showed for our education. The growing recognition of the racism and bigotry in books, plays, art, and society in general would take me years to develop, though it definitely started when I was at Erasmus.

But it was Major Art, so called because it met every day, that was my absolute favorite class in high school. I took it in my senior year, no doubt because I wanted some relief from the constant pressure of academics that defined Erasmus Hall. Major Art was a typical art class in that we drew, painted, and sculpted, but it was unlike any other class I took at Erasmus. Held immediately after lunch, the class was the one time in the day I could let my hair down and get lost in the reverie of art.

High school became more difficult as the years went on. Though I never failed a class and in fact never got anything less than an 80 (save for geometry), I worked hard, always wanting to excel. My most trying year was my junior year, when I had geometry. Mr. Bloom, a rather dour man, was my teacher. I just couldn't make sense of the subject. Even though I had been competent in math until that point, I had never really been enthusiastic about it. And when I got a 25 on my first test in the subject, I was terrified that I'd fail the class, something that had never happened before.

One of my classmates saw the anguish I was going through after I received my test grade. She asked, "Why don't you get a tutor?"

"What's a tutor?" I asked, never before having even heard the word.

After she explained, I asked, "How do I get a tutor?"

"Go to the office and they'll help you," she offered.

It never occurred to me that I would have to pay for this service, something I quickly found out. I went to the office in the Academy Building, where a counselor recommended a college student who was a tutor for other students like me having problems in math. Anna was to save my life, at least my life in geometry. Going home, I had this conversation with Mami:

"Mami, I need a tutor in geometry."

"What's a tutor?" she asked, echoing the question I had asked just a few hours earlier.

"It's someone who helps you understand a subject," I answered patiently, as if I had known this all along. Then I added, "You have to pay them."

Anna, a student at Brooklyn College and an immigrant with a heavy accent, perhaps Russian, explained that I'd have to go to her house, and each session would cost five dollars. When I told Mami, she was astounded it would cost so much but reluctantly agreed to ask my father. After Papi agreed, I began my first tutoring session within a few days. What had seemed so opaque to me became clearer slowly, and within a couple of months, I was passing the class.

As my understanding of geometry improved, so did my test grades. But what really scared me was the Regents Exam in geometry. In New *passed geometry regents @ 100%*

York, then as now, to receive credit for academic subjects, you had to pass the Regents Exams of the high school classes. I was determined not only to pass the Regents Exam but also to prove to Mr. Bloom that, despite what he might think, I was a smart girl.

After a few months of Anna's tutoring, Mami asked me how much longer I would need to see Anna. We had already spent quite a bit of money on these sessions, she said, and it was getting harder to afford. Although she didn't explicitly tell me to stop, she made it clear that this was a burden our family couldn't afford. When I begged her to let me continue until I felt more confident in geometry, she grudgingly agreed. Only later did I recognize that my family was bearing the financial burden for a service that the school should have provided.

By the end of May, Anna assured me I was ready; she had done everything she could, and now it was up to me. To prepare for the exams, I spent three entire weeks sitting in our front room, an enclosed porch, studying for hours every day, Monday through Friday. I locked the door and made sure no one bothered me, including Lydia, who thought I was crazy to study so much. I don't know how I had the discipline, with the weather becoming nice and the outside calling to me. But I stayed there, memorizing, taking practice exams, going over all the theorems, and studying some more. When the day of the Regents arrived, I was nervous but felt ready.

A few weeks later, after classes had finished, I went to Mr. Bloom's classroom to get my score on the Regents and my grade in the class. He looked at me and, with an almost disappointed look on his face, said, "Sonia, you got a hundred on the Regents. Only two other students in the school got that score." This, out of several hundred who had taken the exam. I was on cloud nine when I left his room, but it was clear that I hadn't convinced Mr. Bloom that I was a smart girl. He probably just thought I had been incredibly lucky.

Sister diagnosed w/ ADD)

Lydia had not fared as well as I had in school. Math especially had always been a struggle for her, something we understood only years later, when it became clear she suffered from attention deficit disorder (ADD). Looking back, I now realize that the signs were unmistakable: it was hard for her to focus and even harder to study, and her grades reflected this lack of concentration. But who knew such things then? She failed algebra three times, and each time she came home after failing, I remember that my parents, although frustrated, would say, "You'll do better next time." With me, they were less patient. If I came home with just one 80 on my report card, they'd say, "Why isn't this higher? You can do better."

Lydia had never really planned to attend college. But an incident in her senior year made her change her mind. Although she was extremely intelligent and later became a gifted writer, Lydia had never been an exceptional student. Her goal had been to become either a stewardess or a legal secretary, two jobs romanticized on the television shows we were watching at the time. But when a guidance counselor confirmed what Lydia feared ("You're not really college material, Lydia," and added, "Why don't you become a legal secretary?"), she became so angry that she decided she did indeed want to go to college. She went about getting the help she needed from Jeannie and her family.

For me, Lydia's new ambition was a devastating turn of events. Unlike Lydia, I had for years seen myself as a college graduate. Given her new resolve to attend college, I thought that, being a year older than me and because of our limited family resources, she would then become the only one to attend—that my dreams of higher education would be dashed. The thought that she—who had never even *wanted* to go to college!—would have this wonderful adventure while I would be denied my lifelong aspiration was too terrible to contemplate.

Because college was not a given in our family, once she decided that this was what she wanted, Lydia knew she had to ask Papi's permission. Timidly, she spoke to him after he returned home from the bodega late one night, saying, "Papi, I want to go to college next year." He might have been taken aback by this declaration, but his words betrayed no surprise. Instead, he simply said, "Si te admiten, haremos todo lo que podamos para apoyarte" ("If you get in, we'll do everything we can to support you").

Lydia started college the following fall, in the meantime continuing to give me the support and mentoring she always had. And fortunately for me, a year later, I too achieved my lifelong dream of attending college.

———◆———

LYDIA IS NOT just my sister; she has also been my best friend and my worst enemy. As children, we fought bitterly. Later, as teenagers, we argued incessantly. Even as seventy-somethings, we sometimes bicker, and though our lives have been very different, we continue to be close through life changes in marriage, parenthood, and our professions.

Close in age as we are, Lydia and I did everything together as children, from dressing alike as young children (that was our mother's doing, not ours), sharing best friends, and going to the same university. We even slept in the same bed until Papi bought us twin beds when I was fifteen. I followed Lydia around like a puppy, wanting to do everything she did, from shopping to going to frat parties, from attending movies together to having a crush on the same boy.

Lydia was a pretty child and became a stunningly beautiful woman. Especially when we were adolescents, I was so jealous of her that it left a bitter taste in my mouth. By then, we had fallen into our respective caricatures, the ones that everyone expected: Lydia was the beautiful one, I was the smart one. Obviously, neither characterization was entirely accurate: I wasn't bad-looking, and Lydia was very far from dumb, but we held on to these defining identities for years. I often think I must have soured life for her, coming so soon after she was born and, in some ways, knocking her off her pedestal. But as the middle child and the second girl child, I was never on a pedestal as both she and Freddy were, she as the firstborn and Freddy as the longed-for son.

Lydia was, at the same time, my greatest confidante. Whenever she betrayed that trust, it hurt me to the core and made me angry, sometimes for days. "I've decided," I wrote in my diary when I was fourteen, "that I can't really tell Lydia anything. She always starts making fun of me." Once, she was waiting at home with Jeannie when a date was to pick me up. When my date arrived, they took a look at him and both burst out laughing. "I hate Lydia!" I wrote after that incident. I remember another particular incident vividly: Lydia had promised to go shopping with me. When she reneged on the promise, I was heartbroken and thought I'd never get over it. After that, I was determined never to place such blind trust in anyone again. "I've been crying since I got home from school," I wrote in my diary. "Lydia didn't go shopping with me. I don't think I'll ever really forgive her for this." I did, of course, and we've continued to be sisters and best friends ever since.

Yet we couldn't be more different: I was always a neatnik, she was predictably messy; I was methodical, she was artistic; I was studious, she was intuitive; I worked all the time, she slept a lot and on weekends loved to spend all day watching TV. In a word, if she had ADD, I had OCD. On many days, I thought I'd lose my mind with her messiness. No matter how much I cleaned my side of the room, putting everything away tidily, arranging my dresser drawers with almost military precision, her clothes were strewn all over the place, on the chair, our desk, the floor. When I was sixteen, I decided that I needed to get out of that room. I started to set up our enclosed porch as a bedroom, painting it, buying sheets and pillowcases, staining a new wooden dresser, and selecting a little area rug and artwork. But before I could set it up, the cold weather came and I reluctantly abandoned the idea.

Lydia sometimes made fun of me, laughing mercilessly, driving me to tears. I was soft—"Mantequilla" ("Butter") became my nickname because when I was hurt, I cried often and pitifully—and to my mind at least, she was hard. She would make me furious by borrowing my new clothes before I had worn them, my clean clothes after I had washed and ironed them. She often rifled through my bureau drawers to "borrow" underwear without asking. She even read my diary, the sanctum sanctorum of teen-age girls. At the same time, she was incredibly generous, giving me a perm when my straight hair was beyond hope, or gifts when I least expected them. When I was sick, she sometimes stayed home to take care of me. She fretted about me, and I about her. I once wrote in my diary that I was worried she'd fail her algebra Regents Exam yet again.

But angry at one another or not, Lydia was always my protector and teacher. When we were young children, she taught me English. When we were older, she taught me how to put on makeup, convinced me to abandon my eyeglasses, and helped me select just the right dress or shirt to wear. When I worked at Macy's in college, my supervisor chose me to be on a float. I was to wear a beautiful black velvet dress and a fancy hat with feathers and sequins. Lydia insisted on accompanying me to the parade, leaving our house for the subway station in Brooklyn at five in the morning to get to the float on Thirty-Fourth Street in Manhattan by six. Inside the deserted Macy's, which was open only for those in the parade that day, she applied my makeup with great care and helped me get dressed. To ward off the cold, I had to wear a leotard that was described as flesh-colored. On my skin, however, the leotard was a flaming pink, making the sexy black dress a little less sexy. After Lydia had finished preparing me to her satisfaction, at about seven, she stood in the freezing weather for hours, waiting for the float to pass by so that she could snap a picture for posterity.

Lydia also showed remarkable courage in standing up to authority for me. In my senior year of high school, I got in trouble at school for the first time. I worried that my chances for graduation were ruined. In reality, the incident wasn't a big deal. To me, though, it was enormous because I had always been such a "good girl" at school. Rushing back after lunch one day, I happened to walk on a small patch of grass as a shortcut to the arch on Flatbush Avenue into the Erasmus Hall campus. One of the vice-principals swooped down immediately, grabbing me roughly by the arm, and brought me into his office in the Academy Building.

"What did I do?" I wanted to know.

"You trespassed!" he sputtered.

"What?!"

"And you're insolent to boot," he added. "What grade are you in?"

"Senior year," I whispered.

"This may keep you out of graduation," he said.

My heart sank as he began to write up the terrible infraction of my having stepped on the grass. Was it like the police, I wondered? Do they need to write up a certain number of students each day, like a quota? I was devastated. By the time I got home, I could barely get the words out to tell Mami and Lydia what had happened. As she was intimidated by authority figures, I knew Mami wouldn't do anything, so I didn't even ask.

I never expected that Lydia would take action. By then a freshman at St. John's University, she took the next day off to go to Erasmus Hall. Furious, she stormed into the office, demanding to see the vice principal. I wasn't there, but I imagine she gave him a piece of her mind, telling him what an exceptional student I was, how I had never gotten into trouble, and that I had been recommended for a scholarship and in general making me out to be more than I actually was. Whatever she said, it worked. The so-called trespassing charge never made it to my record, and I went to graduation to hear my name called for a scholarship, all without a hitch.

As an adult, Lydia has continued to protect me. She has become, along with Angel, my greatest fan and strongest advocate. She has gone to more of my presentations than I can count, and always beams when I'm honored

Lydia taught her sister the true meaning of sisterly love.

for *anything*. Lydia has taught me the true meaning of sisterly love, which is more than I could ask of any mentor.

⸻◆⸻

As LYDIA AND I were trying to downplay our Puerto Rican roots, Mami and Papi were also assimilating, if not as willingly as we were, just as inevitably. It took me years to realize that my parents didn't hold on to some of the rituals and traditions that some of our Puerto Rican friends and family members did. Possibly it was because they had already spent years outside Puerto Rico before we were born or because they didn't harbor the dream of returning to the island—a dream that so many other Puerto Ricans held on to. Nevertheless, we didn't grow up with traditions considered indispensable in many other Puerto Rican households. In our home, we never celebrated January 6, El Día de Los Reyes, Three Kings Day, the day on which children in Puerto Rico traditionally receive gifts. I didn't celebrate this holiday until 1967, two days after my husband (who is from Spain, where January 6 is still the preeminent day to celebrate the birth of Jesus) and I were married. After that, it became a tradition for our children. In my family, though, the big holidays were Christmas Day—naturally, with Puerto Rican food and a houseful of relatives—and Thanksgiving.

Nor did we grow up having to ask for our parents' blessing—"Bendición, Papi," or "Bendición, Mami," to which parents responded, "Que Dios te bendiga"—when we went out or came back in the house. Our cousins in Puerto Rico did this regularly. I remember my cousin Tito, who was raised in Puerto Rico but came to the States at fourteen, once telling me that as a grown man, and even if he was upset with his father, he couldn't get on or off the phone with him without asking for his blessing.

My parents also didn't expect us to do much around the house, unlike some of our neighbors, who taught their daughters to cook and clean and iron at an early age. Sons were, of course, exempt from such duties. When I became a teacher, I was amazed to learn that if their mothers worked outside the home, some of my nine- and ten-year-old girls were responsible for cooking their families' entire dinners and for caring for their younger siblings. It gave me a deep sense of respect for these young girls.

As for dating, my parents' expectations of us were much more lenient than those of other Puerto Ricans. I knew girls—some of them my cousins

—whose parents prohibited them from even going on a date until they were eighteen. Even as a teenager, I thought this proscription was the perfect recipe for encouraging girls to escape from their homes and get married at sixteen or seventeen. Mami and Papi placed no such restrictions on us, and though this leniency rather surprised me, when I reached the age of dating, I was grateful. I was a bit delayed in going out with boys, and Lydia even more so—she was so beautiful, she was seen as aloof by all the boys smitten with her. Many of the girls in our East Flatbush neighborhood started dating at the age of thirteen or earlier. As for me, I had my first date at fourteen, something that I celebrated exuberantly in my diary in early 1959: "A new era! A new Sonia! This Sonia has experienced the thrill of going on a date! It's about time." That first date was with a boy named Tom, who decided to take me, of all places, to the Wollman Memorial Ice-Skating Rink in Central Park. Ice-skating? I had never been on ice skates, and I spent half the time on my behind.

We never had a curfew either. Most of the time, we came home at a reasonable hour. There was just one time that we came home outrageously late. I was about fourteen, Lydia, fifteen. Walking back from a party at our friend Mary Ellen's house a few blocks from home, Lydia and I arrived home at 2:30 a.m. As soon as we put the key in the lock, Mami was waiting at the door with a stern, angry, almost anguished look on her face. She must have been sitting in the living room for hours waiting for us.

"What kind of hour is this to be coming home?" she demanded. "Your father has been sick with worry." To be honest, I think my father was asleep. Clearly, she was the one sick with worry, and when I became a mother, I understood her concern perfectly.

Meanwhile, in terms of friends, the situation in the neighborhood was better than at Erasmus Hall. Lydia's best friend, Jeannie Stumpf, became a friend to the entire family, just as my friend Joanne had been. Jeannie lived with her mother, father, and brother just three blocks away from us in a private house across the street from our local cemetery. Although Jeannie was Lydia's friend, they allowed me to hang out with them nearly every day for years, either at her house or ours.

Jeannie lived a solidly middle-class life. I don't recall what her parents did for a living, but both her father and her mother had office jobs, and her grandparents, who adored Jeannie, lived on the first-floor apartment of their home. They made sure Jeannie had cookies and milk after school and took care of all her other needs while her parents worked. Jeannie's family had plans for her to attend college and made sure to help her apply. Because my parents had no experience with these things, we had no such help at our house.

Lydia and I knew precious little about college. The only thing we knew for certain was that the most prestigious college to get into was Brooklyn College. Not only was it virtually free, but it also had an excellent reputation. Lydia, however, knew that with her grades, she probably would not get in. We didn't know anything about other colleges in the city, and leaving New York City to attend college was not even on our radar, much less on that of our parents. Lydia decided instead to apply to St. John's University, largely because Jeannie would be attending. St. John's, with its major campus on Long Island, had a small satellite campus in downtown Brooklyn, reachable by subway or city bus. Although it was not free, SJU, at about a thousand dollars a year, was more affordable than other private New York City colleges. Not knowing of any alternative and with Jeannie's help, Lydia quickly applied and was accepted. And that's how Lydia started college a few months later.

Lydia went to St. John's University

The following year, when the time came for me to ask permission to go to college, I was terrified. It wasn't only because our father was an imposing figure, who (even at five feet three) commanded great respect and even fear. I also thought that it would be virtually impossible for him to afford to send us both to college. I summoned all my courage—I still remember the moment as if it had happened only yesterday—and approached him one evening after dinner.

"Papi, can I go to college?" I asked tremulously.

He responded in nearly the same way as he had with Lydia a year earlier. "If you get in, we'll do what we can to support you." It was one of the happiest moments of my life.

———◆———

As SENIOR YEAR APPROACHED, I made tentative inquiries into different colleges. My guidance counselor, knowing I had strong grades that would get me into Brooklyn College, recommended it as the main place I should apply. The college of choice for most of Erasmus Hall's students, Brooklyn

(Sonia)
She got
into
both
SJU &
Brooklyn,
She ended
up going
with her
sister
—

College seemed the obvious choice for me. With the help of my counselor and my sister, I applied to Brooklyn College and to St. John's, the place I really wanted to go and where Lydia was a freshman. I received acceptance letters from both, but my heart was set on St. John's. My classmates, many of whom had hopes of going nowhere but to Brooklyn College, were astonished at my choice, particularly those who had not been fortunate enough to be accepted.

My guidance counselor agreed, asking, "Are you sure that's where you want to go? It really doesn't have the reputation that Brooklyn College does. You'll get a better education at Brooklyn College."

"Yes, maybe," I said, adding as if this would quiet her implied criticism. "My sister goes to St. John's and I want to be with her."

It's true that a big part of the reason I wanted to go to St. John's was because Lydia was there. But another reason was that St. John's seemed to me a far less serious and competitive place than Brooklyn College and I was ready for less stress and more fun than I had felt in high school. A mile away from Erasmus Hall and with even a higher number of students, many of whom had been my classmates, Brooklyn College seemed like just an extension of high school. I wanted something different.

In hindsight, perhaps Brooklyn College would have been the better academic choice: It was, in fact, far more rigorous than St. John's, and I probably would have gotten a better education there. But St. John's gave me something I might not have received at Brooklyn College: the opportunity to develop those nonacademic skills that have become just as important in my life as my academic skills. In the end, I don't regret my choice.

Going to college became the next step on the path to my Brooklyn dream. I left Erasmus Hall High School with my diploma, a hundred-dollar scholarship from the Flatbush Merchants' Association, a two-hundred-dollar Regents' Scholarship from New York State, my parents' blessings, and the hope for a consequential life, one that would stand for something.

CHAPTER 5

St. John's University

New Friends,
New Horizons

HIGHER EDUCATION, THAT tenacious dream since childhood, became a reality for me in 1961. St. John's University, with about two thousand students, was a third the size of Erasmus Hall and considerably smaller than Brooklyn College. Our classmates were third-, fourth-, and fifth-generation Italian and Irish immigrants, most of them more solidly middle-class than us. Once again, Lydia and I remained two of the only Puerto Rican students at the school. At St. John's, I made fast friends with a wider group of young women. I also began dating a good number of young men, although none very seriously. Lydia, seen as too beautiful and aloof by many (except our sorority sisters), dated little. I, on the other hand, was the proverbial "best friend" to many of the guys and often hung out with them.

I had gotten to know St. John's well while still in high school. I had already accompanied Lydia to numerous Friday night dances, fraternity parties, and other events there. I had met her friends and spent some time at the campus itself, though *campus* is an overstatement. St. John's was a commuter college, the Brooklyn annex of the larger campus in Hillcrest, Queens. Located at 96 Schermerhorn Street in downtown Brooklyn, the annex consisted of an eleven-story building in front of, and connected to two Quonset huts. The huts were probably built during World War II, when such structures were common. Next to the main building, a much smaller two-story building served as our academic library. Our social lives took place mostly at the Quonset huts, where the cafeteria and locker rooms were located. Given the times and the strict St. John's Catholic orthodoxy, women were not allowed to wear anything but skirts or dresses. In inclement weather, though, or when we were decorating the gym for our Friday night dances, we were permitted to wear pants, as long as we scurried into the locker room to change into more appropriate attire immediately afterward. Our classrooms and the administrative offices were on the upper floors of the main building. The gym, where sport games and dances were held, was on the eleventh floor. I reached campus, which was just half an hour from home, either by subway or by taking two buses.

Though my Brooklyn dreams of a higher education did not take me far from home, my time at St. John's was transformative. I went from a quiet and serious high school student to a college student immersed in many aspects of campus life, social, academic, and extracurricular. I remained a conscientious student and did well in my courses, but academics now were decidedly secondary to social life. St. John's had a much more social feel to it than did Erasmus. This difference stemmed from a number of reasons, the major one being the tremendous sway held by sororities and fraternities. As a young woman, you were branded from the start with the imprimatur of one of the sororities: you were either a "Squaw" (the sorority known for its intellectual bent), a Delta Kappa Delta sister (the "beautiful girls"), a Lambda Chi (the artsy girls), or a member of one of three other sororities, each with its own reputation and trademark. Social life at St. John's swirled around these organizations, and it was made clear to all that anyone who wanted to be anyone had to be part of this scene. Lydia and I were no exception. In her sophomore year, when pledging took place, she was already recognized as a prime candidate for DKD and was welcomed with open arms into this elite group. When I entered St. John's, I was briefly torn between the Squaws and DKD, but because Lydia was already in DKD and because DKD girls seemed to have a lot more fun, I pledged DKD when I became a sophomore.

Sorority life, with all its pomp and ceremony, defined my time at St. John's. Looking back, a person might dismiss such activities as shallow, and years later, when I developed more political consciousness, my sorority life made me uncomfortable. But I'm grateful I had the experience. Being in DKD helped me develop the self-confidence I had been lacking in high school. It also, however, taught me about exclusion: during my junior year, the younger sister of one of our sorority sisters decided to pledge the sorority. Some of the girls didn't care for her—I don't remember why—so she was not invited to join. I like to think I voted for her, but I truly don't remember. What I do remember is the shame I felt when the results of the secret ballot became public. Our sorority sister walked by our table and flung her DKD pin in our faces. Empathy is clearly one value we had not yet developed.

———————✦———————

In 1961, something unprecedented happened: *West Side Story* came to the movies. It was the first time Puerto Ricans were represented on the big screen or, as far as I could tell, even on the small screen. Every Puerto Rican I knew, young or old, island or stateside, English- or Spanish-speaking or both, was thrilled. Although some of the major parts were played by non–Puerto Ricans—Natalie Wood as María, George Chakiris as her big brother Bernardo—with most of the lesser roles played by Latinos, it was Rita Moreno, who played Bernardo's girlfriend, a Puerto Rican born in Puerto Rico and raised in New York, who won our hearts. Tiny in real life but bigger than life itself on the screen, Moreno played one of the most important roles, the one for which she won an Oscar that year. She played Anita, the gutsy, fiery, sharp-tongued, strong, unequivocal Puerto Rican, who sang and danced, who fought back and kicked and screamed. Here was a real-life Puerto Rican, just a few years older than me, who had made it big and who for the first time reflected some of our reality on the big screen. After seeing the movie at the age of eighteen, I gushed in my diary entry on January 27, 1962, "It was one of the most wonderful movies I've ever seen! I really saw the uselessness of gangs, and I walked out of the theater in a daze of anger and tears."

At the time, it didn't matter to me that few Puerto Ricans had starring roles or that the story built on some of the worst stereotypes about Puerto Ricans as gang members and criminals. Except for my brief make-believe impression of a gang member in high school, I had never even set eyes on anyone associated with a gang. I had no idea what a rumble was, and perhaps because Lydia and I had been quite sheltered, we knew little of the dangers of the streets. *West Side Story* was a fiction on many levels: no gang members did ballet in the streets, and although we liked to dance and as kids we had lived in a tenement building with a roof such as the one in the movie, we never went up there to dance! Still, it was electrifying for me to see "us" represented in some small way in a movie. The music was unforgettable, and the movie's conceit as a modern-day version of *Romeo and Juliet*, using Puerto Ricans as the prototype, was appealing as well.

But even then, a small part of me cringed when I watched the movie for the first time, wondering why *this* was the first story to be told about Puerto Ricans. Yes, gang life and crime were realities for some Puerto Ricans, but not for anyone I knew. The Puerto Ricans we knew—our aunts and uncles, cousins, and family friends—were factory workers and postal workers, seamstresses and nurses, not gang members. But most of the people we knew were nowhere to be seen in those depictions on the big screen. This is the problem with telling only *one* story: rather than one of many, it gets to be the *only* story that forever defines a community. Unfortunately, the stories that came later, both in the movies and on television, were to perpetuate the stereotype of Puerto Rican men as hoodlums and Puerto Rican women as quiet victims or sultry sirens. A couple of decades later, the movie *Fort Apache, the Bronx*, about crime, violence, and drugs in the South Bronx, continued in the same vein, although with little of the socially redeeming value, hope, or transcendent music that *West Side Story* had brought us. The other difference was that by this time, the Puerto Rican community had become politicized. Boycotts and picket signs, chants and marches now greeted moviegoers at the theaters where *Fort Apache* was playing. The young picketers admonished prospective moviegoers that we were more than what was depicted on the screen.

Interestingly, years later, *West Side Story* again became part of my life, this time in Amherst, Massachusetts, where my family and I had moved in 1975. The year was 1999, and Amherst Regional High School, which staged a musical each year, had chosen *West Side Story* for the spring production. With no overt sexuality, little visible violence, and a more diverse cast than most plays, it seemed a logical choice for an increasingly diverse community that had long been insisting on a more diverse staff and multicultural curricula at all the Amherst schools.

But several students disagreed. Considering the movie racist with stereotypical depictions of Puerto Ricans, they circulated a petition that initially called for a series of workshops to address these issues in the play but that ultimately called for its cancellation. Their reaction was a logical response to the conditions they experienced at the high school, for example, being followed in the hallways by teachers who assumed they were skipping class, constantly being asked for their passes, and so on. As a result, Puerto Rican students, among other students of color, often felt invisible and marginalized.

Opinions on the issue quickly became polarized among students, parents, school staff, and the general community. Some people thought it was high time Latino kids in the school should have opportunities to be represented in school plays, while others thought it would be demeaning for them to play such roles. Others argued that political correctness was at the center of the argument, while still while others said it was instead about social justice. Some decried the call to cancel the play as censorship; others said staging it would add insult to injury.

Amherst is a small town, and it seemed that everyone was engulfed in the controversy. It spurred discussions about such contentious issues as racism, the colonial status of Puerto Rico, and ethnic identity. The story made national headlines in newspapers from the *Los Angeles Times* to the *Christian Science Monitor* and others. The Letters to the Editor section of the local newspaper, the *Amherst Bulletin*, concerned little else for months.

One moving letter to the editor was from a former student of the Amherst schools. She wrote that she was in favor of canceling the play because, as a Puerto Rican student at Amherst public schools, she had felt invisible. The only two times she had heard any mention of Puerto Ricans in the curriculum was once during a cabaret at the high school, when a group of non–Puerto Rican students were dancing and singing "America" from *West Side Story*, with their phony accents ("Ay like to bee in America"), and another time, when a teacher in her high school economics class shared the tidbit that the island of Puerto Rico was the biggest consumer of Velveeta cheese! It was no wonder she was angry.

Ultimately, the school decided to cancel the production, saying that the climate had grown poisonous for civil discourse. I thought about the issue a great deal and came to the conclusion that it was a mistake to cancel the production. Staging it might have given teachers, students, and the

[handwritten margin notes: former P. Rican student wrote letter & got it cancelled. Play ultimately cancelled]

town itself a golden opportunity to discuss some important issues that had been festering, issues such as the lack of a truly multicultural curriculum and the dearth of staff of color in the town's schools. Moreover, canceling the play sent the message that if you don't like a work of art, it should be hidden away. Yet I have learned that no work of art is innocent, that all art reflects a point of view, a bias in favor of or against something or some group. Thus, all art should be viewed critically. There were lots of questions that could have been asked about *West Side Story*, but unfortunately, the town lost an opportunity to wrestle with the kinds of issues children of color face every day.

———————◆·◆·◆———————

BUT IN COLLEGE, as in all my previous schools, there was no mention of anything having to do with Puerto Rico or Puerto Ricans. If people asked, I would admit I was Puerto Rican, but in this enclave of Italian Americans and Irish Americans, there was clearly little awareness or acknowledgment of who Lydia and I were. Which didn't mean we weren't accepted and included; we were. Lydia and I felt very much a part of St. John's. After having felt isolated and somewhat lost at Erasmus Hall, I found that St. John's was a perfect place for us, smaller and friendlier. There, I made good friends and became active in a number of organizations. But no matter how much our friends loved and appreciated us, everything at St. John's was clearly about the Irish and Italians, from St. Patrick's Day and Columbus Day to the Gens Romana and Gaelic Society, the campus organizations that celebrated those heritages.

On the academic side, Spanish was reserved for Spanish class. Even there, the only mention of culture focused on Spain and perhaps Mexico. The literature we read in our Spanish courses included only works by Spaniards and, once in a while, Latin Americans such as Pablo Neruda and Sor Juana Inés de la Cruz. Even later, no Puerto Ricans were mentioned when I studied Spanish and Hispanic literature for my master's degree in Spain. Little wonder then that I imagined there were no Puerto Rican authors of any note. My ignorance of Puerto Rican writers lasted until I sought them out on my own years later, and, lo and behold, there they were, missing in action but significant nevertheless.

It wasn't easy to be Puerto Rican in school, whether it was elementary, junior high, high school or college. Though St. John's was a far more welcoming place than the others had been, my sister and I never felt that we could be completely ourselves. This helps explain why I became "Sunny" while at St. John's. My disposition explains some of it, as it was a good nickname for me because of my—by then—outgoing personality. But in retrospect, another, more disturbing reason was that the nickname was a convenient way of becoming more mainstream, more American, more acceptable.

[handwritten margin note: Nickname "Sunny" more mainstream American]

One incident in particular demonstrates why it was hard to be Puerto Rican at St. John's. One night, Lydia and I were going out with some of our sorority sisters. They came to pick us up, and as we piled into her car, another one said, "Do I have too much makeup on?" Furiously brushing off some of her rouge with her hand, she said, "Oh, God! I must look just like a Puerto Rican!" Immediately recognizing her faux pas, she said, "Oh, I didn't mean the two of you. You're different." The hurt I felt was palpable. After all, here were our best friends, and even *they* didn't think very much of Puerto Ricans.

Meanwhile, my political awareness was very slowly taking shape. Another incident at St. John's made me uncomfortable at the time, though I couldn't really explain why. One day in my junior or senior year of college, a classmate of mine, finding out I was Puerto Rican, seemed surprised. As had happened many times before and was to happen again many more times to the present day, my appearance and behavior challenged her ideas about what a Puerto Rican looked like. The young woman asked me about my family. When I told her a bit about my father and mother, where they came from and where we had lived when I was younger, how Papi worked sixteen or more hours a day while Mami helped at the bodega and tended to the home and to Freddy, she was suitably impressed. "It's wonderful to hear these stories of people pulling themselves up!" she gushed. Years later, I might have told her how patronizing her comment was. But it was, I suspect, something neither she nor I could articulate at the time. At that moment, all I could think to do was smile and act grateful.

[handwritten margin note: example of disparaging backhanded comments by "friends"]

In spite of everything, St. John's University will always have a special place in my heart. It was there that I discovered my voice, timid as it was. I still receive the SJU alumni magazine, and it is astonishing to see how much has changed since I graduated in 1965. There are now photos of reunion events that feature African American and Latino alumni groups. I'm glad to see these changes; I only wish I had witnessed some of them firsthand.

At the end of her junior year, Lydia ran for president of DKD, and as a sophomore, I ran for corresponding secretary. She readily won, but I was crushed when I didn't win, certain I would never get over this defeat. After all, I had visions of being president in my senior year, so being an officer in junior year was almost a prerequisite. I thought my goal of following Lydia as president would be dashed. Some of my sorority sisters, however, told me they had voted not for me but for my opponent because it was a foregone conclusion I would be elected president the following year. They were right. I won the presidency in my senior year, learning *Robert's Rules of Order*, becoming adept at planning the year's activities for the group, and learning how to negotiate with the administration—although, truth be told, not much negotiation went on, as the administration almost always had the last word.

[margin note: Both sister of Sonia became president of sorority]

———◦◦◦———

AT ST. JOHN'S, THE TALK was more likely to be about the next sorority dance or where to hold our forthcoming banquet. Lydia and I took these decisions very seriously. We had gowns made for each occasion by a woman we called Nena (because she was so tiny), the wife of one of Papi's helpers at the bodega. Nena was a fabulous seamstress, and she charged us very little, something our sorority sisters might never have guessed, given the beautiful dresses she made for us. Because of this yearly event, Lydia and I were able to go to some of the very fanciest hotels in Manhattan, namely, the Waldorf Astoria, the Savoy Hilton, the Sherry-Netherlands, and the St. Moritz On-the-Park. One nice thing about these gatherings was that Mami became sort of an honorary member of DKD and was feted at Lydia's final banquet as president. After all, Mami had given two of her daughters to the cause.

There were lots of other extracurricular activities, traditions, and events at SJU, many of them emblematic of the apolitical college scene of the early 1960s. During my sophomore year, Lydia entered my baby picture in the annual Beautiful Baby Photo Contest, and it won first place. In my junior year, several friends insisted I run for the Miss St. John's Beauty Pageant, and I was selected as one of ten finalists that year. All the finalists were interviewed by the president of the Ford Modeling Agency, as well as by Frank Gifford, then a young former football player and sportscaster, and Rocky Graziano, the famous boxer. The contest ended in a banquet where all the finalists were paraded around the dance floor. After dinner, we all stood behind the curtain with our dates, waiting anxiously to find out who would be selected. As each finalist's name was announced, beginning with the ninth runner-up, I prepared to walk out, but to my great surprise, my name wasn't called until nearly the end, when I was named second runner-up. Looking back, it's easy to be critical of these things, but I recognize now that they were almost the only leadership activities available to young women at the time.

Besides the sorority, I also joined the Spanish Club, becoming its president in my junior year. My friend Ed Peduzzi, also in the Spanish Club, urged me to also join the International Relations Club, the bastion of political science and sociology majors. According to the 1964 yearbook, the IRC was one of the most active organizations on campus, "dedicated to educating the members in the area of diplomacy, political awareness and international understanding." One of its fundamental beliefs was that "the development of the student involves not only book knowledge but an understanding of the world which awaits them at graduation." I became the IRC's vice president in my senior year. The club's job was to invite speakers, many from consulates in New York City, to speak to us about what was happening in their respective countries. The IRC also sent students to conferences in the Northeast, generally on college campuses. In this way, I got to see what a "real" college with dorms looked like.

In a way, these activities forecasted the work I would end up doing years later, not in diplomacy but in education and its connection to power and politics. Clearly, my passion for work, languages, and culture began in that eleven-story building at 96 Schermerhorn Street in Brooklyn.

In my junior year, I was also elected vice president of my class. I remember standing on a high ladder, decorating the gym on November 22, 1963, for the junior class dance when someone ran in, breathless and shouting,

"President Kennedy has been shot!" I was shaking and could barely make my way down the ladder. After the initial shock, we officers stood around talking about what to do: Should we cancel the dance? we wondered. We did, of course. All of us then made our way home, anxious to be with those we loved, to try to make sense of this terrible tragedy. Mami, Lydia, Freddy, and I didn't go out for days, staying in our pajamas and staring blankly at the TV set. Even Papi was home more than usual. It was a time of national grief, one that helped define my college experience and separated the carefree times from more serious times to come.

———•◦•———

OF COURSE, I ALSO TOOK classes while at St. John's, but to be honest, that was the least important part of college life for me. As a Catholic college in the early 1960s, St. John's had a curriculum that was mostly uninspiring and repetitive. Whether they wanted to or not, students were required to take courses in religion and philosophy nearly every semester. These frequently included similar content, primarily orthodox Catholic teachings and philosophers. Of course, we also had our regimen of math, science, and English courses. But it was other courses that really interested me. My favorite was a political science class on the American Constitution, a course I found riveting. The professor, a short, wiry man whose nervous energy kept him on his feet throughout the class period, made every class worthwhile. It was the first time I learned what the Constitution—in spite of its warts and blemishes—really stood for.

The education courses were the most interesting for me, not because they were particularly innovative or exciting—the truth is, they were mostly quite conventional—but because they would put me on track to become a teacher, my dream since childhood. In those classes, I got to imagine how my lessons would inspire my young charges and how I would develop caring relationships with them, those things that I knew would be important to me in teaching.

While pursuing my goal of becoming an elementary school teacher, I developed other goals as well: I wanted to travel and see the world, and I wanted to make a difference not only in my classroom but also beyond it. These interests were to define how I approached life after college. Nevertheless, my academic experience was mostly a parochial affair that had little to do with what was going on in the world. Though I went to college in the early 1960s, the turmoil of the era did not begin for me until later, after I had graduated and left home for the first time. My political awareness remained dormant largely because St. John's was light-years away from the concerns of the turbulent 1960s.

An incident near the end of my freshman year of college exemplifies what St. John's University was then like. It was the spring of 1962, and there was a buzz of excitement in the cafeteria that April morning. One of the seniors from the Squaws had married a student from the so-called Indian fraternity who had graduated in January. (I don't think we ever thought to question the use of the terms "Indians" or "Squaws" to refer to these organizations; nor did we bat an eye when referring to the basketball team as the Redmen, a name that has thankfully been now changed to Red Storm). The two students had made the mistake of getting married by a justice of the peace rather than in church. The college administrators considered this an unforgivable offense, and though she was scheduled to graduate that May, she was expelled for it.

S.J.U had strict religious rules

Although we were accustomed to the strict rules of the university, this action nevertheless shocked everyone. But I don't remember anyone starting a petition or organizing a rally to protest the university's action. We were a pretty tame group of people. Civil disobedience was not yet talked about at St. John's. Although by the time I graduated in 1965, the country was in the throes of the civil rights movement and the early stages of protests against the Vietnam War, these things seemed to have bypassed St. John's. The only example of a 1960s-style protest I can remember came in my senior year, when a small, brave group of faculty members went on strike, marching with placards outside 96 Schermerhorn Street. Of the few faculty members involved, the only one I remember seeing on the picket line was Señora Doyaga, a stunning professor from Spain who had been one of my favorite Spanish teachers. Given the repressive culture of St. John's at the time, it must have taken a great deal of courage to grab a picket sign and step into that line. But again, I didn't understand the notion of solidarity at the time. I did nothing but nod in her direction when I passed her on my way into the building.

She grad. around time of protests of civil rights & Vietnam War

In May 1965, just as I was about to graduate, the editorial of our campus newspaper, the *Downtowner*, reflected some of the incipient changes taking place at the campus: "Both student and faculty dissatisfaction reached a boiling point within a period of a few days." According to the editorial, the Students United for Academic Freedom had been formed that year, and the American Association of University Professors had become the voice of the faculty. These were monumental changes for SJU. The editorial ended with an optimistic prediction about the incoming class, those who would graduate in 1969: "They will enter SJU and automatically enjoy a better curriculum and more freedom than we have had until now." I would have welcomed a more critical curriculum and more freedom—even to wear slacks and jeans instead of skirts and dresses—but I missed these long-overdue changes by just a few years.

This is not to say that there wasn't some small level of social consciousness among both faculty and students. There was, for example, an emerging awareness of social injustice and activism among a small number of students. Bob Lynch, one of a handful of Black students at St. John's, had been accepted into the Indians, the premier fraternity. I'm sure the fraternity thought it was a magnanimous gesture and quite a daring action to admit Bob. But even at the time, I wondered how it might have felt to be the only Black student in the organization. Did White girls dance with him at their parties? Did he dare to ask them? It must have been a lonely existence.

Bob and I were buddies. Because we were officers of the International Relations Club and maybe because we were also in the tiny number of "minorities" at St. John's, we were selected to attend a Model United Nations conference in New Jersey. Sometime in 1964, in fact, a big photo of us was featured in an article in the *New York Times* Sunday magazine. Bob knew I was interested in grander issues than just dances and sorority doings, so one day, he asked if I might be interested in going South during the upcoming Freedom Summer. It was the spring of 1964. These actions were taking root in many places, but St. John's proved poor soil for such things. Completely unprepared to take part, I politely demurred, telling Bob that my mother, being afraid for my safety, probably wouldn't let me go. He looked at me for a long time but said nothing, doubtless disappointed that one of the few people he thought might consider doing this

[handwritten margin note: Regrets not taking part in Freedom Summer of 1964]

would decline the invitation. I try not to regret most things in life. That one, though, I can't help but regret.

⬤◆⬤

DURING MY TIME AT St. John's University, my role as Freddy's eventual and inevitable caretaker became more evident than ever. Even before this, as I got older, home began to feel stifling. To add to the weight on my mind, when Lydia and I were children, my mother made sure to remind us that it would become our responsibility to take care of Freddy once she and Papi were no longer around, a terrible burden for young children to bear. And even as a young child, I knew it would be *me* caring for him. Given his disability, I wondered what Freddy's future would be like. The thought of having to care for him throughout my lifetime scared me.

Like Lydia, Freddy had also been a constant in my life, but in a far different way. I loved him deeply and had always been the go-to babysitter for him when he was young. He was a beautiful baby, with thick curls and huge eyes that were quite light, almost yellow. As a child, Freddy spoke only a few words, somehow making us feel confident that he would learn to speak more as he got older. Once, when he was out with Mami, she pointed to a cake in a bakery store window, telling him, "Freddy, vas a comer bizcocho mañana," reassuring him that he would be eating cake the following day, his birthday. He loved cake and was excited at the prospect, so he repeated, "Bizcocho mañana, bizcocho mañana, bizcocho mañana." That became his way of saying "cake." He knew our names, saying "Mami," "Papi," "Lydia," and "Sonia," all followed by "ya" (soon), probably because Mami had once told him that one of us would be coming home *soon*. He also said good-bye and a few other words, and he understood (and still understands) both English and Spanish. This ability made me even sadder, thinking that somewhere inside, he knew what was happening but couldn't express it.

Largely because of Freddy's condition, Mami and Papi had no social life. That he was usually confined to the home and could not go to public school changed our family life irrevocably. For several months in the 1950s, when he was about eight, they sent him to a special school in Brooklyn, spending the unheard-of sum of $150 a month, a small fortune for them in those years. There, he might have improved, but they had to take him out because the cost was prohibitive. Though my father and mother never went out very much to begin with, and then only to visit family and close friends, their lives became more constrained than ever.

After I returned from my graduate year in Spain when I was twenty-three years old and a new teacher, my gift for their twenty-fifth anniversary was dinner at Casa del Sol, a Midtown Manhattan Mexican restaurant then quite popular. I don't believe that my parents had ever gone out to dinner before, or after that. Perhaps that's why, when Mami lived in Massachusetts years later, her favorite activity was going out to dinner with us every weekend. Since I had already experienced some of the benefits of having a job, including going out to dinner, this observation troubled me greatly. It made me realize what a circumscribed life they led.

In the late 1940s, when Freddy was born, there were no support groups, no special education, no real help of any kind for children with mental retardation or autism. Mami devoted her life to Freddy, fiercely and completely, staying home with him or taking him to the bodega when she went to work with Papi. Freddy was a handful. No doubt bored, he got into all sorts of mischief. At home, when he wasn't rocking back and forth on the couch, he would unroll an entire roll of toilet paper and plug up the toilet with it or empty the bottle of dishwashing liquid into the sink. At the bodega, he would fling newborn kittens—the offspring of the cats Papi kept in the store to fend off mice—on the walls, inadvertently killing them.

With my mother already in her early fifties and Papi even older, it became clear that they couldn't continue to have Freddy at home full time. When he was about eight years old, my parents placed Freddy in an Upstate New York psychiatric hospital, but heartbroken about the conditions there, in short order they took him out. As he got older, Freddy became more difficult to control. Mami waited on him hand and foot. With all the physical and emotional care he required, though, she was always stressed and grew increasingly impatient. I remember her screaming a lot, something I know distressed her but which was understandable given the state of her nerves. I don't know how she managed as well as she did.

When Freddy was a teenager, Lydia and I encouraged our parents to try another hospital. Hoping he would finally get the help he needed, they agreed and placed him in Kings Park Psychiatric Center in Upstate New York. It too ended up as a short-lived stay. In the brief time he was there,

[margin handwritten note: *my parents did not have social life - big thing was going out to eat.*]

[margin handwritten note: *Freddy huge handful*]

the whole family would visit each Sunday, spending the entire day with him. The drive took several hours, and we'd pack the car with Freddy's favorite foods that Mami had spent many hours cooking. But seeing him in that hospital, sometimes bruised and wearing raggedy clothing—as his good clothes were often stolen shortly after we left—made my parents even more unhappy. I apparently didn't notice these things as much as they did, or I chose to focus on the few positives of institutionalization, because as inevitably happens with a disabled child in the family, particularly when little help is available, family life becomes very challenging.

I longed for relief not only for me but also for my parents and Lydia. A journal entry during that time, when Freddy was in the psychiatric center and I was in my second year of college, says a lot about how much Freddy was on my mind as I entered young adulthood. I lamented what I described as Mami's selfishness. Because her life was totally devoted to Freddy, for years this had left me and Lydia feeling abandoned, though as a mother years later and facing a similar dilemma of having to give most of my attention to one daughter over the other, I understood and could empathize with my mother.

Heartsick and disturbed by conditions at the hospital, my parents brought him home after just several weeks. Freddy remained at home until the mid-1970s, when he was in his thirties. Ultimately, we did find an appropriate living situation for Freddy when he was an adult, but that is getting ahead of the story.

Tried for years to find appropriate hospital for Freddy finally did

———◆———

I STARTED MY WORK LIFE quite young. My first job, though unpaid, was working in my father's bodega. I must have been no more than six years old the year he bought his first bodega, and I started working at the bodega shortly afterward. I put away the cans and other provisions as they were delivered, fixed the shelves, and, because of the ever-present cockroaches and mice, regularly cleaned the tops of cans with a dish towel to remove any droppings the creatures might have left. As I got older and became more adept, I waited on customers, putting my bilingual skills to good use, while weighing produce and making change.

@ age 6 Worked @ Papi's bodega also babysat

I also began to babysit at a young age. Because I was pretty good at it, I had a steady stream of customers who had heard about me from their friends. It was good to have my own money, something I got used to quickly. In one of my diaries, I wrote about how Titi had called me one day and told me, hesitantly, that she had no money. I can only imagine how difficult that was for her, a woman in her fifties who had always been able to fend for herself. I gave her fifteen dollars, probably all the money I had. But it made me realize I liked having the independence to decide when, where, how, and on whom to spend money.

At the age of sixteen and the summer before my senior year of high school, I got my first real job as a clerk at our local branch of the Brooklyn Public Library, about a mile from home. I was always ambitious, and I believe I got the position by knocking on doors. I didn't know anyone else who had a job, but somehow I knew that I would always work. And since that first job at sixteen, I always have. Taking the library job was my way of showing my parents that I could help pay for college and that, as they got older, I would take care of them. In any case, I was concerned about these things even at that age and in 1959, when most girls weren't thinking about professional careers—at least not until after they had children.

I continued to work in college. In April of that first year of college, a couple of my friends at St. John's suggested I apply to work with them in Lower Manhattan. So off I went to Merrill, Lynch, Pierce, Fenner, and Smith. In those years, this stock brokerage company was on Pine Street, one of the narrow, historic streets of Lower Manhattan in the Wall Street section of the city. Along with other college kids my age, I worked on Thursday evenings and all day Saturday. We were assigned to a room in the sub-sub-basement, a room about twelve feet high and filled floor to ceiling with wall-to-wall file-card-sized cabinets that held index cards with the names of all the company's stockholders, of which, to us, there seemed to be millions. The nearly bare room included only a big table for us to write on, stiff chairs, and ladders to climb to the upper reaches of the cabinets. Our job, insane as it sounds now, was to hand-address envelopes for the stockholders, informing them of upcoming meetings, votes, proxy votes, and other actions and deliberations. This was, of course, way before computers did these things. It was a menial and unsatisfying job but one that I was happy to have. It gave me the cash I needed to buy books, clothes, lunch, and an occasional dinner when I stayed late at St. John's for some function or another.

Because of my heavy course load in the first semester of sophomore year, I decided not to work for a few months. By the spring of that year, though, I had started looking through help-wanted ads. Having no luck, I decided during the summer between my sophomore and junior year to place an ad in the *New York Times*. I don't know how that idea occurred to me. Nor do I remember the exact wording of the ad. I imagine it was something like, "College student seeking part-time job. Enthusiastic, energetic, and bilingual in Spanish and English." It seems that by then, I had realized the benefit of being bilingual and touted it. I was also becoming more self-assured and assertive.

None of the leads for jobs worked out, but I kept looking. Finally, a few weeks into the summer, I landed a job as a salesperson at Macy's on Thirty-Fourth Street. It was a long forty-five-minute subway ride from Brooklyn, but, happy to have a job, I didn't complain. I worked on the third floor fitting room in the bathing suit department. It was exhausting. Why do women try on so many bathing suits? Do we think that one of the garments will magically get rid of all our imperfections? Whatever the reason, customers would try on five, six, or even eight bathing suits and then leave them—no hangers, bikinis without their match—in a heap on the table where I was stationed. Sometimes, I couldn't even see over the pile. I would start trying to organize them when the next flock of customers would throw their five, six, or eight bathing suits on top of the ones I was trying to place on hangers. It would take me hours to put them back correctly on hangers, then even more time to return them to where they belonged. It sometimes drove me to tears. I swore that from then on, I would never show such disregard for a fitting room attendant, and I've kept that promise. Even more than my stock brokerage work, the Macy's job taught me to have empathy for working people, especially those who deal with a public that can be callous and condescending.

After my first few months at the job, James Doyle, my supervisor, told me he was impressed with the work I was doing. He said he saw that I was a "very smart girl" who learned easily, and he decided to promote me to his office on the third floor. I loved that job, elated to have the chance to work in an office after the stressful fitting-room experience. I filed, kept the office organized, and answered the phone, learning phone etiquette and customer relations while also troubleshooting any problems that surfaced.

(margin handwritten note: She was on a Macy's Day parade float)

(margin handwritten note: graduated & left Macy's)

It was often quiet in the office. This gave me the time I needed to do homework or read. It was certainly a step up from working in the women's fitting room during bathing suit season. Mr. Doyle also happened to be the grand marshal of the Thanksgiving Day Parade, a huge honor and an enormous responsibility. He was the one who gave me the plum post on the float in the parade I mentioned earlier. Being on television that day for a few seconds was my fifteen minutes of fame when I was twenty-one years old.

I left Macy's the summer of 1965 after I graduated from St. John's University with my bachelor of science degree in elementary education. On my last day, Mr. Doyle and my co-workers gave me a beautiful leather and needlepoint flight bag from The Little Shop, the boutique department that catered to women with more expensive tastes and more disposable income than the customers in the general women's departments. A gift I cherished for many years, it was the only thing I ever had from The Little Shop.

MEANWHILE, BEFORE THAT SUMMER, my time at St. John's was coming to its inevitable end. In my last two years, I was finally focusing on what had been my dream since childhood: becoming a teacher. My junior and senior years were filled with courses in education: educational psychology; child psychology; health education; library education; methods courses in social science, reading, and math; and more courses in Spanish, which I had settled on as my minor. In those years, most universities, including St. John's, offered only a brief practicum of student teaching. So except for one semester, we had little experience in actual schools. I chose to do my student teaching during my final semester, a decision that made for a very busy several months. Besides doing my student teaching, taking an accompanying seminar and a course in Spanish literature, getting ready for graduation, and applying to graduate school, I was vice president of the IRC and president of DKD, responsibilities that kept me extremely active. That semester remains a blur.

For my student teaching, I was assigned to an elementary school in Flatbush, a short bus ride away from home. It was a solidly middle-class school whose population was almost completely White, reflecting the neighborhood at the time. All the teachers and administrators were also White. For the first half of the semester, the school assigned me to a sixth-grade class with a woman whose name I don't recall, for good reason. She was a disagreeable and bitter woman who either had stayed in the profession well beyond the time she should have left or was never meant to be a teacher in the first place. With strict rules and a no-nonsense way about her, she showed little affection for her charges. They in turn, when not terrified, seemed sad to be in her class. The only thing I remember about my time in her classroom was a dream she shared with me. This was the era when most classrooms had six rows with immovable seats, something that featured prominently in her dream.

"Sonia, last night I had a dream," she said.

"Really?" I asked, feeling somewhat awkward that she would share this fact with me.

"Yes, I dreamt that I was in my classroom and I said, 'Row one, stand up.' When they stood up, I said, 'Drop dead,' and they did. Then I said, 'Row two, stand up. Drop dead,' and they did."

She went on like this until she had covered all six rows, reveling in telling me how all the children had dropped dead. I was speechless. I never did learn anything of value from this woman.

Fortunately for me, my second student teaching experience, in the fourth-grade classroom of a woman named Mrs. Adler, was much more satisfying. She was about the same age as the sixth-grade teacher in whose classroom I had previously been placed, but the two women couldn't have been more different. Partly because of her influence, I decided that fourth grade would be my favorite grade to teach, and it was. Always a sharp dresser, Mrs. Adler was energetic, focused, and warm. She demanded the best from her students, yet in her personal interactions with them, she was easygoing and pleasant. Through the lessons she planned, the infectious excitement she had about learning, and even the way she walked around the classroom, it was clear she loved her students and her job. Something Mrs. Adler told me one day has always stayed with me: "I'd rather teach than eat!" she said, making it clear why she was a teacher.

Mrs. Adler was always on her feet, moving about the room enthusiastically, seldom using the teacher's desk that was piled with papers in the corner of the room. I don't remember her missing even one day of work, although she once came in with laryngitis. She couldn't speak, so she made a game of writing everything down on the board to communicate with the students. She wrote that she had come into work even though she couldn't speak, because she loved being in school and didn't want to miss a minute of it. Mrs. Adler inspired me to want to become a good teacher, one who would treat all children fairly, see the good in each child, and be a learner for life. I went home exhausted every day, but my desire to be a teacher was reinforced by being in her classroom.

When I graduated from St. John's University, I thought I would be a fourth-grade teacher forever, but I recently came across a May 14, 1965, article in the *Downtowner*. The piece foreshadowed my dreams of continuing beyond college, of becoming an academic even. Highlighted in the article were a number of graduating seniors, including me. Under my photo, it said, "A scholarship to the University of Madrid signifies a promising future for Sonia Cortes, president of DKD . . . After completing her education, she may teach on the college level, but who knows what will happen after a year in sunny Spain." Who knew, indeed! My year in sunny Spain turned out to be a fateful one, not only for my career but also for my personal life.

Received a scholarship to the Uni. of Madrid

Becoming an Educator

CHAPTER 6

NYU

Interlude in Spain

It was not until I left Brooklyn to study for my master's degree in Spain that I would really be away from home. Ed Peduzzi, my good friend and fellow St. John's student, was a Hispanophile and Spanish major, having spent time in Puerto Rico, where his aunt and uncle had an Italian restaurant. He was enthralled with the idea of traveling to Spanish-speaking countries, so when he found out about the program offered by New York University in Madrid for master's degree students, he immediately applied and encouraged me to do so as well.

"Come, Sunny!" he urged. "We can travel there together, live near one another, and hang out. It'll be fun!"

The idea of studying and living in Spain was electrifying. Except for a couple of trips to Puerto Rico, the furthest I had been from home was Philadelphia. Although I couldn't have put it into words at the time, life at home was suffocating. Knowing that I would eventually be counted on to take care of Freddy and perhaps even my parents within a few years, I was anxious to get away while I was still young and relatively carefree. Even though I had loved my student teaching experience—at least, the second part of it—and I was anxious to begin my teaching career, I decided to put it on hold for a year. It was one of the most fateful decisions I would make in my life.

The winter before graduation, I filled out the application for the NYU master's degree program of study in Spain, praying I would be accepted. A couple of months later, I received a letter saying I had been placed on a

[handwritten margin note: worried about having to be Freddy's care giver—drove her away to Spain]

117

waiting list and asking me to call the program office to make an appointment for an interview. On the appointed day, I was anxious as I took the
subway to Washington Square. There I met with Dr. Stamm, the director
of the program, who explained that I hadn't been immediately accepted
because I wasn't a Spanish major, having only minored in Spanish. He
wanted to make sure I could speak Spanish and that I was familiar with
some Spanish and Hispanic literature. Thanks to Señora Doyaga and my
other professors of Spanish at St. John's, I was. I made certain to mention
as many Spanish and Hispanic authors as I could cram into our conversation, regaling him with my knowledge. At the end of the interview, he
simply said, "Okay, Sonia, you're in. Congratulations!" That remains one
of the most joyful moments of my life. I floated out of Dr. Stamm's office,
imagining myself like Eliza Doolittle's would-be suitor in *My Fair Lady* as
he sang, "I have often walked down this street before, but the pavement
always stayed beneath my feet before." That day, my feet definitely floated
above the pavement as I crossed Washington Square Park to catch the
subway home.

Mami, however, was not as thrilled. When I got home and shared my
elation at having been accepted, she sank down on a chair by the kitchen
table, put her head down, and cried.

She just wasn't ready to let me go yet. I, however, was more than ready
for this next adventure. I reassured her that it was a wonderful opportunity and that I would return. But it was hard for her to lose the daughter
she most relied on, the one with *capacidad*. She loved Lydia, perhaps even
more, but it was me my mother turned to when she needed something
done. In spite of her reluctance to see me go, she rose to the challenge,
helping me prepare for the trip in every way she could. Papi didn't show
as much emotion, but I knew he too was sad. After all, we had never lived
away from home, and now both Lydia and I would be leaving.

Lydia was already twenty-three and would soon be moving to Rome.
That summer, just after I had graduated and she and two friends had finished their first year of teaching, they had traveled together to Europe.
There, she had met Franco, a handsome Italian who was an extra in the
movies. Lovesick and enamored not only of Franco but also of Rome, she
abruptly quit her teaching job and moved to Rome to be near him. Living
together was out of the question at the time, but she rented a small apart-

[handwritten margin notes:]
Sonia's mom did not want her to go

Lydia fell in love & moved to Rome

ment and found a job at a shoe store. She was living there when I went to visit at Christmastime.

This was shortly after I left for Madrid, so you can imagine what a blow it was to my parents to have us both abandon the nest at almost the same time. The thought of a house without us and with only Freddy probably gave my parents pause.

Ed and I coordinated our plans for Madrid, booking passage on what we later learned was the smallest ship allowed to cross the ocean. It was an Italian ship bound for Le Havre, France, with nine hundred students from ages sixteen to twenty-two on board. What now takes four or five days to cross the ocean took nine full days in 1965, at least on that small ship. Everyone—Mami, Papi, Lydia, Freddy, Titi, and a good number of my SJU friends—showed up at the dock on September 9, 1965, to bid us bon voyage. I was more than a little nervous, but happy to have Ed as my traveling companion. Everyone cried, including me, but what really shook me was that Papi cried. In my journal, I wrote that I felt like getting off the ship then and there, adding, "Is this 'self-realization' of mine worth all this?"

The decks on the ship were divided according to gender, some for men and others for women. The cabins were airless and stuffy, so we spent as little time in them as we could. There were four of us in my cabin, which had two double bunks—I slept on a lower bunk—with a tiny sink and an aisle separating them. Despite how crowded it was, we were fortunate, as some cabins had six, and others eight, people in each. We shared the bathrooms on our deck and had to learn to live with little privacy among people we didn't know. For most of the students, the setup was old hat, as they had gone away to college. For me—though I had shared a room with Lydia my whole life—living with strangers was a new experience. Coming from a conservative Catholic college, I was also shocked to hear some of the girls talking about their sexual exploits. One sixteen-year-old loudly explained that her mother had put her on the Pill before the trip. Birth control pills were just becoming available at the time. Most of the young people on the ship had not been as sheltered as I had been, but for us Catholics, it was a sin to even think about such things. There was lots of folk singing and guitar playing on the trip, also a new experience for me. I was more accustomed to rock 'n' roll and salsa music than to Peter, Paul, and Mary, so for me, it was truly the start of the 1960s. Despite some of the inconveniences, the trip was eye-opening and exhilarating.

The nine-day crossing felt like months. The newness of every experience made the voyage seem like a long journey. Two of our new friends, Carla and Gary, joined us as we made our way to Madrid. After docking at Le Havre, we spent about a week exploring Paris, getting rooms in cheap pensions and, for our meals, following the suggestions in *Paris on $5 a Day*. I was overwhelmed by the beauty, writing in my journal, "Paris is dazzling—can't believe a Flatbush girl is really here." I fell in love with Paris and vowed to return. Ed too was awed, saying, "Miss Cortés, do you realize we're in Paris right now? Wow!" I was the only one in our group of four who spoke any French at all, so I used my best high school French, which helped us get around. The people with whom I spoke invariably told me I spoke well; the reality—thanks to Mr. and Mrs. Fried and my other French teachers at Erasmus Hall—was that I had a good accent and knew thousands of words, but, truth be told, I couldn't put many of them together to make any sense.

Moved
to Madrid

MY FIRST IMPRESSION OF Madrid was decidedly unfavorable. Aside from the caricatures of bullfights and flamenco, I had little idea of what Spain would be like. Perhaps I expected it to look like the pictures I had seen of whitewashed houses with red tiled roofs drenched in sunlight. Although some towns like this exist in southern Spain, Madrid was nothing like it: here everyone lived in apartment buildings, and because we arrived on a rainy, gray day, everything looked dark and gloomy to me. I thought, *What have I done? How can I bear to live here for a whole year? And without my family?* At that moment, I was sure I had made the biggest mistake of my life. Instead, for many reasons, it turned out to be one of the best decisions I ever made. Getting away from home was good for me. I still lived with a family, but in Madrid, I had a great deal more freedom, fewer responsibilities, and more exploits—none of which would have been possible had I stayed put, begun my teaching career, and married one of the boys back home.

My home for the next year, on the fourth floor of an apartment building near the center of Madrid, had a somewhat worn but stately look. I boarded with a widow by the name of Doña Emilia, whom we all called Señora. Also in the household were her sixteen-year-old son and their maid, also Emilia, who took care of our every need: she cooked, served us our meals, set and cleared the table, drew our baths, and cleaned the apartment. Our only job was to make our beds and pay attention to our studies. It was clear the Señora had known better days, but as a widow, she had little recourse but to have students in her home to make ends meet. Our schedule there was set: breakfast was served at 8, lunch—when we were home—at 2:30, and dinner at 10:30 p.m. It took some getting used to eating dinner so late at night, so my apartment mates or Ed and I would often go out at 7 or 8 in the evening for tapas and wine or beer.

My classmates and I attended classes at La Universidad Complutense de Madrid, at the time the country's premier public university. On nice days, Ed would walk over from his apartment about a block away, and we would walk the mile or so to the university. Most of our classes were held in the Facultad de Filología, the language department, whose building was one of the last bus stops on campus. We would head to the café in the basement for coffee or even wine and tapas, something that would have been unimaginable not only at St. John's but at any other university in the States. Our professors were the regular faculty members in the department, but the classes were just for our cohort and the curriculum was vastly more interesting and demanding than our coursework at St. John's. Although I hadn't really gone to Spain for the literature but rather for the adventure, I became a lover of literature nevertheless. It became an area on which I focused later in my professional career, studying Puerto Rican children's literature and, later, language and literacy in general.

Studying in Madrid was thrilling and frightening at the same time. Even though Spain was still in the grips of the Franco era, a thirty-year fascist dictatorship that would last another ten years, my time there was nonetheless a liberating experience for me. The police presence and the ever-visible Guardia Civil, the dreaded police with the tricornered hats, made Madrid a very safe city, as was all of Spain during those repressive times.

I received a scholarship from New York University and had taken out a loan for eighteen hundred dollars—a huge sum at the time—to help offset the rest of the cost of the program. Mami and Papi always sent me something

She realized how her education distanced her from family in experience

as well. Mami wrote often. Papi, with his limited education, never wrote, but he always sent his love. Because they had never been out of the country except to Puerto Rico, which is part of the same US postal system, Mami once sent a bunch of airmail stamps, saying that Papi had bought them so I wouldn't have to spend my money on stamps. What he didn't realize was that US postage stamps were useless in Spain. This was another indication to me that my education had further distanced me, not in affection but in experience, from them. I sent the stamps back, telling my parents that now they would have lots of stamps to keep writing to me.

Because I didn't want to depend on them for money, I meanwhile looked for a part-time job. A sign on the street advertising a position as a tutor for a Spanish couple drew my attention. I called immediately. The couple, Señor and Señora Loperena, lived just around the corner from me and wanted to learn English because their daughter was about to marry an American. I went to their apartment every day for several months. They were a delightful pair and eager to learn English, and the job helped to ease my financial burden.

An unforeseen consequence of going to Spain, ironic as it may seem, was that I became comfortable with, and even proud of, my Puerto Rican identity, something that had happened neither in Brooklyn nor in Puerto Rico. My Spanish was passable but not great; it was what I've called "kitchen Spanish," the kind of Spanish a person uses at home, that is, the *pasa la mantequilla* and *¿es la hora de comer?* level of Spanish. By the time I was a teenager, I spoke mostly English with my parents and other family members. The only time I spoke Spanish was in my Spanish courses at the university. The saving grace was that I was one of the few Latinas in the graduate program, so my Spanish was quite a bit better than most of the others. Other students had learned the rules of grammar and might have read more literature, but I had the intuitive language of a native speaker. That helped a lot.

I was pleased that I had little trouble getting around Madrid, that most Madrileños were friendly and eager to help, and, indeed, that from the beginning, I was accepted very nearly as a compatriot. I remember clearly at least one person who, upon finding out I was Puerto Rican, said,

"Oh, then you're one of us!" At the time, many Spaniards saw Americans as superficial and American girls as fast (remember, this was during the Franco era, when both sex and politics were forbidden and the Catholic Church reigned supreme). There were downsides to being Puerto Rican, too: being from the *madre patria*, many Spaniards held patronizing attitudes toward their former colonists. In general, though, I found people genuinely interested in me *as a Puerto Rican*. This was a first for me.

My studies included more than coursework. While in Spain, my friends and I took every opportunity to travel around the country and beyond. By this time, I had become incredibly homesick, longing for the familiarity and warmth of the holidays at home. So, that Christmas, Ed and I, accompanied by two other friends, decided to travel to Rome. Ed and the others stayed in a pension, and I stayed with Lydia in her apartment. She helped me get over that bout of homesickness. She also took us sightseeing. We were lucky because she had already become quite fluent in Italian, showing us the sights almost like a native.

Whenever we had a vacation or a *puente* (the Spanish word for "bridge" is also, appropriately, a term for a long weekend), Ed and I, along with a revolving cast of friends, traveled to other places in Spain, including Sevilla, Córdoba, and Granada in the south, and to cities closer to Madrid such as Segovia, with its two-thousand-year-old (and, at the time, still operative) aqueduct, and Toledo, with its gorgeous architecture and fascinating history. We even managed to go to neighboring Portugal on a *puente*.

By March, with very limited funds and an increasing school workload that left little time for travel, I still had an insatiable desire to see everything I could before returning home. In my remaining time in Spain, I decided to take one-day trips close to Madrid. Susan, one of my housemates and a junior in the NYU program, joined me on one of those short trips. Together, we decided we would travel to Cuenca, a city about a hundred miles east of Madrid, on Saturday, March 19, 1966. We selected Cuenca even though we knew nothing about it, because we hadn't been there before. Also, we could get there and back in a day. It turned out to be a fateful decision.

Little did we know that March 19, St. Joseph's Day, was a national holiday that at the time was also celebrated as Father's Day in Spain. In addition to the usual ways of celebrating the holiday, in Valencia, a coastal city on the east, the day is also known as Las Fallas. On that day, elaborate wooden structures are built and then burned in spectacular fires. Cuenca is situated halfway between Madrid and Valencia. As a result, the trains were very busy that day. Susan and I bought the remaining two seats on the train, and we almost didn't make it. We rushed into the train car and took our seats. Within a moment or two, a young man walked over with his ticket in hand.

"Excuse me, señorita, but you're sitting in my seat," he said, showing me his ticket.

I took out my ticket, which had the same seat assignment, and showing it to him, I said, "No, I think this is my seat."

"No se preocupe" ("Don't worry yourself"), he assured me. "I'll go find someone who can help figure this out." He came back a little later with a new seat assignment and sat in front of me for the duration of the trip.

When we got off the train, Susan and I quickly made our way to the local tourist office. From previous excursions, we had learned that tourist offices were the best places to get information, maps, posters, and advice. Each town has such an office, which is usually well advertised. Walking the three or four blocks to the tourist office, we were disheartened when we arrived to see that it was closed. We should, of course, have known: it was Father's Day, and everything was closed for the holiday. Because we had gotten up at dawn, Susan and I were exhausted. And even though it was a gorgeous, sunny day, it was also blustery and cold. We stood there, freezing, wondering what to do, when the young man from the train happened along.

"You're the señoritas from the train, aren't you?" he asked innocently. "You're looking a little lost. Can I help out?"

He went on to offer his assistance, saying that even though he was on his way to visit his aunt down the street, he'd be happy to serve as our guide for the day.

A seasoned New Yorker, I had learned not to trust strangers. "I don't know about this guy," I said to Susan.

Susan, a native of Ohio, was much more trusting than I was. "Oh, come on, Sonia," she said. "What can happen? Besides, it's cold, we're hungry, and he's cute."

I reluctantly agreed to have this handsome stranger accompany us for the day.

And that is how I met Angel Nieto, the love of my life, my best friend, my first and only boyfriend, and my husband of forty-eight years. Anyone who knows Angel, shy and reserved as he is, realizes it must have taken tremendous effort on his part to offer us strangers his company. That we were assigned the same seat on the train has always seemed like destiny to me.

Met Angel— her husband

he followed her oboe the train

It was only after we were married—a scant nine months later—that Angel confessed he didn't just happen to be walking down the street that day. He had *not* been going to pay a visit to his aunt, but had actually followed us from the train. I had piqued his interest.

We spent a magical day together, Susan, Angel, and I, exploring all of Cuenca on foot. Cuenca is a gorgeous city whose *casco*, or historic center, includes an iconic cathedral; narrow, winding streets (some impassable by car because they have steps); stunning views of the new part of the city and surroundings; and quaint houses painted a bouquet of colors, from ochre to pumpkin to dark pink and lilac. There are also sixteenth-century houses called Las Casa Colgadas (the Hanging Houses) that literally appear to be hanging in midair but are built into the stones. When we tired of walking, Angel took us *de tapas*, going from bar to bar to have a glass of wine and a bit of an appetizer before we made our way back home to his parents' house for a sumptuous lunch. Even though he was an impoverished student (which we didn't know), he didn't let us spend even one peseta all day.

When he brought us back to the train station that evening, Angel tried to convince us that we should stay the night at his parents' house—that a mere day didn't do justice to his beautiful city. He was home for Father's Day and could accompany us back to Madrid, where he too lived, on the following day. Knowing we had a slew of work to do, we demurred but not before Angel gave us his phone number in Madrid, insisting we call him for anything we might need. In 1966, accepting a young man's phone number was, I had been taught, unseemly, so I instead gave him the Señora's phone number, which he quickly wrote down. He then disappeared into the little store at the station, returning a couple of minutes later with a small bottle of Resoli, the city's home-grown liqueur, for each of us. To this day, that little bottle (by now empty, of course) sits on my kitchen window sill.

Looking out the window as we left the station, I thought, *I think I fell in love today.*

———◆———

THINGS MOVED QUICKLY AFTER THAT. Within days, we started dating. Before two weeks were up, we had professed our "I love you" to one another. I was captivated by Angel's shyness and his looks, of course, but also by his intelligence, the respect and care with which he treated me, and his generosity, maturity, and kindness to everyone he met. As I got to know him better, I was also impressed with his courage, how much he knew about the world, his passion for what was right and just, his disdain for pettiness and arrogance, his rejection of cruelty of all kinds. These are the qualities that have always defined Angel and have endeared him to me from the beginning.

We spent a glorious spring being in crazy love, the kind of love that takes your breath away, where you can't think of anything else. Could anyone in the world have ever felt this passionate, consuming love? I didn't think so at the time, and as much as Angel—always more realistic than I—tried to disabuse me of this idea, I couldn't believe that ours was a typical experience. We dated every day I had left in Spain. I went to classes, trying to concentrate on my studies, but it was becoming more difficult with the distraction of love in the way. Angel worked from 8 a.m. to 2 p.m. at the Iberia Airlines offices. From 3 to 7 p.m., he attended classes at the Ministry of Tourism. He would pick me up afterward, and since we had no place of our own and very little money, we'd make our way by bus or metro to an outdoor café or some other public place. More often, though, we'd pick up a bottle of wine, some cheese and olives, and a crusty loaf of bread and go to a public park, where we'd feast on these simple pleasures.

Angel made me feel good about myself in many ways, including my being Puerto Rican. He also became my political and cultural mentor. Always politically aware (his father had sided with those who opposed Franco's fascist insurrection that led to the Spanish Civil War), he defined himself as an anarchist, but really, he was closer to what I'd call a democratic socialist: he believed in collaboration and solidarity with others, ideals that are still among his major values. He was also incredibly well read and smart, having consumed every book in his father's extensive library. We'd spend hours talking about politics, art, literature, everything. His political ideas began to influence me as soon as we met and have continued to do so to this day.

The months from late March to late June were a whirlwind of love and adventure, falling in love with Angel and with Spain, and a growing boredom with school. In late June, I reluctantly left for what was supposed to be a six-week trip through Europe with my friend Carol Ahrens, something we had arranged before I had met Angel. It was hard for me to leave, not because I didn't want to go; in fact, I was looking forward to seeing Carol. But the love bug had done a good job on me, and I wanted nothing but to be with Angel. By this time, Carol's young marriage was in trouble (she and Harry had married at twenty-one, as was typical for our classmates at SJU) and she wanted some time away to think about the future. I went on the trip willingly, of course, wanting to explore more of Europe, but I soon realized I was miserable without Angel. I put a little photo of him on my alarm clock and stared longingly at it every night. Carol, meanwhile, was also missing Harry. So, after visiting Paris, Luxembourg, Rome—where we stayed with Lydia—and Athens, we decided to shorten our trip, forgoing Germany and England. Returning home a couple of weeks earlier than anticipated, I had sent Angel a postcard with the news. He surprised me when I got off the train at Atocha, Madrid's major train station, coming up from behind to embrace me and hand me a little bouquet of flowers. I remember our reunion still as one of the happiest moments of my life.

It was now the end of July. Anxious to stretch my time in Madrid as much as possible, I decided to stay an extra month. I secured a flight to New York on September 3, just a few days before I was to begin my career as a teacher. Angel and I spent every moment we could together, going to our old haunts, visiting his family in Cuenca one last time, and making plans to have him visit me in New York in the fall. I was twenty-two years old, soon to turn twenty-three. He was twenty-six.

CHAPTER 7

JHS 178

The First Year of Teaching

THE ADJUSTMENT BACK HOME was hard. After Madrid, Brooklyn seemed boring and dreary. Where were the outdoor cafés? The tapas? The beautiful wide boulevards and the charming narrow streets? I even missed hearing Castilian Spanish, different from my Puerto Rican Spanish but an accent to which I had become accustomed and even picked up for a time. Whereas I had been terribly homesick when I first arrived in Madrid a year earlier, I was now terribly homesick for Spain. I had a feeling I didn't really belong anywhere and perhaps never would.

Seeing Mami and Papi was, of course, wonderful. I had missed them a great deal. They couldn't have been happier to have me home, especially since Lydia was now living in Rome to be near her paramour and there was no telling when she would return. Just turned sixty-five, Papi retired later that year and could then help out at home with Freddy, who was becoming more difficult to handle, though my presence helped. By the time I returned home to begin my teaching career, my identity as a New York–born Puerto Rican, what later became known as a Nuyorican, had been strengthened. I also resumed speaking only Spanish with my parents.

Angel came to visit for a couple of weeks in November. Although I was working, we managed, by taking advantage of a couple of Jewish holidays and Veterans Day, to squeeze in lots of time to explore New York City and reignite our relationship. I took him to see the usual sights—Times Square, the Empire State Building, Rockefeller Center, St. Patrick's Cathedral, Greenwich Village, Wall Street, the Metropolitan Museum of Art, and the Museum of Modern Art. Since the tallest building in Madrid was then just about twelve stories high, Angel, like a typical tourist, couldn't stop staring up at the skyscrapers. One day, we had a romantic walk across the Brooklyn Bridge in the rain. It was a magical time. On the few days I worked during his visit, Papi brought Angel to the *bodega* to help out. I think that's when Papi fell in love with Angel too.

———————◆◆◆◆———————

It was now time to start the career I had been dreaming about for so many years. I had looked forward eagerly to teaching fourth grade, the same grade for which I had done my student teaching when I was in Mrs. Adler's class a year earlier. As it turned out, my first job was at JHS 178 in the Ocean Hill–Brownsville community of Brooklyn, teaching English, ESL, Spanish, and French to sixth through eighth graders. At the time, teachers had no choice but to go where they were assigned by the New York City Board of Education. Though junior high was the last place I thought I'd end up—after all, I had been trained as an elementary school teacher for grades 1 through 6—there was a shortage of teachers. And since JHS 178 had a sixth grade, technically it was permissible for the board to place me there. I was assigned to the school, along with a half dozen or so other elementary-trained teachers and about thirty other new teachers who had been trained to work at the junior high level.

During my first few years of teaching, seeking inspiration and advice, I read all the education books I could get my hands on. There was no shortage of books on public education in those years. Urban education had become a hot topic. It was the 1960s, after all, and more time and attention were being paid to issues of justice and equality, including in urban public education. The civil rights movement was now in full swing. The nightly news featured stories of dilapidated schools where poor Black and Brown children were cheated out of a decent education, and of the ever-present conflicts between the United Federation of Teachers (UFT) and community groups, something I was to experience firsthand during my first years in the classroom. I read some of these books before I started teaching, but most of them after I started. All of them helped me understand my own role as a teacher differently from my previous, idealized notions about teaching. I began to understand that teaching was not just about personal fulfillment—mine or my students'—and not just about sharing exciting lessons and discoveries. It was also about commitment, service, courage, and love.

I found Bel Kaufman's book *Up the Down Staircase* (1965) both hilarious and bizarrely realistic. Herbert Kohl's *36 Children* (1966), documenting his first year as a teacher in a school in Harlem, paralleled my own experience in Ocean Hill–Brownsville, and Jonathan Kozol's *Death at an Early Age* (1965) painted a picture not too different from JHS 178. Years later, I would meet both Herb and Jonathan, and I now consider them not just revered authors but also colleagues and friends in the same struggle. Their insights and compassion for children denied a decent education because of bureaucracy, racism, and neglect have been inspirations to my own work.

The one saving grace of being assigned to JHS 178 was that as serendipitous as it was in a system with almost a thousand schools, my friend Carol Ahrens (whom I had met on my first day at St. John's, who was my best friend through my four years there, and with whom I had traveled in Spain) and I were assigned to the same school. Besides sharing some of the same books, we counted on one another as sounding boards, neophytes, friends, colleagues, and confidantes that first year. We would commiserate as we sat in her classroom or mine for lunch, as we had given up on the teachers' lounge, an oppressively negative place, almost as soon as the school year began.

The school year started just a few days after I returned from Spain. To say that the first year of teaching was difficult is an understatement. Adjusting to the United States after being away for a year, having to live at home again—in spite of being happy to be reunited with Mami and Papi—and living without seeing Angel every day, not to mention starting my profession as a teacher: all these seemed, at the time, insurmountable challenges. I started having a recurring dream: I would climb some very steep stairs, barely able to keep up. Every time I climbed a step, more steps appeared; it was relentless, and I could never reach the top.

School started for new teachers a couple of days before it started for students, a day before the returning teachers came back. I remember the first day well. After going over the expectations for new teachers (no staying after school—it was dangerous; no going above the first floor until classes started, for the same reason; clocking in and out every day; getting all paperwork in on time; having lesson plans ready for inspection every Monday; and so forth), Mr. Feld, our assistant principal, told us we would be joining the returning teachers, thirty-five in all, the following day. This meant that *half* the teachers were new, a situation he told us was typical of the turnover at JHS 178. I later found out that it was also typical of many other schools in poor communities. It still is.

As I had expected, I was the only Puerto Rican teacher—in fact, the only Latina. This didn't surprise me at all as I myself had never met a Puerto Rican teacher. I was something of a puzzle for my colleagues: they also had never met a Puerto Rican teacher before. Acquainted only with Puerto Ricans who lived in poverty, they appeared surprised to meet an educated and by now middle-class Puerto Rican, one returning from Spain with a master's degree. They didn't know what to make of me. They must have wondered, *Is she Puerto Rican? She doesn't look it. Is she Spanish? How exotic!*

We were assigned our classes that first day. Besides reading, Spanish, and French, I was also assigned to teach the so-called NE classes. NE stood for non-English, meaning students who didn't yet speak English. As the NE teacher, I was labeled NE right along with my students. That I would be teaching beginning Spanish was a logical assignment. Teaching French was a stretch, considering I hadn't taken a French class since high school. Had I been teaching in a middle-class school, the situation would never have been tolerated. But I was the only person in the school who could remotely be expected to teach that language, so whenever she visited, the district supervisor of French would observe me, quietly correcting my grammatical and spelling errors.

As new teachers, we had our work cut out for us. Ocean Hill–Brownsville sounds far fancier than it is. Then, as now, it was an impoverished community, not in spirit or culture but in resources and infrastructure. Most of the housing consisted of either decaying tenement buildings or newer but rapidly dilapidating projects. Nearly all the residents were African American and Puerto Rican, the unemployment rate was sky high, and there were few activities for young people in the community. In spite of these problems, a newfound optimism was apparent as the political

[handwritten margin note: She taught reading Spanish French "NE" classes "non English"]

activism of the 1960s reached Brooklyn and the schools. Parents and other community activists were waking up, and among their demands was a better education for their children. Given the deteriorating condition of many public schools, the dismal failure rate of students, the irrelevant curriculum, and a largely unprepared, overwhelmingly White teaching staff that was often uninterested in teaching these children, the community's anger and demands were reasonable. Instead of decaying schools, disinterested teachers, and a dumbed-down course of study, community leaders demanded newer schools, caring teachers, courses that were more challenging, and what would many years later be called a *culturally relevant curriculum*, a field in which I would specialize decades later.

Given the disillusionment following the results of 1950s and 1960s desegregation efforts—demands that led instead to more White flight and increasingly segregated schools throughout the nation—the community was now insisting on more local control of the schools, more Black and Hispanic administrators and teachers. Rather than "Desegregation Now!" the new rallying cry was "Community Control!" Having left St. John's (a conservative Catholic university on the brink of change) in 1965 and Spain (still in the grips of fascism), a year later, I was unprepared for the activism of 1966. This was the political context in which I began my teaching career.

[handwritten margin note: Began teaching career during politically active time.]

I WAS ASSIGNED A CLASSROOM on the second floor of the building. Children were assigned to classes presumably on the basis of their ability, which in those days was most likely defined by a combination of previous grades, teachers' recommendations, and perhaps IQ tests, then routinely used to classify students. Besides two small ESL and reading groups, I also taught language classes to several classes twice a week, specifically, 6-1, 6-2, 6-3, 6-12, 6-13, 7-1, 7-2, and 8-1. Tracking was especially crass in those days, with little room for doubt about students' placements. The feeling was that intelligence was fixed, something that you were born with and that never changed. Tracking continues to this day, in some ways even more crudely, but at least nowadays, that assumption is under question. It took Jeannie Oakes's brilliant 1985 research on tracking, years after I started teaching, to demonstrate that tracking was inequitable, based as often on social class and race as it was on intelligence and merit. Once assigned a particular track, a student faced enormous odds to get out.

Assigned to the top three sections in their respective grades, most of my students were considered "smart." Foreign language classes were generally reserved for "smart" students, because students who were unable to keep up with their own regular subjects of reading, writing, science, math, and social studies supposedly would have a hard time keeping up with a new language as well. But that year, administrators had decided to launch an experiment of sorts. They assigned some of the "slowest" students to study Spanish. That's why I was also teaching Spanish to Class 6-13. This group became one of my favorites that year. The students seemed genuinely grateful to be learning Spanish, a privilege previously denied them. They liked saying and practicing the new words and writing them in their notebooks. The children of Class 6-13 were also among the best-behaved I taught that year.

In general, though, it was an agonizingly difficult year, especially the first few months. Like many new teachers, I felt unprepared to teach. This was a new feeling for me. At St. John's and during my student teaching, I felt ready and eager to tackle teaching. Since the age of five or so, I had wanted to be a teacher, always certain I would be good at it. Whatever self-assurance I had now quickly dissipated: I became uncertain of my ability to teach the range of subjects I was assigned, unsure of my skill to motivate students, and unprepared for the many discipline issues, ranging from plain old sassiness to outright violence. This situation was particularly hard for me to swallow because, as a Puerto Rican who had grown up in what I had thought were similar circumstances, I had always assumed that I would immediately and instinctively be able to reach my students, that I would be a big hit right from the start. This certainly is not what happened, at least not at first.

Those first few months on the job even made me question my lifelong desire to become a teacher. What most distressed me when I started teaching was that I became unrecognizable to myself. I was not at all the teacher I had envisioned myself to be. I always thought I would be a patient, loving, self-confident, and accomplished teacher. Instead, I found myself screaming all the time, even losing my voice a few weeks after starting the

[handwritten margin note: Foreign language usually reserved for smart students]

school year. I regularly sent students to the assistant principal's office for their behavior, because of my inability to control it. I could not even turn my back on my students without a minor rebellion. How was this possible? *I had been one of those students*, I thought. I knew what their lives were like. But as I was to find out, this was not really the case.

It took me some time to realize that the environment in which my students lived was quite different from what mine had been. Drugs were now rampant in urban areas, and the level of inequality seemed worse. There were more family stressors than even a couple of decades before. The unbridled optimism and enthusiasm of immigrants like my parents were not as visible among newer immigrants from Puerto Rico and other parts of the world, or among African Americans, whose earlier hopes ignited by the civil rights movement for the promised equal education for their children had been dashed. The kinds of jobs available to unskilled workers like my parents were becoming less abundant, as was affordable housing in New York City. Single mothers were becoming a more prevalent phenomenon, placing added emotional and financial strain on struggling families. This was not at all what I had experienced. My family certainly had not lived in luxury: a car, television set, or telephone was not even introduced in our lives until we had moved out of Williamsburg. But we never went hungry. Our poverty had been manageable, primarily because ours was a stable family with a wide support network. Many of my students, on the other hand, had more complicated childhoods, both financially and emotionally, than mine had been.

I HAVE VIVID MEMORIES OF that first year. Discipline problems were, to my mind, epic. Besides frequent fights between students, cursing in the halls, disrespect, and inattention, there were the kinds of behavior for which my courses at St. John's had not prepared me. Students talked back or ignored me. Many of the lessons I meticulously planned were a flop. Spitballs were common, student fights ubiquitous. It wasn't unusual for students to simply walk out of class when they felt like it. One day, a student decided to hang out the second-story window, nearly falling out. Another time, Rodney, a student in my 6-12 class, in a fit of anger, cracked a desk in half with a karate chop. He became so incensed when he was suspended after

I sent him to the assistant principal's office that he kicked in my door at the end of the school day, shouting, "Fuck you, teacher! I'm gonna get you after school!" I was grateful that Papi picked me up after school that day, so I never got to see if Rodney would be true to his word.

In spite of having a difficult year, I tried not to pin things on the students, at least not completely. That's why I found the talk in the teachers' room so intolerable. There always seemed to be a lot of bitching and moaning, with some teachers saying incredibly negative things about the kids. "They're really animals today!" or "These kids will end up pregnant or in jail." One teacher I took to calling Madame Defarge, the fictional character in Charles Dickens's *Tale of Two Cities*, because she was always knitting as she calmly made the most venomous comments about the students. One day, no doubt believing she was being constructive, she said, "You know, these kids are good with their hands, but not with their heads." Ironically, she said this as she was working with her hands.

Since I didn't yet drive—a skill Angel taught me after we moved to Massachusetts—I usually took the subway to work. Occasionally, I got a ride from a group of other teachers, a practice I soon discontinued because I found the conversation in the car overly cynical. Most of the talk was as disconcerting as the talk in the teachers' room: it was either about the results of the stock market the previous day or about how uncivilized the kids were. Although I too was frustrated, the racism in their comments was conspicuous. As the only Puerto Rican teacher and one of a handful of teachers of color in the school, I thought, *They could be talking about me or my sister or my cousins.*

What was I to make of such statements? Besides convincing me to stay clear of the teachers' room, the negative comments also soured me on the motives of some who had entered the profession. *How could they have decided to become teachers*, I thought, *if all they can do is say hateful things about the kids?*

There are still teachers who blame their kids, the community, and the culture for all the problems having to do with education today, but there's more awareness about what is acceptable to say, or "politically correct," if you will, so that such comments are now generally more tempered. And while teacher education courses, textbooks, and the media have dramatically improved our understanding of cultural differences and diversity in the past forty years, and the number of educators of color has increased as well, we still have much room for improvement.

I would often resolve to go into school with high hopes and a smile on my face. By the end of the school day, I would drag myself home and start weeping from frustration and discouragement. But in truth, another part of what made that first year so difficult was that I missed Angel. Once home, I would write my daily letter to him—this was long before email— then settle down to plan my lessons for the following day. Every evening after dinner, I would listen to two records Angel had given me before I left Spain, *El Concierto de Aranjuez* and Chopin's Second Piano Concerto, and cry.

Sprinkled among the frustrating times in the school year were also some laugh-out-loud moments, some endearing incidents, a few real breakthroughs, and, in the end, the firm conviction that I had indeed made the right career choice: that I was meant to be a teacher. For one thing, I got to see a couple of phenomenal teachers in action, and I learned a lot from them. Despite the poverty, the growing tension in the school—a tension that grew exponentially the following year—and other difficult conditions, some teachers seemed to work magic. Carol and I often wondered why Mr. Scott, an African American colleague who taught in the same corridor as ours, had absolutely no discipline problems. Students in his classes sat ramrod straight and paid attention, while in our classes, they couldn't even sit still in their seats. You could hear a pin drop when you walked by his class, with all students engaged and enthusiastic. Miss Roberts, another new teacher, also African American, was as frustrated as I was. Like me, she thought the students would automatically relate to her. As in my case, that would take some time.

Besides Mr. Scott, there was Mr. Seidman, a social studies teacher. Noticing that I was struggling, he invited me into his eighth-grade history class. This was Class 8-13, supposedly the most intellectually challenged class among all eighth graders. When I stepped into his classroom, I was astonished to see the class, all boys, about fourteen or fifteen of them, engaged in a sophisticated Socratic conversation about American history. Unlike Mr. Scott's class, where all the students sat up straight in their seats, listening quietly, in Mr. Seidman's class, the students were much less formal, sitting on chairs or desks, talking without raising their hands, and

[handwritten margin note: She was impressed by some teachers ability to teach]

These teachers loved their subject and had a true belief in children

equally engrossed in the topic at hand. These two teachers demonstrated excellence in quite different ways, but what they had in common was a belief in their students, a love of the subject matter they taught, and a refusal to accept the prevailing stereotypes about the young people they taught. These teachers gave me hope that I might someday become a good teacher.

Change is always slow to come to schools. When it does come, it's usually in the form of mandates and regulations. No such mandates about diversity were sent from the New York City Board of Education to its city teachers. In fact, the first I even heard mention of African Americans—who surpassed Puerto Ricans in New York City schools in numbers in those years—came in *Africa in the Curriculum*, a book by Beryle Banfield (1968). She was a curriculum specialist at the New York City Board of Education and, in 1966, a founder of the trailblazing Council on Interracial Books for Children, an organization for which years later I was proud to write. For a young teacher, Banfield's book was like a breath of fresh air. No similar book was created about Puerto Ricans or Latinos while I was a student in the New York City schools. Around this time, it began to dawn on me that much of the curriculum was irrelevant to the students' lives.

Sonia realized that much of the curriculum was irrelevant to the children's lives

This revelation was well before the words *multicultural education* were ever spoken or written about, but several incidents made me realize that students had a wealth of experiences that were not being tapped into and that I could use in my teaching. For example, one day, I asked the students in one of my classes what they'd be eating for Thanksgiving. They gave all the expected answers: turkey, gravy, mashed potatoes, stuffing, and so on. When I mentioned that at my house, we were having some of those foods, along with rice, beans, and *pernil*, some of the Puerto Rican children stared at me in disbelief.

Once she opened up to her children about her Latin heritage there was change

"*You* eat those foods?" one child asked incredulously.

"Sure," I said, "I'm Puerto Rican, like you."

That moment proved to be a step forward in my relating to my students. At that point, some of the other children, both Puerto Rican and African American, began to open up about what they would *really* be eating on Thanksgiving: tostones, arroz con gandules, collard greens, okra, Southern-style macaroni and cheese, among other things. It was one of my most successful lessons up to that point.

Another memorable moment occurred a couple of months into the school year. A monumental spitball and paper airplane fight had begun at the start of class and lasted the entire period. The floor, in the end, was littered with paper from wall to wall. When class ended, one of the students, a little slip of a boy named Terrance, one of those antsy kids who couldn't sit still, came over to me. "Miss Cortés," he said, "would you like me to clean up the floor?" Although I had been furious and upset by the students' antics, and Terrance had been a willing participant in the melee, his gesture of kindness and humanity shook me to my core. I began to cry. Probably embarrassed for me, Terrance said, "Oh, don't cry, Miss Cortés. They don't mean it."

"They don't mean it"

"They don't mean it." Four simple words. I knew then that I wasn't seeing students at their best. Like all teachers, I needed to find ways to help my students tap into their better selves. This was probably the most important lesson I learned that year, one that stayed with me throughout my teaching and teacher education career.

THOUGH ALL MY CLASSES were difficult, my most challenging group that year was Class 6-12. I found the children unruly and disrespectful; they seemed unable to sit still long enough for me to teach even one simple lesson. I remember one student, Kyla, calling me "Miss Kotex" rather than Miss Cortés, and everyone bursting into laughter.

Our assistant principal, Mr. Feld, had received multiple complaints about Class 6-12. It wasn't just me, a neophyte teacher, who was having problems with them. A couple of months after the school year began, and because of their many disruptions, Mr. Feld decided to shadow the class for an entire day, sitting in the back of every class the group went to, to figure out what was happening. Mr. Feld was the school's major disciplinarian, and the kids were afraid of him. As a result, on that day, they were a model class. I was shocked when I saw them approach my classroom: rather than a noisy ragtag group of kids, they marched into the classroom single file, quietly took their seats, and brought out their notebooks. That day was the first time I was able to get through an entire reading lesson with them. Even more surprising, the children seemed really to enjoy it. The experience gave me an inkling of the teacher I could be; it gave me hope. I went home elated. I think it also gave the students an idea of who they could be.

As new teachers, we were supposed to be observed several times during the first three years, the years of our "probation." To be efficient and so that the day wouldn't be a total loss in terms of his other responsibilities, Mr. Feld used the occasion to formally observe all the teachers who taught Class 6-12 that day. We teachers had not been given prior notice of his visit; luckily for me, I prepared my classes every day, even though I usually couldn't get through half my lesson plan. A week after Mr. Feld's visit, on November 30, 1966, I found his observation report in my school mailbox. "I was very impressed with your teaching methods," it began. Further on, he wrote about the "fine class atmosphere," noting, "Your remarks such as 'John, try to read the story; we'll help you' were commendable." He added a couple of minor suggestions, but the final sentence was what captured my attention and filled me with joy: "I'm sure you will become a Master Teacher." When I read these words, they brought tears to my eyes. That single sentence kept me going for the rest of the year.

I was thrilled with the observation. In some ways, though, it made me feel like a fraud. How could Mr. Feld, I wondered, *know* I would be a master teacher? I had only begun my teaching career two months earlier, and to say those two months were marked by disappointment and frustration would be an understatement. It made me wonder, too, about the other thirty-five new teachers in the school: Were they feeling as vulnerable as I was? Did they have any moments of redemption amid the unrelenting harshness of the situation in which we were working? Still, I figured I was one of the lucky ones because Mr. Feld had decided to shadow Class 6-12 on that particular day. This simple act changed my year, my future as a teacher, and, in reality, my life. It also taught me how serendipitous life can be. Because of the supportive words of one kind individual, I had regained hope. I was far from being a master teacher, but holding out this possibility, Mr. Feld had given me a picture of my still-possible future self.

For me, the most important statement on that first observation, aside from the "Master Teacher" comment, was this remark: "A feeling of warmth and congeniality prevailed." Yes! This was exactly what I had always wanted to be, a warm and caring teacher. From the beginning, I knew instinctively that far more important than the content I taught, and for the content to make sense, I had to have authentic relationships with students. The first couple of months in the classroom, I was disheartened that it was not happening. Rather than affection and concern for my students, I had felt mostly frustration and anger. The ability of one unplanned observation to make such a difference made me realize the importance of school leaders with faith in their teachers: just as students need to be reminded, from time to time, of their better selves, so do teachers.

The students in Class 6-12 never really went back to their old ways. If not a model class, they at least became a fairly respectful and engaged group of students. I actually looked forward to seeing them every day. I figured out who was who, and I got to know more about them. As I became more comfortable with them, they also became more comfortable with me. Kyla of "Miss Kotex" fame became one of my favorites. Feisty and fresh, she was also smart. As it turned out, she just needed attention. She also became one of my greatest supporters and, as a natural leader, was an enforcer of good behavior among her peers.

One day in particular stands out in my mind. I had to write something on the board, and seeing that there was no chalk in the room, I told the students I was going next door to borrow some from another teacher. This was something I would never have dreamed of doing before Mr. Feld's fateful visit. I returned a couple of minutes later to a silent classroom, all twenty-five students working intently. Moved and overjoyed, I asked them to stop working so we could talk. I told them how proud of them I was and asked what had changed from a few weeks earlier, when bedlam would have prevailed. "Miss Cortés," Kyla spoke up, "the thing is, you respect us. And if you respect us, we respect you." As simple as that.

Another breakthrough: Rodney, the boy who had kicked in my classroom door after being suspended for breaking a desk, became another of my favorites. Clearly, he was a child living in difficult conditions, with multiple challenges, both learning and emotional. But underneath that hard exterior, he was also sweet and loving. For example, since I often arrived at school about an hour early anyway, I had started an open-door policy a few months into my teaching: students could come up to my room before school to do homework, talk, or just hang out. (This was, of course, completely against school policy, something administrators would have frowned upon had they found out.) Rodney became one of the regulars. Right before the Christmas break, he gave me a toiletry set with cologne, talcum powder, and body lotion with a note that said, "To Miss Cortés, by Rodney." My guess is that he couldn't spell "from." Another student later told me Rodney had stolen the gift from the corner pharmacy.

Despite how incredibly difficult that first year was, I learned many valuable lessons that have stayed with me. I learned to love my students, of course. Even more to the point, I learned to respect and understand them. There are plenty of teachers who love their students yet may not believe in them or understand who they are. Both sensibilities are needed.

I learned the significance of having colleagues and administrators who support you, not just when things are going well but especially when they're not. New teachers need consistent mentoring, a pat on the back when they're doing well and a caring critique when they still have a lot to learn. I was fortunate to have some of these things in that first job.

* * *

DURING MY FIRST TUMULTUOUS year as a teacher, my personal life changed dramatically too. I had told Lydia about my feelings for Angel, but to my parents and friends, all I said was that Angel was a friend. Although I was hoping for the best, I was afraid that, given the distance and other obstacles, nothing might come of our relationship. How my friends and family could miss the lovelorn look in my eye, however, is beyond me. In the meantime, I saved my money to return to Madrid to spend Christmas with Angel. My parents were disappointed, because it would be the second year that neither Lydia nor I would be home for the holidays. For me, though, the upcoming trip kept me going all fall.

I arrived in Madrid on Christmas Eve. In those days, you could walk right up to the airplane gate, so as soon as I got off the plane, there was Angel, anxiously waiting for me. When I reached him and we embraced, he simply said, "We can't go on like this. Let's get married." Not a typically romantic proposal, but it was more than good enough for me. Right after Christmas, we went to the US Embassy to see whether it made more sense to get married in Spain or in the United States. We decided on Spain because the embassy staff told us if we got married there, Angel would get his green card sooner than if we married in the States. We spent the next week and a half visiting his family in Cuenca to let them know of our decision, getting a marriage license, having our blood tests, and taking care of other red tape. We also bought our wedding rings, thin 18-karat gold bands, mine costing five hundred pesetas (about eight dollars), and Angel's, eight hundred pesetas (about twelve). Because this was during the Franco era in Spain, no marriage could only be civil; we would also have to have a church ceremony. That dashed my hopes that we might actually have a church wedding in the States when we returned, especially because I knew Mami would be deeply disappointed if we didn't. The only way, then, was to elope. We set the date for Wednesday, January 4, 1967.

I called home the night of January 3 to let my parents know I was getting married the next day. The discussion with my parents could be the subject for an entire book, but I'll leave that for the future. Lydia actually did write a funny and poignant story about our elopement and the call home I made, and she read the story on our twenty-fifth anniversary celebration. Suffice it to say that my parents were shocked ("*Who* are you marrying?" Mami asked). As I had guessed, she was disappointed—after all, she wanted me to have a nice wedding with all the trimmings. I know Papi was happy because, as he told me later, we had decided to settle in the States. He had already assessed Angel's character, and even though Angel and I had only been seeing one another for about four months (the rest of the time, we were separated by an ocean), Papi instinctively knew he was the right man for me. In fact, Angel was uncannily like Papi in so many ways that I often said I married a younger version of my father.

We had a memorable, if unconventional, wedding. Angel picked me up at the Señora's house (where I was again staying), and we made our way to the church, Nuestra Señora de los Dolores, just a couple of blocks away, first stopping for tapas and a glass of wine at a couple of bars along the way. Once we arrived at the church, we waited for a long while. "You weren't wearing a white dress, so I didn't realize you were the bride," said the priest, explaining why he hadn't come out to greet us. I wore, instead, a brown suit, and Angel, a dark blue one. My Señora insisted it didn't matter what I wore, but flowers were a must, so she gave me a glorious bouquet of

[handwritten margin note: Mom wanted to give wedding Dad happy cause he knew Angel was right guy]

gladiolas, the same kind my mother had carried at her wedding a quarter century earlier. Isa, the owner of the apartment where Angel lived, lent me her beautiful black mantilla.

Just thirteen people attended the ceremony: besides our respective landladies, there were a couple of friends; Angel's mother and two brothers, who had come from Cuenca (his father stayed home); a couple of cousins and their spouses who lived in Madrid; and a few of the ubiquitous old women dressed in black who seem to live in Spanish churches. Because there had been a wedding right before ours, a professional photographer happened to be present. He took beautiful black and white photos to document the occasion. Unlike other brides in similar situations with last-minute qualms, as I walked down the aisle, I felt this was the best decision I had ever made. As it turned out, I was right.

We had a four-day honeymoon in Aranjuez, a historic royal town near Madrid, staying at an inexpensive pension with a bathroom down the hall, but it didn't really matter to us where we were. We were ecstatically happy and grateful for those four short days together. While other couples have a favorite song, our favorite piece of music was, and continues to be, *Concierto de Aranjuez*, recalling those joyful days. On January 9, Angel took me to the airport to return to New York, assuring me he'd be joining me within a couple of weeks. Saying good-bye was heartbreaking. The pain was relieved, though, by the certainty that we would be soon reunited, this time as husband and wife.

Unfortunately, it wasn't as soon as we had expected. I returned to my parents' home in Brooklyn, busied myself with work, searched for an apartment for Angel and me in Brooklyn, and attended to all the preparations for our new life together. Angel, in Madrid, spent every minute he could at the American Embassy trying to secure his green card. He would show up every day and take a seat and a number. Each time, there was another delay. In his daily letter, he would tell me how frustrated he was, how desperate to join me. On February 4, exactly a month after we were married, his mother, only fifty-four years old, had a stroke and died in her sleep. This turn of events was a terrible loss for Angel. He had been his mother's favorite son and a constant source of strength to her. He often helped her in the kitchen. That's why, unlikely as it was for a Spanish male at the time, he already knew how to cook. His mother's death also caused him tremendous guilt at leaving his father and young brother, Antero, then only twelve, behind.

———•◦•———

BACK AT SCHOOL, MY COLLEAGUES congratulated and enthusiastically welcomed me back. Rather than Miss Cortés, I returned as Mrs. Nieto. Some of the students had a hard time with the change. Jaime, a sixteen-year-old eighth grader who had been left back a couple of times, came up to me on the day I returned to work. A tough kid, he sported a moustache and was reported to be a neighborhood pimp, though with me he was always sweet and protective. In the hall between classes, he looked me straight in the eye and asked, "Is it true what they're saying? Did you really get married?"

"Yes," I responded. "Isn't it wonderful?"

Not for Jaime. He just shook his head sadly and walked away, perceiving yet another disappointment in his life.

My second semester was much calmer and more rewarding than the first. Life was easier now: I had my routine, I knew all the students, and I was much happier in my personal life. Discipline, not trouble-free, was at least much more manageable. Though not yet a master teacher, I was definitely becoming a more confident one.

On the evening of March 9, 1967, exactly two months to the day that I had left Spain, Angel showed up unannounced at my family's front door. I was, of course, elated but also shocked. *What happened?* I asked myself. *How did he manage to make it to New York?* Apparently, Angel had almost given up waiting, so he decided to take matters into his own hands. As he had every day since we eloped, he showed up at the American Embassy on March 8, went straight to the clerk at the front desk with tears in his eyes, and claimed that his new bride had been in a terrible car accident, was hospitalized, and in grave condition! Somehow, they bought his story. They gave him a visa on the spot. He then made his way back to his office at Iberia, where he bought a ticket for the following day.

I called Mrs. Young, the woman from whom I had rented an apartment a month earlier, telling her the good news. I had packed a bag more than a month before. Saying a quick goodnight to my parents, Angel and I made our way to our small furnished basement apartment a couple of miles away. When we arrived, Mrs. Young met us by the side door, our entrance to the basement apartment, to say hello, meet Angel, and tell us to look in the fridge. There, she had put a bottle of champagne for us to enjoy on our first night together. As you might have guessed, I took a personal day the following day.

Within a few weeks, Angel had learned how to navigate not only our new Brooklyn neighborhood but the New York City subway system as well. While I went to work, Angel went job hunting, searching through newspaper ads, filling out applications, pounding the pavement. As he barely spoke English, finding work was not easy. Jobs for non-English-speaking immigrants, education notwithstanding, were scarce. Angel was becoming disheartened, but finally, in late May, he received a call from the famous New York Waldorf Astoria Hotel, where he was offered a job as an elevator operator. Though it was a low-paying job, the supervisor said he recognized Angel's obvious intelligence and was certain that after a while, Angel would make his way up the hierarchy, no pun intended. Angel went off to work on that first day with great enthusiasm. When I returned home that afternoon, I found him sitting in the dark, disconsolate. The work had proved not to be a good choice for his first job in the United States. As someone who suffered from motion sickness, he had gotten ill with all the ups and downs. He left the job immediately, never claiming the pay for the three hours he had worked.

Shortly afterward, he went to the Spanish Tourist Office on Fifth Avenue in Manhattan, just a stone's throw from Rockefeller Center. There, he was offered a job as office manager. He was the only person there who had actually studied tourism. Although he was paid Spanish wages—much lower than US wages at the time—he was happy to have a job and to contribute to our household.

We quickly established a regular routine: Every morning, we walked to the subway station together, then parted ways, he to Manhattan and I further south in Brooklyn. On Saturdays, we did our weekly food shopping at all the local shops, went to the bank, cleaned our small apartment. In 1966 it was unusual for a man to be an equal partner in domestic responsibilities, but from the start, Angel cleaned right along with me. In fact, throughout our marriage, he has always shared the housework and child-rearing. Sundays were reserved for visits to my parents' home. Papi would often be waiting for us on the stoop, embracing and kissing both of

Sonia taught Angel looked for jobs

Job as office manager @ Spanish tourism office

us when we arrived. Angel had become as important a part of their lives as he was of mine.

By the end of the school year, I had accumulated several other glowing observations ("excellent rapport," "a comfortable and easy-flowing relationship with the pupils," and so on), and a final review where the "excellent" ratings outnumbered the "good" ones, ending with "Mrs. Nieto is a pleasant, competent, enthusiastic teacher whom we are very glad to have on our faculty." Far more than I would have expected at the beginning of the year.

In April 1967, after Angel joined me, Lydia returned from Rome, her boyfriend Franco to join her a few weeks later, to plan their wedding in Brooklyn. I was, of course, the matron of honor, and Angel the best man. For the next few years, Lydia and Franco moved back and forth between Brooklyn and Rome, but divorced when their son Jimmy was six years old. She stayed in Brooklyn, where she was a teacher and later a supervisor working for the New York City Board of Education. Her real love was writing, to which she has dedicated her life since retiring at fifty-four. A poet and short-story writer, she is always a big hit at readings in the New York City and Charleston, South Carolina, poetry scenes and beyond.

Meanwhile, I returned to school in September, determined to become a better teacher. But controversies continued to erupt. The political situation at JHS 178 and throughout the rest of the New York City schools had deteriorated considerably. Because in my first year of teaching my attention had been almost completely focused on my own struggles as a novice teacher, I had been rather oblivious to what was happening politically in my district and in the New York City schools in general. I knew, of course, that there was widespread discontent and frustration on the part of both the Ocean Hill–Brownsville community and, though for different reasons, the United Federation of Teachers, the teachers' union. For the general community, it was clear that the decades-long struggle for desegregation led by African Americans, Puerto Ricans (who then made up the vast majority of Latinos in New York City), and progressive Whites had gone nowhere. Few tangible benefits of the civil rights movement had reached Ocean Hill–Brownsville. In spite of the many needs in the community,

[handwritten marginalia: Lydia got married moved back & forth between NY & Rome then divorced]

[handwritten marginalia: Sonia went back to teaching much political discourse]

few social services were available to residents. In terms of the schools, the quality of education for kids of color was abysmal, with low literacy rates and an astoundingly high dropout rate of 70 percent. One year, it was reported that just *1 percent* of the community's high school students graduated with an academic diploma (Wielk, 1969). The number of teachers of color was, in addition, extremely low, and the number of administrators of color, minuscule.

As a result, community activists were now focusing on the control of public schools by the communities in which they were located. While community control is typical in middle-class areas, it was unusual in poor communities such as Ocean Hill–Brownsville. Power lay in the hands of an entrenched White bureaucracy, including an almost entirely White local school board. The recipients of services such as education had little or no power. There was a virtual war between community members and activists, mostly African American and Puerto Rican, and the UFT, with a mostly Jewish membership. At times, it turned ugly.

The struggle for community control was felt most keenly in several New York City communities, and JHS 178 was one of the key schools affected. Bowing to pressure from community groups, the New York City Board of Education had established three decentralized school districts, of which Ocean Hill–Brownsville was one. In July 1967, the Ford Foundation awarded the district a grant to create and begin managing the newly established district. The new district operated under a governing board elected by community members, and the board had the power to hire and fire teachers and administrators. This power to hire and fire was non-negotiable to community members, who believed that many of the teachers assigned to the schools had no commitment to the students and no desire to be there. The powerful UFT, however, considered this a union-busting strategy. The union also opposed the new community superintendent, Rhody McCoy, whom it considered a Black Nationalist and therefore too militant. These changes were occurring at the height of the Black Power movement, signaling a sea change in the Black community and its relations with Whites. The governing board, community activists, and the African American Teachers' Association (ATA) also opposed a clause in the UFT contract. Called "the disruptive child clause," it would give teachers the right to have disruptive children removed from their classrooms and placed in special schools. For the governing board, it was nothing more than a way for the schools to rid themselves of children who had never received a fair chance at a good education.

The stage was set for a confrontation. The UFT called a strike for the first day of school in September 1967. The new governing board, for its part, voted to keep the schools open. As a fairly new teacher, I was torn. At twenty-three, I still felt like a greenhorn regarding political issues. Carol and I both joined the strike, but the handful of teachers of color were divided. A few joined the strike; most broke rank to keep the school open. The strike lasted fourteen days, casting a pall over the entire school year and creating considerable tension and resentment among the faculty.

In the next couple of years, Ocean Hill–Brownsville schools experienced strikes, demonstrations, transfers of teachers and administrators, walkouts by teachers and students, and even arrests. A report written a couple of years after these incidents summed up the situation:

> If the confrontation and strife have produced nothing else, it has made Ocean Hill–Brownsville a community. Once apathetic and politically powerless, Ocean Hill has emerged as a symbol of the black man's desire to control his own development. It has become the arena from which to attack the entire educational malaise which has gripped the public school system. (Wielk, 1969)

Back then, I was generally too immersed in the challenges of becoming a teacher to understand the politics of these events. Within a couple of years, as my political consciousness grew with my greater experience as a teacher, Wielk's assessment would make sense to me. At the time, however, the situation made me anxious and disheartened.

In spite of the chaos at the school and in the district, I learned and improved quite a lot that year. I knew all the students, and they knew me. Even though there was still a 50 percent attrition rate among faculty, the return of some of us gave the students a sense of stability that made our job easier. My pedagogy had improved. I felt more comfortable with my curriculum and my relationships with my students. Somehow—this was always true when I taught young people—I seemed to gravitate to the kids considered the most problematic or rebellious. Angel also got to know them, and he and I would sometimes take students to museums or dinner or even bring them home, activities that would be frowned upon today. Connie, one of my eighth graders, was a particular favorite. She was smart and sassy, and I thought if I could introduce her to different possibilities, it might give her a different perspective on life. A year later, when I was no longer at the school, she called me at home one day to tell me she was pregnant. I was distraught thinking about what her life would be like: a fifteen-year-old with so much promise but little education and even less hope. It was one of those moments when I realized that no matter what an individual teacher does, we can't change the conditions in which our students live. That, however, doesn't mean we should give up on them. Maintaining your hope in the face of incredibly difficult conditions is what makes teaching so hard. At the same time, I began to understand that political activism was as important as hope and perseverance.

THE OCEAN HILL–BROWNSVILLE community had for years pressured the New York City Board of Education for a new school, so we began the academic year with plans to open a brand-new school, Intermediate School (IS) 55, to which the teachers and students of JHS 178 would be moving. JHS 178 would be, in turn, converted into an elementary school. A steering committee of parents and teachers was set up to plan for the opening. Moving the entire school in the middle of the school year brought its own challenges and disruptions, not only for the students but for the teachers as well. The move came in January 1968. There we were, students, teachers, and administrators carrying boxes of books, supplies, and equipment two blocks to the new school.

The political unrest, constant references to the community's schools in the media, and the turmoil of opening a new school all took their toll on me. In addition, the camaraderie and goodwill among faculty—what little of these remained—were eroding, and the downslide was having a devastating effect on me. I began to dread going to school each day to face the turmoil and hostility. I was having trouble sleeping at night, had a hard time focusing, and was feeling more and more anguish at the situation. At the time, I didn't understand what I was experiencing, but anxiety is a good word for it.

Given the situation, I decided to take an indefinite leave of absence that spring. The decision surprised everyone, including me, who had never dreamed that I would leave the profession. This was a low point in my life, both personally and professionally. It left me disheartened and profoundly sad. The leave was to last half a year. At the time, though, I thought seriously about leaving teaching altogether.

Sonia took a leave of absence due to stresses of teaching

CHAPTER 8

PS 25

The Bilingual School: ¡Somos Pioneros!

NEW YORK IN THE LATE 1960S was a hotbed of both traditional politics and identity politics. Like everyone else, I was caught up in all the emotions and turmoil of the time. As a teacher and, later, as an instructor in the Department of Puerto Rican Studies at Brooklyn College, I was surrounded by conflict and debate about everything from the Vietnam War to civil rights to gender and racial/ethnic identity. People who had never before been out of their shells began marching and proclaiming "Black is beautiful!" and "Brown Power!" Women burned their bras as army recruits burned their draft cards. It was a heady time. At the same time, the assassinations of the Reverend Martin Luther King Jr. and Senator Robert Kennedy in 1968, as well as the Democratic Party convention in Chicago in 1968 raised to a fever pitch the political upheaval of those years.

Though my political awareness began after I met Angel, it hadn't yet taken root when I had started teaching, because the chaos and conflict I was experiencing daily in Ocean Hill–Brownsville had been so raw and uncomfortable. One thing was certain: in those first two years of teaching, I saw firsthand that my students' fortunes were determined not solely by their intelligence, hard work, or determination but rather by their race, where they happened to live, as well as their lack of access to the kinds of opportunities regarded as the birthright of more privileged young people.

Prior to teaching at Ocean Hill–Brownsville, I had swallowed the meritoc-racy myth whole. A person's hard work, I thought, was what mattered. I had been a successful student, so it seemed to me that anyone else could be as well. My students—many of whom were smart, curious, and deter-mined—quickly disabused me of that idea. I began to understand meri-tocracy as little more than a myth.

Began teaching ESL to adults

After I left IS 55, I took a couple of weeks off to take stock of my life. I also began looking for another job. In late spring, I was offered a position as an ESL teacher in an adult basic education program in mid-Manhattan. Although I was working with adults, the job gave me some degree of com-fort that, yes, I *was* a teacher, regardless of the ages of the people I taught. I enjoyed my students, all immigrants from countries around the world who believed desperately in the American Dream and were working hard to make it happen.

Angel, still working at the Spanish Tourist Office, was just a few short blocks away. We met for lunch every day that spring and summer, often at Bryant Park in front of the majestic main branch of the New York Public Library. Given my ongoing distress at no longer being a classroom teacher, meeting Angel for lunch was one of the few bright spots of my days.

———◆———

Received job interview @ bilingual school

In July 1968, I received a phone call from Hernán LaFontaine. He identi-fied himself as the inaugural principal of PS 25, the Bilingual School, a new school that would be opening in the Bronx. I was excited to get the call but also surprised: at the time, teachers were assigned by the central Board of Education, not hired by principals of specific schools. But PS 25 was to be a very different kind of school: it was the first totally bilingual school not just in New York City, but in the entire Northeast. PS 25 was preempted only by a school that had opened a year earlier in Miami Dade County and that served the children of Cuban refugees. Since all teachers needed to be bilingual, a job at PS 25 required an actual interview.

The school was located on East 149th Street, about a block from the subway station and the heart of the Puerto Rican community in the South Bronx. An imposing structure built in 1897 that looked its age, the school had been scheduled for demolition. A new school had been built just a block away to house the students of the former school. But community demands for bilingual education led by a militant parent group, the United Bronx Parents, and other community members had convinced the district superintendent to keep the older building open as a bilingual school, a true experiment. Hernán LaFontaine, a Puerto Rican raised in New York, was hired as its principal.

Back then, it was almost unheard-of for a New York City principal to be both so young and Puerto Rican at that. But Hernán was up to the task. Several years old than me—I was now twenty-four—he was impressive: a community activist with experience as a teacher and an administrator, he had made his commitment to bilingual education clear. He was a natural choice for principal.

I like to think Hernán saw something in me that day despite my interview: frankly, I couldn't have impressed him very much with my responses to his questions. I knew nothing about bilingual education. I wasn't even sure it was a good idea, and told him so. He also asked me about parent involvement, another pillar on which the school was to be founded. I said I wasn't convinced parents *should* be involved in their children's education. After all, I said, "*I* made it and *my* parents weren't involved in my education." I had believed the story about the success of European immigrants without questioning whether it held true for other immigrants. "My people made it without [bilingual education, welfare, affirmative action, or whatever other so-called benefit poor people were receiving]," the argument went, "so what's wrong with your people?"

Only later did I come to understand the weaknesses in this argument. Puerto Ricans, and most other people demanding bilingual education, were among the first people of color to immigrate to the United States. Because of their race and ethnicity, Mexicans, Puerto Ricans, and other immigrants of color were not accepted as readily into US society as European immigrants had been. Also, these newer immigrants were unwilling to give up their language and culture as previous immigrants had done. They generally believed they could be *both* American *and* Puerto Rican, Mexican, or whatever their national origin happened to be, and that this diversity would enrich the nation. Most importantly, the kinds of jobs available at the beginning of the twentieth century, when all you needed to succeed was a strong back, were quickly disappearing. My knowledge of these issues would come later, after I had been a bilingual teacher for a while.

Poor interview or not, Hernán hired me. Overjoyed and eager to be given this second chance, I was equally ecstatic to be working as a teacher again, especially after I found out I would be teaching my beloved fourth grade!

THE SCHOOL YEAR, HOWEVER, did not start smoothly. In the fall of 1968, the UFT called another strike. Ocean Hill–Brownsville again lay at the center of the controversy. The strike began as a protest against the involuntary transfer of ten White teachers by the largely African American Community School Board the previous May. Lasting thirty-six days, the walkout was the longest teachers' strike in New York history, with 93 percent of the city's teachers out of school (Pritchett, 2002). This time, though, I was glad to be on the side of history. The words *social justice* didn't yet flow smoothly from my lips, but I knew I was changing. My dawning political awareness, the excitement of participating in a brand-new school as pioneers in the bilingual education experiment, and being surrounded by like-minded teachers, administrators, and community members all made for a dramatically different atmosphere than that of my initial two years of teaching. Working at PS 25 was an extraordinary experience, one that changed my ideas about teaching, learning, culture, and politics.

Bilingual education, both as policy and practice, was new for all of us. As a result, we teachers were required to participate in two weeks of training before the opening of school. The Friday before the strike was set to begin (and schools were scheduled to open), one of the teachers asked Hernán what we should expect. "Will PS 25 be open?" the teacher asked. "Should we come? Should we picket? Should we stay home?"

"The decision to show up is an entirely individual one," Hernán responded. "As for me, I'll be here."

The following Monday, every single staff member showed up. Of over nine hundred schools in New York City, only PS 25 and three other schools remained open during the strike. The decision to keep the school open also had the unqualified support of the local Puerto Rican community.

[handwritten margin note: PS 25 stayed open during strike]

But it wasn't only the teachers' strike that would keep schools closed. The janitors' union had voted to physically close the schools in support of the teachers' strike. This meant that keeping PS 25 open would be tricky. The dilemma was resolved when Hernán and several male faculty members decided to sleep at the school overnight to keep it open for the duration of the strike. Every teacher and administrator worked during those days, and in contrast to the conflict that had characterized my time in Ocean Hill–Brownsville, there was a great sense of solidarity and collective purpose at PS 25.

While working in Ocean Hill–Brownsville, especially toward the end of my year and a half there, I had felt an overwhelming sense of helplessness, not just about the contentious political situation but also about the reality of the students' lives: poverty, substandard schools with few resources, and crushing odds for success in life. I was becoming more aware of just how the cards were stacked against the children and their communities.

PS 25 changed all that. Starting work there was a like getting a new lease on life. Given the priorities of the school, I soon became a staunch supporter not just of bilingual education but also of the benefits of parent involvement. My educational philosophy changed dramatically as a result. Learning to value Spanish as a resource and strength, I also learned about doing serious and respectful outreach to families. The school made its values obvious in many ways. There was a parent lounge—formerly a classroom—right next to Hernán's office, a clear indication of the prominence parents had in the school. They were welcome to come and relax, read, learn crafts, attend workshops on advocacy or English, and join in a host of other activities. They were also invited to volunteer in classrooms. As for me, I began regularly visiting my students' homes, where I was always received with great respect, even reverence. I was in awe of my students' lives and the responsibilities they assumed or were given at such tender ages. One of my students, my namesake Sonia, all of nine years old, not only took care of her younger siblings after school but also prepared dinner for the family every night.

[handwritten margin note: School had a parent lounge - invited to volunteer in classroom]

My colleagues and I knew there was something special about PS 25: there was a palpable sense of adventure among us, all of whom, from the principal to each of the teachers and counselors, were bilingual. Nothing epitomized that sense of adventure more than our school song, "Somos Pioneros, We Are Pioneers," written by some of my colleagues that first exhilarating year. In both English and Spanish, the song extolled the virtues of being bilingual: "Somos pioneros, somos los primeros"—as pioneers, we were the first. All the children and staff learned the song and sang it at every school event.

We are often victims of our own experience. Since it's the only one we know, we are inclined to think that our own experience must hold for everyone else as well. Throughout my young life, it had never occurred to me that speaking my native language in school would be possible or even a good thing. Having had to learn English as a child with no support, I had believed that everyone else should have to do so as well, even if it was *a la fuerza*, or forced. That idea dissipated almost as soon as I began teaching at PS 25. There, I saw the benefits of learning in two languages, the importance of culture in teaching and learning. Having never studied bilingual education, though—there were no university bilingual programs at the time—we educators were inventing the program as we went along, much like learning how to fly a plane without a manual.

The model we followed was designed by Hernán LaFontaine and Muriel Pagán, the assistant principal. Classes were designated as *bilingual*, *Spanish dominant*, or *English dominant*. Children were assigned according to their level of proficiency in one or both languages. Incoming Spanish-speaking students new to the country could be accommodated in Spanish-dominant classes. Those who spoke little or no Spanish—whether they were Latino/a or not—would be placed in English-dominant classes. The school was overwhelmingly Puerto Rican, with about 15 percent African American students. Since these students spoke no Spanish, they were placed in the English-dominant classes, along with Puerto Rican and other Latino/a students who spoke mostly or only English. Conceivably, African American students who excelled in Spanish could be placed in bilingual classes, but most of the students in the bilingual classes were Latino/a. There was also one Chinese American student in the entire school. He probably became trilingual. My class was designated as a bilingual class, meaning that I would teach some subjects in English, some in Spanish, and some in both. I taught reading in English on some days and Spanish on other days; math was in Spanish and social studies in English. The model didn't always work, but the administration made adjustments as we went along, and the school soon found its rhythm.

———◦———

My colleagues at PS 25 were mostly young and inexperienced, but what they lacked in experience they made up in enthusiasm. All were bilingual. The group was about a third Latino/a, a third Black, and a third White and, as a result, a much more diverse group than the general profile of New York City teachers at the time. With still much to learn, we found very soon after opening the school that we shared a strong commitment to the ideals upon which the school had been founded. As the teachers' strike raged on in schools all around us, we soldiered on, happy to be united with the community. Even the students had this sense of mission, aware as they were that all the other schools in the community were closed, including the new one just a block away.

Across the hall from me were Herminio Vargas, who became like a brother to me, and Luis Cartagena, a teacher recently arrived from Puerto Rico. I invited Luis to Thanksgiving at Mami and Papi's house that November because he had no family in the States. Luis would become the principal after Hernán left PS 25 several years later to become the founding director of the Office of Bilingual Education of the New York City Board of Education. I also became good friends with Evelyn Colón, a gifted first-grade teacher who later married Hernán. Their two children, coincidentally, have the same names as my own daughters, Alicia and Marisa.

I loved my students from the first day. All Latinos, they were predominately Puerto Rican, but a few were Panamanian and Dominican. All spoke both Spanish and English to some degree, and most were able to follow the lessons in either language. Teaching in Spanish, for me, was a true adventure. Who would have thought I would be able to do so in a New York City public school? I also learned a great deal about the difference between teaching reading in English and in Spanish, and about Puerto Rican history and how to incorporate it into my curriculum.

I likewise became more courageous in exploring new methods and materials. About halfway into the year, for example, I had tired of the basal reader and initiated instead a program of independent reading so that children could select books they were interested in, rather than just those

[handwritten margin note: Allowed Students to read what they wanted]

I assigned. It was something I had read about but had never done before. As with everything else we did that year, I learned how to do it by the seat of my pants. I got my hands on all sorts of books for my students, buying some, obtaining others from teachers and friends. Reading what they wanted rather than simply what they were assigned to read turned out to be a very good way to teach reading, and my students loved learning this way. I got to know more about them by reading with them individually while getting to know their tastes, goals, and habits more deeply. I also was learning how to effectively expand my curriculum to include other topics and perspectives. Although these attempts were rudimentary, they nonetheless foreshadowed my growing interest in literacy, equity, diversity, and culture.

I learned that culture is not an impediment to learning, despite what I had been taught at St. John's. There, the message, explicit or not, had been, "Leave your cultural baggage at the door." At PS 25, I learned that doing so was not just an impossibility, but also a lost opportunity for teaching and learning. The renowned educator and philosopher Paulo Freire once said something that solidified for me the impossibility of being culture-less. "I *am* my culture." He added that it would be as difficult to leave his culture behind as it would be to shed his skin. This didn't mean, he said, that culture is destiny, but rather that culture influences who we are, what we value, and what we do.

[handwritten margin note: I am my culture - culture influences who]

I saw the reality of this truth every day that I taught at PS 25. Each day, I brought my class downstairs for dismissal. All my girls, and even some of my boys, would line up to kiss me good-bye, asking for *la bendición*, my blessing. To this typical Puerto Rican custom and sign of respect, I would give the expected response, "Que Dios te bendiga" ("May God bless you"). Having given up going to church shortly after returning from Spain, I wasn't at all religious. But I didn't see this as a religious ritual, but rather a cultural one. Given the current sanctions about hugging, kissing, or even touching of any kind, this practice would no doubt be seen in a negative light today, but I would still do it. This doesn't mean everyone should. I've often cautioned teachers that becoming culturally responsive doesn't mean you should do things that feel uncomfortable or unnatural. Becoming culturally responsive most of all means becoming familiar with students'

[handwritten margin note: Would Still perform culture rituals]

cultural practices and trying to respect them. We might not always be able to do so, of course, because we all have our values, which are sometimes in direct conflict with the values of others. This is what makes teaching with a multicultural perspective difficult. I've always said that teaching in a monocultural way is easier yet, in the end, less effective.

Shortly after beginning my job at PS 25, the school received a grant that would pay tuition for teachers to study for master's degrees at New York University. I had already earned my MA during my year in Spain, but I still took advantage of the opportunity to take several classes at NYU. All these classes would help me become better informed about the nascent field of bilingual education and increase my meager salary. One course was on Puerto Rican history. Not only was it the first course of its kind I had ever taken, but its instructor—Luis Cartagena, who, as I mentioned earlier, would succeed Hernán as principal—was the first Puerto Rican teacher I had ever studied with. The class was an riveting experience. Here, finally, was what I had been hungering for: I learned about the people who had previously been invisible to me, Puerto Rican men and women who had made history, fought for their freedom, created stunning works of art, and changed the lives of their people on the island and in the States. They weren't all heroes, but they *were* all consequential.

This experience made me reflect seriously on what I had been missing in my education. I was both angered and saddened by what I was learning. More importantly for me as a teacher, it made me aware of what our students were missing. While we made sure to include cultural knowledge and history in our curriculum at PS 25, I wondered, *What about children in all the other schools? What did they learn?* And I wasn't concerned only about Puerto Rican kids; by this time, I was developing an awareness that all children—indeed, all adults too—needed to know more about the multicultural history of our nation and the world. Although I didn't yet know the term *multicultural education*, my classroom practice was already changing to become more inclusive.

My political awareness grew along with my increasing cultural knowledge. For us at PS 25, *community control* and *parent power* were not alien or negative terms as they had become in other parts of the city. They were realities we lived every day. The Young Lords, a militant Puerto Rican

P. Ricans pride parade

group much like the Black Panthers, were not just a name in the news. In 1970, my third year at PS 25, they led a group of thousands of marchers with Puerto Rican flags and fists held high in the air and signs proclaiming "Proud to be Puerto Rican!" and "Puerto Rican Power!" in New York City's annual Puerto Rican Day Parade. The parade was previously known primarily for its floats and salsa music, its beauty queens, and its mainstream politicians walking the route and shaking hands with potential voters. But in 1970, the parade became much more, a proclamation of political and cultural awareness and pride. All of these events made a deep impression on me as both a Puerto Rican and a teacher.

As calls for bilingual education became more prominent, we had many visitors curious about it. Some wanted to begin their own programs. Hernán often sent visitors to my room, as well as to the classrooms of other teachers he thought were doing a good job. One man, I vividly remember, visited my room and stayed for quite a long time. Before leaving, he remarked, "You have such a wonderful way with the students. It's easygoing, but they also respect and love you and know you expect a lot from them." That statement meant more to me than all the formal positive evaluations I received as a teacher. It reinforced what I already knew and had learned from my brief experience: that strong relationships are the basis for successful teaching and learning.

Teaching fourth grade that year was the happiest experience I ever had as a classroom teacher. I learned a lot from my students, and they from me. One of the most important lessons I learned was that I needed to form my own judgments about students rather than rely only on previous records or other teachers' experiences. I remember one student in particular, Angel, my husband's namesake and a boy just as sweet as my Angel. After having taught him for several months, I was stunned to read his cumulative record. Although he was one of my brightest and best-behaved students, his file read like that of an impending juvenile delinquent! Another student, Wanda, was one of my most challenging: she needed constant attention and was always after me for one thing or another. Wanda was talkative and loud. One day, she lit a fire in the classroom. It was good to get a rest from her in June at the end of the year. But when I had my first daughter, Alicia, the following November, Wanda was the one student who somehow found my home address and sent a beautiful bath towel for the baby. I was touched. We kept that towel for many years.

ANGEL WAS STILL WORKING at the Spanish Tourist Office in Manhattan when, as I had often done during my first year at PS 25, I went to meet him there after work one day in April 1969. I wanted him by my side when I called Dr. Martens's office to get the result of the pregnancy test I had taken a few days earlier. I was nervous as I dialed the doctor's number. Angel and I put our ears to the phone and heard the good news together: yes, I was pregnant, and the baby would be due in early November. Elated, we immediately started planning: What name would we choose if it was a boy? A girl? What about furniture? And where would we live? We were, at this time, living in a small furnished apartment in upper Manhattan, having moved to be closer to work. We loved it there, but we also knew we'd need more room when the baby came.

Though I wasn't due until November, I would have to take a maternity leave beginning in August. Women then were not allowed to work until right before they gave birth; nor was paid maternity leave an expected part of most jobs. Because I wouldn't be getting a paycheck for almost a year, our biggest concern was how we would live on Angel's meager salary. One of his coworkers at the Spanish Tourist Office suggested he teach Spanish at the Berlitz School of Languages, a job he started part-time while I was pregnant. He soon left the Spanish Tourist Office and began working full-time at Berlitz.

The end of the academic year was bittersweet. I knew I would not be returning to PS 25 for nearly a year and was sad at leaving the students and by now close friends with whom I had spent a year. It had been a very successful year for me, my students, and the school. A personal handwritten note from Hernán ("Thanks for your outstanding efforts in making our new program a success") made me feel vindicated as a teacher, satisfied with the progress I had made, and happy to be in the vanguard of what we at PS 25 considered a grand experiment.

That summer and autumn were exciting times of expectation and planning for Angel and me. We were deliriously happy to be expecting. During the summer, we found an apartment on the second floor of a private home

Had baby "Bilingual Baby" Alicia

in Flushing, Queens, but wouldn't move in until October, right before the baby was due. Papi, who had offered to buy us a living room set, came shopping with us and bought us not only living room furniture but also an entire dining room set. We bought our first car right before moving to Flushing. In our new car, we did a couple of practice runs to New York Hospital in Manhattan.

When the day came, Angel rushed us to the hospital, where I had a short labor. He stayed with me the whole time, from labor to delivery room. Having dads in the delivery room was then a daring experiment in only a few hospitals. Angel's having attended Lamaze classes with me was also a fairly new practice. Alicia was born on November 4, 1969, giving Angel and me one of the happiest moments we've had as a couple. She was a gorgeous baby. Though I was twenty-six and in some ways still felt like a baby myself, Alicia quickly taught me to build the self-confidence I needed as a mother.

As the first baby born to a staff member at PS 25, Alicia was henceforth known as "The Bilingual Baby." My colleagues regaled us with baby gifts. A particularly special one was a poem written in Spanish by my friend and fellow fourth-grade teacher Herminio Vargas. "Bilingual Baby" was an apt name for Alicia in other ways, too, as she was bilingual from the start. We had decided I would speak only English to her, Angel only Spanish. She thus grew up hearing and speaking both: her first words, after "Mamá" and "Papá," were "agua" and "water."

Our lives changed irrevocably of course, as a result of becoming parents. Angel and I still joke that our lives went from whispering sweet nothings to one another, to asking the essential question of the day, "¿Ha eruptado?" ("Has she burped?") As young parents, we doted on Alicia. Except for a couple of months in her infancy, when she was colicky in the late evenings, she was an easy child. And Angel, ever the gentleman, was the one to get up with Alicia in the middle of the night. When she became fussy, he also took to staying up with her until nearly midnight, as together they watched reruns of *Perry Mason*.

———⦿———

ALTHOUGH I LOVED BEING with Alicia, housework bored me. I knew then that I could never be a stay-at-home housewife and mom, though it was a fairly typical choice for my contemporaries. I realized rather quickly that I needed to work outside the home, not just for the money but for the joy and fulfillment of working. I missed the stimulation of being around other people, I missed the kids, I missed teaching, and I missed learning.

I returned to PS 25 three months after Alicia's birth, working as a substitute teacher for one to three days a week. One of the greatest insights I had after becoming a mother was how much parents love their children, how that relationship colors how we see the world. When Alicia was an infant, I remember thinking I wanted to protect and keep her from harm always, not wanting her to suffer for even one moment. This goal is, of course, not possible, but I'm sure every parent feels this way. Years later, Alicia followed in our footsteps and became a teacher. When, several years later, she became a mother herself, she talked about this feeling in an interview for one of my books:

> When I became a parent, everything changed for me as a teacher. I realized that every kid in my class is someone's child or grandchild, it's someone's *special person*. Just the thought of anyone saying or doing anything that made my son feel uncomfortable or sad in class broke my heart. That really transformed my teaching. (Nieto, 2013, p. 71)

Again, one of the constant and enduring themes in my life—public education—reemerged. Like Alicia, becoming a mother also transformed my teaching and reinforced my commitment to make sure that my daughter, and whatever other children and grandchildren I was to have, would get the best education possible. I feel the same about everybody else's children and grandchildren. This meant making sure, as much as I could, that my own children and my students would be loved, respected, and honored for who they were. At PS 25, this desire was primarily evident through our curriculum, our pedagogy, and our relationships with students and their families.

———◆———

Our greatest need at PS 25 was for an appropriate curriculum and materials. As only the second bilingual school in the country, we had few resources available to us. Most of our texts were from either Spain or

[handwritten margin notes: "Went back to work 3 mos later"; "Everyone is someone's child ✱"; "✱ At that time few cultural bilingual resources available"]

Mexico and had little to do with the students' cultures and experiences. Even the few textbooks we had from Puerto Rico—despite being in Spanish and including illustrations of palm trees and beaches—in other ways, were uncannily similar to the old Dick-and-Jane-type readers I had read as a child: they featured neat, middle-class, private houses with White-looking children in White-looking, nuclear families. Our students, on the other hand, lived in poverty, often in intergenerational families in cramped apartments in a Northeast urban ghetto. There were no palm trees or beaches to be seen. Like the Puerto Rican community in general, the students ranged from dark-skinned to light-skinned, often with many skin tones in the same family.

The lack of curricula and materials meant that we teachers had to develop most of our own. Early every morning before the students arrived, we would congregate by the mimeograph machine to crank out copies of the materials we had created, inevitably ending up with purple ink all over our hands. It was inventive but not the most efficient way to develop materials. Hernán, meanwhile, was busily writing proposals to get us some needed help. In 1970, we received the good news that the school had received one of only eight federal grants in the nation for bilingual programs. Several projects, including the hiring of staff to develop curriculum materials, were to be funded.

As I readied to return to work in September 1970, Hernán asked me to accept a new position as curriculum specialist, a position made possible by our federal grant. I was excited to be asked but unsure about my ability to do the job. I had developed a curriculum for my own classroom, but what did I know about the theory and practice of curriculum development in general? Fortunately, Hernán had enough confidence in me for both of us. I was also concerned that although I wanted to work, I didn't want to leave Alicia with a babysitter every day, all day; instead, I suggested to Hernán that I work part-time so I could stay home with Alicia the rest of the time. He agreed, and I began working three days a week as a curriculum specialist. Happily, there were two positions and Herminio was hired as my partner. Nothing could have been more ideal.

Learning to be a curriculum specialist, like becoming a bilingual teacher, was a trial-and-error process. We first had to figure out what was available and then fill in the gaps. We ordered some materials and created others, experimented with various designs, and asked teachers to try out the lessons in their classrooms. We also asked them for feedback and other help in figuring out what we should focus on. As when we were in the classroom, we had numerous visitors anxious to know what we were creating and how they could use the materials (since the materials were produced for a federal grant, they were freely accessible).

At the end of that first year, Hernán asked me to come back full time; we would otherwise be losing some of the grant money. Angel and I had a serious talk about this. We had been fortunate in finding good babysitters for Alicia on the days I worked—all the caretakers were loving and conscientious South American women who spoke Spanish with her—but we didn't want her to be with babysitters every day. Angel was working countless hours at the Berlitz School, sometimes teaching as many as ten or twelve classes a day with a five-minute break between them. Although he was a talented teacher and enjoyed the work, it was exhausting and not well compensated. Since my salary was substantially higher, it wouldn't have made sense for me to stay home while he worked full time. Angel offered to stay home with Alicia while I worked the full workweek. This arrangement was highly unusual for the era. But it was just the first of three occasions that Angel would be a full-time stay-at-home dad. The next time was with our daughter Marisa several years later, and the third, with our granddaughter Jazmyne, whom we raised.

I remained at PS 25 from 1968 to 1972, some of the most significant years of my life. During this period, I honed my skills as a teacher, learned a lot about curricula, became much more confident of myself and my abilities, and developed a good deal of political awareness.

I've HAD SEVERAL IMPORTANT mentors over the years. Hernán LaFontaine has certainly been key among them. His support during the four years I was at PS 25 not only helped me grow as a teacher, but also increased my self-assurance. The first year I was there, a camera crew from a local television station came to visit the school. My fourth-grade classroom was one of those to which Hernán sent the crew. Watching myself with my students on the TV news later that evening with Angel made me feel good about the work I was doing. In subsequent years, Hernán would invite me and other teachers to meetings in the district or universities that were beginning graduate programs in bilingual education or to hear speakers address issues of importance to our work. He once invited me to accompany him to hear Vera St. John, an eminent scholar in the growing field. Starstruck at meeting a published author and researcher, I remember thinking, *Wow, she's a real person! I wonder if I can ever do that?*

Hernán involved the entire staff at PS 25 to organize the very first bilingual conference in the nation. Held at Columbia University in 1969, it featured Francesco Cordasco, an Italian American scholar who had written the first book on the education of Puerto Ricans in the United States, as keynote speaker. As one of the instructors in our master's program at NYU, Hernán gave my classmates and me the option of either being on the planning committee for the conference or doing a final exam; we all chose the former. A lot more time-consuming and demanding than taking a final exam, the committee assignment was also worth the time and work because we learned a tremendous amount. We spent many hours organizing workshops, setting up registration, sending out notices, and recruiting attendees. The conference was a great success. We also had a hand the following year in organizing a conference that was the catalyst for the eventual launch of the National Association for Bilingual Education (NABE). Held at New York's Waldorf Astoria Hotel, the meeting drew people from around the country. Although the Columbia conference had been more or less local, the Waldorf conference was national in scope. We were proud to have had a hand in organizing it. Thanks to the hard work of the organizing committee, the first NABE conference followed in Chicago in 1971.

At the end of my third year at PS 25, as I was completing my first year as a curriculum specialist, Hernán called me to his office and offered me the job of head of summer school.

"What?" I asked in disbelief. With absolutely no administrative experience and being only twenty-seven years old, I didn't think I could do it.

"I have every faith in you," he assured me. "You'll do a great job. In any case, I'll be here all summer. If you have any questions or if anything comes up that you don't think you can handle, all you have to do is come to my office."

We needed the money, and, excited for the opportunity, I took the job. I handled it with no major problems and developed a great deal of confidence that summer.

I will always be grateful for Hernán's confidence in me and for his insistence that I do things I had no idea I could do. Both he and Evelyn Colón, my former colleague who later became Hernán's wife, have gone on to impressive careers in education. I'm glad to say that Angel and I have remained friends with them.

⸻◆⸻

ONE DAY DURING THE LATE spring of 1972, my fellow teacher and curriculum specialist Herminio came to me and said excitedly, "Missy [the title by which many Latino kids call their female teachers, and his particular nickname for me], I've just been offered a job in the Puerto Rican Studies Department at Brooklyn College! It's to teach courses in bilingual education, and there's another position available. Please, por favor, apply for it!"

Apply for a job at a college? Impossible, I thought. But he kept urging me to do so, saying, "We can still work together! Imagine!" So I finally agreed. Going to the interview that summer day, I was more than a little anxious. Angel waited with Alicia outside in the car for what I thought would be just an hour or so. The small conference room of the Department of Puerto Rican Studies was crammed with faculty and students that afternoon. They peppered me nonstop with questions about bilingual education, my philosophy of education, my political ideology, and my thoughts on the status of Puerto Rico; there were no holds barred. I emerged three hours later as an instructor of Puerto Rican studies, to begin in two months.

Ironically, I would end up at the place I had studiously avoided attending for college a dozen years earlier, only to cut my teeth as a professor there. A whole new adventure awaited.

CHAPTER 9

Brooklyn College

An Activist in Academia

I KEPT A JOURNAL THE YEAR I went to Spain to study for my master's degree. I hadn't reread it until recently, forty-eight years later. When I did, I was struck by how young I was, how open to the world, how impressionable, and, sometimes, how judgmental. One particular entry made me chuckle: in late January 1966, after being in Spain for half a year, immersed in the study of Spanish and Hispanic literature, I declared my aversion to academics:

> I have decided that the scholarly world is not for me. There are simply too many phonies there making up their own world, explaining everything away with their trite little phrases, scorning everybody and everything else . . . What brought this on? A *merienda* at the house of the Resident Director of NYU in Madrid, Professor Stamm. After a few glasses of sangria and lots of talk ("Tell me, what do you think of Joe Schmoe's interpretation of the philosophic element present in 'Mother Goose'?"), I decided that this is not for me. I want an *alive* life, not a dead one. I love literature—this year has helped me realize that—but I hate phonies and so-called "erudites."

Ironically, within a few years of writing these dismissive words about the "phonies" in academia, I ended up a professor, first at Brooklyn College and later, after completing my doctoral studies, at the University of

Massachusetts. I would remain in the academy for over thirty years. But let me begin with Brooklyn College.

When I left the interview at Brooklyn College that fateful summer day in 1972, I was trembling with excitement because I walked out an instructor. Poor Angel and Alicia! They had been waiting for me for hours, but Angel was always patient and Ali was an easy baby and hadn't fussed very much, he assured me. We drove to a nearby restaurant to celebrate. Angel was so proud, and even Alicia, at two and a half, seemed to know that something big was happening. I thought about Papi and Mami: "Wait until I tell them!" I told Angel. "They won't believe it!" I was filled with gratitude for them, knowing how much they had sacrificed to enable me to get to this point. I thought about Papi's sixteen- to eighteen-hour days at the bodega, Mami's struggles with Freddy, and everything they had given up to give Lydia and me the opportunities we had gotten. Landing a job at a college, in spite of the protestations in my journal six years before, had in truth been a lifelong, secret desire. Nonetheless, I was still in shock that it was happening. I was twenty-eight years old.

The bilingual education program at Brooklyn College, set to begin that September 1972, was a joint effort between the Department of Puerto Rican Studies and the School of Education. The faculty in the Puerto Rican Studies Department were fortunate that Carmen Dinos, who had been a longtime teacher and advocate for the education of Puerto Rican students, was a professor in the School of Education and worked closely with us.

I didn't at first understand why a bilingual program would be housed in the Department of Puerto Rican Studies, but the reason soon became apparent. During those years in New York City, "bilingual education" was synonymous with "Puerto Rican." The civil rights movement begun by African Americans had spawned numerous other movements for social justice, including the Latino civil rights movement. Activists in the Puerto Rican community were a major force behind the demands for bilingual education. As the largest Spanish-speaking community in the city at the time, Puerto Ricans had seized on bilingual education as a major way to improve educational outcomes among their children. Self-determination was a crucial cry in those years. So, it was logical that Puerto Ricans would want to control not only the K–12 implementation of bilingual education but the content that preservice and practicing teachers would be learning as well.

*P. Ricans were a major force behind the demands for bilingual ed

Like ethnic studies, bilingual education was born of struggle and agitation. Improving K–12 education had been the central issue uniting African Americans, Puerto Ricans, and progressive Whites. Attention now shifted to include higher education. In 1972, a university program in ethnic studies and another in bilingual education were not just unique but nearly revolutionary. The City University of New York (CUNY) system, with its various urban campuses, was the most affordable and accessible way for young people from working-class and poor families in New York to aspire to a college education. Going to a CUNY college cost practically nothing in those days. Many previous immigrants had benefited from its low cost and accessibility. The rigorous entrance demands, however, put many CUNY campuses out of the realm of possibility for most Puerto Ricans. Still, by the late 1960s, a few Puerto Ricans had made it to Brooklyn College and to other CUNY campuses; these students were among those who had been in the forefront of demands for Puerto Rican studies departments. Brooklyn College was one of the first campuses to establish such a department. Today, over forty years later, the department remains one of the strongest in the system.

By the late 1960s, a trickle of reports, articles, and books concerning the dismal state of the education of Puerto Rican children in the United States had been published. One especially distressing and powerfully written study was *The Losers*, by Richard Margolis. The author explained the idea behind the title in this way:

> "Losers" refers to us all. The children are losing all hopes of learning or succeeding; the schools are losing all hopes of teaching; and the nation is losing another opportunity, perhaps its last, to put flesh on the American Dream. (Margolis, 1968, p. 1)

Finding this report a few years after it was published, by which time I was at Brooklyn College, was a revelation. I felt as if a blindfold had been removed from my eyes and I could see clearly what I had only dimly understood before: it wasn't that I was special because I had succeeded in school; instead, I had been one of the few Puerto Ricans to survive the education system, mostly unscathed, through a combination of luck, family support, determination, light skin, and some good teachers and especially because my family had moved to a middle-class community when I was in junior high school. For others, I was a quintessential example of the American Dream made visible, but by then, I knew that it was neither so simple nor so sanguine.

In the 1970s, the growing pressure from the Puerto Rican community and especially the small but rising number of Puerto Rican professionals led to an increasing number of reports, studies, and commissions devoted to the topic of education among Puerto Ricans. Remarkably, a minuscule number of the authors of these publications were Puerto Ricans. When I edited a book on the topic, *Puerto Rican Students in US Schools*, over three decades later in 2000, by contrast, all but one of the authors were Puerto Rican.

The year I was hired was the launch of the bilingual program. I was, once again, present at the creation of something new and exciting. Besides Herminio and me, María Engracia Sánchez, a longtime ESL teacher and supervisor in the New York City public schools, was also hired for the program. In the 1960s, María had been among the small group of pioneer Puerto Rican teachers in the city's schools. Her friendship would be invaluable to me in the years ahead. She'd often say, "We went from SAT to RAT." She meant that as a teacher of ESL, she was one of the first to earn the title of substitute auxiliary teacher (SAT). What could be less significant than a substitute *and* an auxiliary? After some lobbying by political activists and teachers, María and some colleagues were among the first regular auxiliary teachers (RAT); hence, from SAT to RAT. They were the trailblazers, teachers who taught English to the growing population of Puerto Rican students in the city and among the first educators to advocate for these children.

In all, we were eight faculty members in the department, half of us without a doctorate (not surprising, given the tiny number of US-based Puerto Ricans with doctorates at the time). In addition to Herminio and me, there was Antonio Nadal and Richie Perez, all of us in our twenties. María and our department chair, Josephine Nieves, were older, in their forties. Although they, too, lacked doctorates, their extensive professional experience earned them the professorial rank. Josie had been appointed by President Lyndon Johnson to the US Department of Labor. The highest-ranking Puerto Rican in his administration, she had directed the federal Office of Job Training and Development. An excellent administrator, Josie also shared the students' political vision.

"SAT" to "RAT" teachers explained

The three other professors, all from Puerto Rico, had doctorates. This, too, was not surprising. Unlike the younger faculty, who had been raised in the States and came from poor or working-class families, these three professors had been raised in Puerto Rico and mostly came from the middle class. I and the rest of the US-raised staff felt that although the three professors brought prestige and experience to the department, they probably were not as committed to the US-based community. They benefited from much higher salaries, sometimes two or three times higher than they were earning on the island. It was not unusual for them to accept positions in ethnic studies departments in the States for one, two, or three years, then return to Puerto Rico.

I grew especially close to María, her husband, Miguel, and their daughters, Ana and Madeline; to Tony Nadal, a colleague in the department, and his wife, Milga Morales, who worked in the SEEK Office (the Brooklyn College department that provided African American and Latino students academic, financial, and counseling support); and, of course, to Herminio Vargas. These colleagues and several of the most active students became like members of our families. At Ana's wedding a few years after I started at Brooklyn College, Tony, who has a beautiful voice, sang "Mi Niña Bonita" (the Spanish equivalent of "Daddy's Little Girl"). Our daughter Alicia, then nine years old, immediately declared that she wanted Tony to sing it at her wedding. Twenty years later—even though we were now living in Massachusetts and hadn't seen Tony in years—he did.

———◦◦———

I TRULY FELT LIKE a fish out of water when I started my job at Brooklyn College. Unlike some of the faculty, I had not been apprenticed into academia through a doctoral program. Scheduling courses, preparing syllabi, holding office hours, serving on departmental and college-wide committees, doing research, and publishing: these were all new to me. Elected to the Faculty Senate in my second year on the job, I remember thinking, *Who, me?* Nearly all the members of the senate were older White males; few women and only one other person of color were members. I had to remind myself to heed Angel's advice, "Sensación de poderío!" ("Walk in as if you own the place!"). I tried but it wasn't easy. My own advice to myself during those early years in academia was, *You belong here just as much as anybody else does.* In subsequent years, I grew into that advice, making myself comfortable—more or less—wherever I went, whether it was sitting on a panel with Rosa Parks in 1983 or receiving the six honorary doctorates I've been honored with.

Politically, working at Brooklyn College was a baptism by fire. I thought I had learned a lot in the turbulent climate of the late 1960s and early 1970s, but it was nothing compared with what was to come. The three years I was at Brooklyn College, from 1972 to 1975, were a blur of on-the-job political education, rallies, demonstrations, takeovers, and even arrests. This explosion of political activism was the result of the growing pains of ethnic studies and the apparent threat the field posed to higher education. Because the discipline—or, rather, the interdisciplinary endeavor—was new and untested, there were powerful vested interests lined up against it. Ethnic studies, at its core, was a direct challenge to higher education's Eurocentric curriculum, its until-now stranglehold on defining what knowledge was most important. New and critical voices were contesting the previously agreed-upon notion of what it meant to be an educated person. No longer limited to Shakespeare, Faulkner, and Hemingway, the new curricula included Morrison, Neruda, and de Burgos. History was no longer simply about the conquests and achievements of Europeans and Americans; it now included the study of imperialism, colonialism, and exploitation as well.

My political, social, and cultural awareness took a giant leap forward that first year at the college. Although I was hired as an instructor, I was equal parts learner. In a course I took at New York University, I had learned about Puerto Rican island history; at Brooklyn College, I was introduced to the history of Puerto Ricans in New York and the Northeast. I learned that we weren't just victims or, to use the current jargon, "takers." We were doers, creators, and initiators. It made me value, more than ever, my parents' courage in journeying to the States—individually and without much support—to start a new life. The photo of my father sitting on the dais at the St. George Hotel as president of the Puerto Rican Merchants' Association made me immeasurably proud. As one of those in the first wave of Puerto Ricans in a city and country that had neither welcomed nor accepted him, his meager fourth-grade education notwithstanding, he had

As Sonia learned more & started college she became increasingly proud of parents- who came to US & started a new life w/ no help - thoughts of pic of dad @ St George Hotel as president of P. Rican Merchant Assoc.

nevertheless persevered and made a significant contribution to the growth and development of his community.

From María Sánchez, I learned about the courageous teachers who were the first Puerto Ricans to teach in the New York City public schools. By the mid-1960s, of the fifty-five thousand teachers in the city's public schools, there were now a few dozen Puerto Ricans. I learned about Antonia Pantoja, a true Renaissance woman and the catalyst for several significant Puerto Rican organizations in New York, including the Puerto Rican Forum and Aspira, the latter of which promoted and facilitated higher education among Puerto Rican youths. I learned about Dr. Helen Rodríguez Trías, a New York-based Puerto Rican pediatrician, independence supporter, and women's rights and community activist in New York City who was the first Latina president of the American Public Health Association. I met Puerto Rican activists and musicians who came to speak and perform at the college. Working in the Department of Puerto Rican Studies taught me more than what I could teach my students— though I think I did a pretty good job of that as well. My experience at the department taught me that we were not invisible, that we had stories to tell, that we had made, and were making, history. It was a riveting time for me.

She took classes about P. Rican history and taught classes

Our students were instrumental in all curricular, personnel, and other decisions in the department. They served on all departmental committees, indeed sometimes as chair, often outnumbering faculty; they also represented the department on college-wide committees. Both the students and some of the faculty were far more radical than I had ever been. My colleague Richie Perez, for example, had been a member of the Young Lords. Even though my experience during those three years was exciting and eye-opening, it was also terrifying as it challenged the good-girl persona I had always cultivated. Participating in rallies, signing petitions, speaking at demonstrations, serving as a member of various negotiating committees— these were all alien activities to me. Even while I participated in them, I held my breath.

Brooklyn College was a remarkable learning experience in other ways as well. Through research for the courses I taught, I also learned a great deal about bilingual education because, although I had learned the prac-

[handwritten margin notes: learned practical from PS 25 immersed in theory & research @ Brooklyn College]

tice of bilingual education at PS 25, I became immersed in the theory and research at Brooklyn College. I learned as well what life in academia was like, though I knew, even then, that ours was not the typical academic experience. The activities that I would become involved with—political education efforts, picketing, almost weekly demonstrations, and the take-over of offices—were not usually associated with academia, though they were fairly typical activities in those years. I also learned skills that aren't necessarily regarded as consistent with academic life. I became adept at speaking in public, for example, not at professional meetings to present my research, but at rallies on the quad! We organized so many demonstrations, we joked that we should start a business that in those years would have probably been quite lucrative: Rent-a-Demo, where we would pile poster paper, Magic Markers, bullhorns, and other paraphernalia associated with community organizing and political activism into the trunk of a car and go around the city renting the stuff to organizations and groups that needed it.

PAPI HAD BEEN DIAGNOSED with lung cancer in 1972, just after I started my position at Brooklyn College. The doctor had called me to tell me the diagnosis, which I shared with Lydia. I was heartbroken, not only because I adored Papi but also because it was a heavy burden for Lydia and me to bear. As was the custom in those years, we decided not to tell either of our parents. They must have figured it out, of course. Papi had been a smoker for many years but had given up the habit several years before the diagnosis (we still, however, smelled the telltale signs of tobacco in the bathroom whenever he sneaked a smoke). By the time he gave it up, it was too late.

In the summer of 1973, some of my colleagues and I took a group of Brooklyn College students to Puerto Rico. Angel and I had decided to go on the trip, thinking Papi's health wouldn't deteriorate so quickly. With Alicia, who was then just three years old, we stayed at the University of Puerto Rico at Río Piedras Guest House on the beautiful campus. In the tropics, rain often comes quickly and surprisingly, sometimes lasting just a few minutes before the sun peeks out again. I remember one day when the water workers were on strike, leaving us with no water for our daily shower. As soon as one of those serendipitous rain showers started, Angel put on a bathing suit and grabbed Alicia in his arms for an impromptu shower, complete with soap. I looked out to see them soaping up and laughing on the terrace.

On that trip, we heard lectures, deepened our friendships with faculty and students, took trips around the island, and participated in a couple of pro-independence demonstrations. One such rally was a counterdemonstration to the official celebration of the Fourth of July. Isn't it ironic, we thought, that colonized people are celebrating the independence of their colonizer? As in our Rent-a-Demo times back home, we brought poster paper, Magic Markers, and other supplies to make signs and share them with others.

Angel, Alicia, and I also visited family who still lived in Puerto Rico. For me, it was a homecoming of sorts to be able to reconnect with my roots. I hadn't been back to Puerto Rico since I was a college student. Seeing the aunts, uncles, and cousins I had stayed with when I spent the summer there with Lydia when I was eleven, I felt as if the years hadn't made a difference. My cousin Virginia, who had moved back to Puerto Rico from New York, insisted on keeping Ali for a weekend; I thought, yes, we're home.

A couple of weeks into our trip, Papi had to be taken to the hospital. We returned home just a few days before he died. It was almost as if he had held on, waiting for us to come home. We visited him in the hospital every day. Alicia still remembers climbing into his hospital bed to lie with him. He was not only a wonderful father, but also a fiercely devoted grandfather to Alicia and to Lydia's son, Jimmy.

We were all there—Angel, Mami, Lydia, Freddy, Jimmy, and Alicia—on the night of August 22. When everyone left, I stayed back, wanting to stay with Papi for a bit longer. As I said good-bye, ready to join the others downstairs, Papi, in a barely audible voice, asked me to stay with him. The others were waiting in the car, so I told him I had to leave but assured him I would be back the following day. I left, and he died shortly thereafter. He must have known it was the end; I only wish I had realized it so that I could have spent the last few minutes of his life with him, holding his hand. Another of those moments I will always regret.

I got the call from the hospital as soon as Angel, Alicia, and I got home. That night, I thought I would die too. Even though I was twenty-nine years old, the words "Sometimes I Feel Like a Fatherless Child," my take on the African American spiritual "Sometimes I Feel Like a Motherless Child," kept repeating themselves in my head. I was not ready to see him go yet. Decades later, I still have dreams about him as if he were still alive.

When Papi died, Mami became catatonic, unable to do much of anything. She had relied on Papi for so many years; I'm also certain she couldn't imagine how she would manage with Freddy by herself. And Freddy took to throwing drinking glasses out the window, smashing them on the sidewalk. He also started tearing the labels off all his clothes. Lydia said it may have been his way of mourning. I guess we'll never know.

Milga and Tony took Ali to stay with them for a few days while Angel and I made the final arrangements for the wake and funeral. The wake was held at a local funeral parlor. All of Papi's remaining brothers from Puerto Rico came, as well as his sister and brothers from New York. Many nieces and nephews, from both Puerto Rico and the States, also came. Papi had been the patriarch of the family, the elder everyone looked to for advice and support. Former customers and helpers from his bodega, and some of our neighbors came as well. To our surprise, his old friend Willie Sacconino from the Jewish deli days many years before also showed up. And my colleagues from Brooklyn College were there throughout.

———◆◆◆———

OUR LONGEST AND MOST successful campaign at Brooklyn College started after my first year there and lasted through my third and final year. At the end of my first year, when Josie Nieves had fulfilled her commitment as department chair for three years, the faculty and students quickly decided that María Sánchez should be our next chair. We knew, even before Sonia Sotomayor coined the term some thirty years later, that María was the quintessential "wise Latina." Not only did María have extensive supervisory experience, level-headedness, and a singular ability to get along with a wide range of people, including politically active faculty and students impatient for change, but she was also adroit at forming both respectful and authoritative relationships with the administration.

Because our department was only three years old, our dean, Bruce Birkenhead, wanted to establish the department's credibility in the university and thus wanted to control the search for the department chair. He formed a search committee with two faculty members from our department, two from other departments, and himself as chair. Richie Pérez and I were selected by the students and faculty to be our department's representatives on the search committee. Luckily for us, Carmen Dinos from the School of Education was one of the outside members and was also sympathetic to our department and our cause.

After lengthy recruiting efforts, the search committee agreed on two final candidates: María Sánchez and Elba Lugo Luis-Deza, a Spanish language and literature professor from the University of Puerto Rico. After a lengthy interview process, the search committee voted three to two in favor of María. Carmen Dinos, under consideration for tenure that year, proved the swing vote. It was no secret that her appointment to the search committee had been a cynical move by the administration to pressure her to accept the candidacy of Lugo over María. Carmen, however, chose principle over personal gain and voted for María.

Professor Lugo, of course, had the right credentials (a doctorate from a US-based university, research experience, and a reasonable number of publications), all of which María lacked. But Lugo knew little, either personally or professionally, about the largely working-class urban Puerto Rican community in the United States—knowledge that the committee saw as essential to the position.

We were already accustomed to locking horns with the administration, but what happened next surprised even us: despite our recommendation, Dean Birkenhead unilaterally sent Lugo's name to President John Kneller as the top choice. The decision was met with outrage by students, the department's faculty, and other supportive faculty throughout the college. As the departmental representative to the Faculty Senate, I was charged with reading at the next senate meeting a long statement condemning Birkenhead's action and demanding that María be named immediately as chair.

In the weeks that followed, I joined my colleagues and students in protest, doing everything from marching outside the president's office, to signing petitions, to marching and chanting, "Kneller, you liar! We'll set your ass on fire!" and other like ditties on the quad. I helped organize students and called faculty members from other departments to solicit their

Department recommended 1 person for chair. President elected other person for chair. Caused major protests support. Putting aside my discomfort with some of these actions, I had to learn to become more courageous than I'd ever been.

My constant support and role model throughout all these activities was Angel. He was then taking courses at Brooklyn College and became very active in our struggle. Always present at our meetings, he was also a terrific organizer and was fearless and principled. From time to time, Alicia, at three and four years old, also joined us in the public demonstrations.

In September 1974, the dean and president dug in their heels and decided to bring Elba Lugo to campus as the new chair. She arrived with a police escort, but the students blocked the department door office with tape, refusing to let her in. Eventually, the administration set Lugo up in an off-campus office.

When it became clear that President Kneller would not back down, the students and faculty from our department took over his office on Friday, October 18, 1974. Tony and I represented the faculty in another round of negotiations with the administration, and everyone agreed to a ceasefire of sorts.

By the following Monday, when Kneller was clearly not budging from his position, we decided to take over the registrar's office, just down the hall from our department offices, to make an even bigger statement. In round-the-clock meetings that weekend, some of them in the apartment close to campus where Angel, Alicia, and I lived, we had planned every detail meticulously, from publicity to food for the protesters.

The staff members of the registrar's office were stunned and nervous as two hundred of us walked in, asking them—very politely—to vacate their offices. We promptly set up operations, defying a temporary restraining order from the New York Supreme Court. In addition to all the department's faculty members and dozens of our students, other university staff and students, as well as local community members and others from around the country, supported us by either participating in the takeover, demonstrating on campus, bringing supplies to the offices, or sending messages of support. Various media were on campus daily. Meanwhile, Angel spent hours with us every day, bringing food, blankets, and other provisions and going home at night to take care of Alicia.

We joked that our takeover was a strictly Puerto Rican affair: not only did we not destroy any records, but we also swept the floors and took

[Handwritten margin notes: Lugo - new chair arrived w/ police escort - Students blocked door & would not let her in - she was set up in off campus office. They took over the presidents office]

out the garbage daily. We even brought in an iron to press our clothing! I remember one student insisting on having a perfect crease in her jeans; without it, she said she simply couldn't go out to the daily demonstration. In a word, we left things exactly as we found them, and even better. Some staff members from the registrar's office remarked that their offices had never looked so good.

The takeover lasted four days. Finally, at 4 a.m. on Thursday, October 24, 1974, forty-five law enforcement officers, about half of them armed, descended on the campus. We marched out, fists in the air, chanting, "Black, Latin, Asian, White: for our rights we will fight!" I was arrested as one of three faculty members and forty-one students. From that moment on, we became the BC 44. After several hours at the courthouse, where we attempted to sleep on hard benches and waited for a judge to show up, we all pleaded not guilty to disturbing the peace and received sixty-day suspended sentences.

Despite the rough night, we immediately headed back to Brooklyn College and were surprised to be greeted by a boisterous crowd of about two thousand on the quad. When I was asked to speak before this very loud and energetic crowd, my remarks, like those of the other speakers, were met with thunderous applause.

Along with other photos of protesters and police, an image of me, fist held high in the air, appeared on page 1 of the Brooklyn College student newspaper. There was widespread support for our protest. Even the Alumni Association and the Professional Staff Congress, the organization that represented most faculty on campus, gave us their support. That day's editorial took President Kneller to task for stonewalling and threatening the delicate balance between the administration and all students, not just Puerto Rican students.

Within a few months, members of the administration agreed to appoint María as our chair. To save face, they did so with some stipulations: she would be appointed only as "interim" and would be on probation for a year or two. María proved to be an exceptional leader, serving as chair for several years. She was also an important mentor to the young faculty she brought to the department in subsequent years. As the department's reputation grew, more young scholars were recruited. With the number of Puerto Ricans with advanced degrees climbing steadily, all new hires had doctoral degrees. Our program was eventually recognized as one of the strongest Puerto Rican studies departments in the CUNY system.

———◆◆◆———

AFTER THE ARRESTS AND accommodations with the administration, life settled down into an uneasy peace. Conflicts of all kinds continued to erupt, though without the constant tension of before. But there were always issues: Will our courses be approved? What about new faculty? How many will we be able to hire? Who will decide? Will a major in Puerto Rican studies be approved? The adrenalin that had pumped us up for so long was unsustainable. Though I was still young—thirty-one—I was finding it difficult to fulfill both my responsibilities as a faculty member, wife, and mother and the demands of perpetual conflict. We had meetings round the clock, and I often got home late at night. Angel was always understanding; in fact, since he too was involved, we were often together at meetings and other activities. Alicia too was affected. I laugh to think of it now: rather than play house, Alicia played "going to meetings." More importantly, during those years, I never did research, nor did I publish anything; I presented my work at only one national conference, the 1974 NABE conference, with Herminio. There was simply no time for any traditional scholarly work.

As I had decided that being a teacher educator would be my life's work, this lack of traditional scholarly activity was a problem. My job at Brooklyn College was satisfying every dream I had ever had about my life as a teacher. Preparing prospective teachers was exhilarating and inspiring. Though I had loved my elementary and junior high school students in Brooklyn and the Bronx, it was as a teacher educator that I felt most complete. I had always been attracted to intellectual pursuits, and I believed that working at the university level would satisfy both this desire and my commitment to remain in the field of education. I loved preparing and teaching my classes, reading and learning, building strong relationships with students, pushing them to question conventional wisdom, sharing what I knew about teaching, and learning from their insights and experiences. Most of my students were Puerto Rican, a good number of them preservice teachers who wanted to put their bilingualism to good use. Many believed that their work as bilingual teachers would fulfill their com-

mitment to working with Latino/a students to help improve the students'
lot in life and the community's future. I wanted to continue this work.

At the same time, I knew that if I was to become an academic, I
needed a doctorate. But there was no way I could simultaneously study
for a doctoral degree and be a full-time faculty member at Brooklyn College; there simply wouldn't be enough hours in the day to do both and to
have a life with Alicia and Angel. I would no doubt face new challenges at
the college—all of them probably exciting—but after three all-absorbing,
exciting, and contentious years, I was ready for some peace and tranquility.
I knew that the only way to remain in academia would be to leave New
York City. Otherwise, I would be immersed in every political skirmish in
the city involving Puerto Ricans. At this point, we decided to leave the city
so that I could pursue my doctoral studies.

Deciding to leave Brooklyn College was painful. María, Tony, Milga,
Herminio, and several of the students had become como familia to me and
Angel. We shared birthdays, weddings, as well as good news and bad with
them. These were also the friends who comforted me when my beloved
Papi died in the summer of 1973. At Christmastime, we turned the Puerto
Rican tradition of *parrandas* into an urban New York affair: we would go
to apartments and houses in different sections of the city, in frigid temper-
atures, bringing our maracas, guiros, *cuatros*, claves, and other instruments
to sing our favorite Christmas songs outside their doors until they let us in,
offering us the typical holidays foods.

Wanted to pursue doctorate outside of NYC

By THE END OF 1974, I started making inquiries about graduate programs
outside the city. Angel also started making plans for our move. Although
he had been taking courses simply for the joy of learning, I convinced him
to look into a Brooklyn College program that validated life experience and
prior education. As it turned out, he needed just a couple of courses more
for a BA, which he received in May 1975, shortly before we moved.

At about that time, the Ford Foundation was beginning a program to
support the doctoral studies of African Americans, Mexican Americans,
Puerto Ricans, and Asian Americans. One of my departmental colleagues,
Loida Figueroa, an eminent historian from Puerto Rico, would be reviewing applications to the Ford program and suggested I apply. I did and, as a

Support for P. Rican Studies

semifinalist, was invited to the Ford Foundation offices in Manhattan for an interview. There, I met Arturo Madrid, the distinguished scholar who was the director of the program. Within a few days, I found out I had been selected as a Ford Fellow. I was thrilled. But, oops! I hadn't yet applied to a university, meaning the process was, as a result, slightly reversed.

Intrigued by the idea of our family moving to Massachusetts, I decided to apply to both Harvard University and the University of Massachusetts. I had heard from a colleague at Brooklyn College that UMass had a cutting-edge school of education. Given my background as a curriculum specialist at PS 25, I decided on curriculum as my specialization and sent in my application to the University of Massachusetts. In a few days, I received a call from Robert Sinclair, director of the curriculum program. He invited Angel and me for a visit to meet with him, his family, and some of the doctoral students in the program and to perhaps sit in on a class. Angel, Alicia, and I drove up on a cold, blustery February day in 1975 and stayed at a local inn. Weather notwithstanding, our visit convinced us that this was the place for us. Not only was I impressed with the UMass program, but Angel and I also immediately fell in love with the Amherst area. What a difference from the busy, crowded streets of Brooklyn! What a delight to drive through town and not have to face bumper-to-bumper traffic! How lovely the homes looked! Everything was so different, so bucolic, so peaceful—just what we were looking for. Since Angel's arrival in New York, we had often traveled to New England during the summer months. We had gotten hooked on concerts at Tanglewood and dance performances at Jacob's Pillow, both in the Berkshires, and we found Massachusetts in general to be more restful and soul-satisfying than New York City.

Alicia too, at age five, was captivated by the idea of living in a real house, not an apartment with no back yard. For months after our visit to UMass, Alicia drew pictures of the house she imagined we would live in once we moved. After visiting Amherst, I decided I wouldn't even apply to Harvard's Graduate School of Education—its curriculum program seemed much more traditional and not as cutting-edge or exciting. As a result, UMass became my only choice. Besides, the thought of living in a small town was intriguing.

During our February visit, Bob Sinclair had alerted Sylvia Viera, director of the new Bilingual Education Program in the School of Education,

[handwritten margin note: applied UMass,]

about my visit. When I went to meet her at the Bilingual Education Program offices, I noticed a list with names of prominent people in bilingual education. Imagine my shock at seeing my own name included! Apparently, my experience as a teacher and, later, a curriculum specialist at the first bilingual public school in the region and as an early faculty member in a groundbreaking bilingual education programs at a university was qualification enough. Nevertheless, except for the curricula Herminio and I had written at PS 25, I had never done any research or published anything except some book reviews for the *Bulletin of the Council on Interracial Books for Children*. I had loved the writing, but I also knew I had a long way to go to become an academic.

Shortly after we returned to New York, Professor Viera called me, offering me a Title VII (bilingual education) fellowship. I will always be grateful that Bob put me in touch with Sylvia, because I began my studies at UMass with two full fellowships. These paid for my tuition and books and even covered our living expenses for four years. The financial awards also enabled us to buy our first home, a modest cabin by a lake in a neighboring town.

Went to UMass w/ 2 full fellowships paid for everything

AFTER LIVING IN BROOKLYN all my life, except for my year in Spain, I knew the decision to leave would be difficult. How could I say good-bye to my Brooklyn College colleagues and leave Mami in New York alone with Freddy? How could we leave Lydia and her son Jimmy—more like a brother than a cousin to Alicia? At the same time, I knew that something more was out there for our family. Ever my booster, Angel readily agreed to the move.

How, though, to break the news to everyone? When we explained to Mami that we were moving so that I could continue my studies, she was, naturally, heartbroken. Nevertheless, she was proud of the reason. She must have also been worried about her own situation: especially after Papi's death a couple of years earlier, she had grown to count more than ever on Angel and me. Besides visiting every Sunday, we also took her shopping and ran errands for her, and Angel fixed everything in the house that needed fixing. To make our decision easier for her to take, we promised to visit at least once a month. Still, the news came as a blow to her. Lydia, who was teaching full-time, raising Jimmy by herself, and without a car,

Had to explain to family of leaving to UMass

couldn't give Mami the same level of attention that we had. Leaving Mami, we knew, would be our biggest challenge.

When it came time to tell my colleagues, I was concerned that they might react negatively. I was afraid my commitment to the department, our students, and ethnic studies in general would be questioned; I even fretted that they might see me as a traitor to the cause. Nothing of the sort happened. From the beginning, they completely embraced my decision to leave and supported it. As for me, I knew I had given the department, the students, and my colleagues everything I could and was ready for a new chapter in my life.

<hr>

As we prepared to move to Massachusetts, I had mixed feelings about leaving Brooklyn College. My time there had been incredibly enriching. But looking back, I also saw the tremendous toll political activism had taken on the program, the faculty, and especially the students. Only a few of the most active students, for instance, ever managed to graduate with a degree, although some did graduate and even went on to successful careers. Those who did not graduate had gained a valuable experience, but only these students would know if the experience helped them in the long run. The faculty and the program, for the most part, did well, though it did take some time for the Department of Puerto Rican Studies to come into its own. Thanks to the vision of María Sánchez and, later, of the renowned historian Virginia Sánchez Korrol, who followed María as chair, the department was placed on firm organizational and intellectual footing. But, again, this took time.

Several of my colleagues went on to do significant work in ethnic studies. As I write this, Tony Nadal, a highly respected faculty member in the department for forty years, has just retired. Milga Morales, who began as a counselor at the college, is now vice president of student affairs, and also planning to retire soon. The department, though, went through several more difficult and contentious years after our victory in 1974. There were several ugly incidents and disturbances, some of them internecine conflicts involving vying political interests among the faculty and students.

Our early struggles at Brooklyn College yielded uncertain permanent gains. Most Puerto Rican studies departments have, in fact, survived. But their existence has always been precarious, and they have had to struggle for legitimacy and recognition. Many of the original departments have evolved to embrace a more pan-Latino identity. This evolution is as it should be, given the changing demographics in New York City, where Puerto Ricans are no longer the majority Latino group. While the number of Puerto Rican and other Latino students at CUNY colleges has grown substantially, the same is not true of the number of Puerto Rican faculty throughout the CUNY system. The year with the highest number of Puerto Rican faculty was, indeed, 1975, the year following our triumph. A policy brief from the New York Latino Research and Resources Network documented that between 1970 and 1974, the number of Puerto Ricans on the CUNY instructional staff increased by 173, or approximately 70 percent (Pimentel, 2005). Just a year later, the number of Puerto Rican instructional staff reached 245, CUNY's highest number ever. Since then, the number has declined steadily to only 131 in 2002. At Brooklyn College specifically, Puerto Rican tenure-track, full-time faculty represented a meager 1.9 percent of the total faculty in 2002.

Puerto Ricans at CUNY have, in fact, fared worse in terms of faculty representation than any other federally protected group. This, despite the substantial increase in the number of Puerto Ricans who now have doctorates since 1972, when I began as an instructor at Brooklyn College. The same policy brief reported that in the 1970s, 0.2 percent of the total number of US doctoral recipients were Puerto Ricans on average; by 2002, the proportion had improved to 1.2 percent. Though this increase should also be evident in the number of Puerto Rican full-time, tenure-track and tenured faculty, that is far from the case. The report concludes that "the Puerto Rican fulltime faculty is 'vanishing' little by little since not enough new hires are replacing those who are retiring or leaving the institution" (Pimentel, 2005). Perhaps it's time for a return to the militancy of the early 1970s.

LEAVING BROOKLYN COLLEGE made me realize that I would never be the same Sonia Nieto as before. My whole outlook on life changed as I developed a more critical consciousness about life, education, culture, and politics. I could no longer watch the news on TV or read anything without

Brooklyn College made her realize that she would never be the same — she had changed

thinking about the political implications. Issues of colonization, patriar-
chy, and race would always be on my mind, particularly as they related
to education. I learned to be more courageous, more direct, less afraid of
upsetting the status quo. Through my classes and interactions with students, at the same time, I learned that my job was not to teach others to be
like me but rather to open their eyes to different perspectives, to *educate* in
the truest sense of the word.

Brooklyn College also taught me I would never be as radical as some
of my colleagues and many of the students, although they probably aren't
as radical now as they were back then either. I also decided that I could
never be a revolutionary, ready to take up arms or engage in violent acts of
any kind, as some of my colleagues seemed to be. I did, however, continue
to take part in more than my share of demonstrations and picket lines
in subsequent years. I would go on to sign many petitions, contribute
financially to international and local political and social justice organizations, and hold signs for political candidates for everything from local
school committee elections to presidential candidates like Jesse Jackson
and Barack Obama. I would support with time, money, and legwork many
organizations focusing on diversity and equity and serve as an advisory
board member or a trustee on numerous boards working for a more inclusive and just society.

The focus of my political work became clearer. While some of my colleagues focused on the independence of Puerto Rico, I did not. Though
I sympathized with the cause, I knew that no matter how Puerto Rican I
felt, I would always live in the United States. It is my country of birth and
upbringing, the place where my siblings and children live. With my growing consciousness, I also realized that—although I might not yet have had
the language to adequately express it—social justice, equity, and diversity
would define my life's work. My focus then became, and has been ever
since, the education of students for whom the US public education system
has not worked equitably. My goal was to help change that.

CHAPTER 10

UMass and the Che-Lumumba School

Learning to "Read the World"

Angel, Alicia, and I moved to Amherst, Massachusetts, on August 19, 1975, a month shy of my thirty-second birthday. Our first place was what in New York City might be called a two-story private house but in Massachusetts is known as a duplex apartment, that is, attached on both sides to similar apartments. Even though it was small, I was thrilled that for the first time in my life, I would have a second floor and two bathrooms, as well as a sliding glass door to the little patio outside our living room.

After living in a big city all my life, being in a small town seemed like a dream: clean streets, no traffic to speak of, plenty of parking, little shops, no hassle getting to and from everything, lots of places for Alicia to run and play, and numerous small-town community events. In addition, though Amherst was not as ethnically and racially diverse as it is now, the town surprised us with more diversity than we had expected, particularly among the graduate students at the university. It didn't take long for Angel and me to decide that this was where we wanted to establish roots and raise our family.

I was anxious to begin my classes, and after moving in, getting to know the town a bit, making our way to the local farmers' market (*How quaint!*

we thought), opening a bank account, registering Alicia for first grade at our local public school, and sundry other moving-in tasks, I was ready to begin my doctoral studies. The first course I walked into was Foundations of Multicultural Education, taught by Bob Suzuki. Bob's class changed everything. Little did I realize then that the topic of this course would become my life's work.

The UMass School of Education (recently renamed the College of Education) was a fascinating place in those years. Regarded as notorious by its critics and innovative by its supporters, it had been transformed by the forward-thinking dean, Dwight Allen, from a fairly traditional program to one that challenged most of the conventions of schools of education and even the rest of academia. For one thing, about a third of the faculty Dean Allen recruited were from other disciplines. This is how Bob Suzuki, an aeronautical engineer by training and formerly a faculty member in the Aerospace Engineering Department at the University of Southern California, had come to UMass. The GRE (Graduate Record Examination), a requirement for admission at most major universities, was not required at the School of Education. Dean Allen also recruited the most diverse faculty and student body the campus or the town had ever seen. In 1975, greater diversity among faculty and students was something that was just beginning to be demanded at other universities, but the UMass School of Education had been working toward it for several years. The school might have never again reached as high a level of diversity, among both students and faculty, as when Allen was dean.

The courses taught by faculty members and graduate students were innovative, not only in content but also in format, meeting from just once a week for five weeks, to meeting for several weekends, formats that are typical today but were new at the time. Doctoral students, in addition, were encouraged to design and teach courses in the topics that most interested them. We were also expected to create independent studies of our own design. Also—and this was one of the most significant differences between the UMass School of Ed and others—there were no grades. All courses were taken pass/fail. For all that, I never worked so hard in my life. Nor have I ever gotten so much out of my studies as during those years of doctoral study. Part of it had to do with the absence of pressure for grades. This experience changed how I thought about learning. I became convinced, and still am, that learning is most meaningful when connected to intrinsic rather than extrinsic rewards. My intrinsic reward was learning; I couldn't get enough of it.

The School of Education also sponsored exciting and innovative conferences and other events that put UMass on the map. In my years as a doctoral student, we hosted scholars from Buckminster Fuller to Paulo Freire, among many others. Unfortunately, when Dean Allen left the school just a month before I arrived, many of his innovations began to slowly erode. By my fourth and final year as a doctoral student, some of the push for experimental courses had disappeared, replaced by more traditional topics and formats. When I retired as a professor thirty years later, many more of the earlier innovations had disappeared. Unchanged, however, was the school's and university's stated commitment to social justice. At a time when these words were rarely heard at a college or university or in relation to public education, social justice was already entrenched at UMass. It is what drew me to and kept me at UMass, even years later, when I had numerous opportunities to go elsewhere. If that commitment was not always strictly honored in deed, it was widely recognized as a commonly shared value, and that itself is significant.

⟫◆⟪

As a doctoral student, I was privileged to have mentors who changed not only my thinking but also the course of my life. As mentioned earlier, Bob Suzuki was one such mentor. He also left a significant imprint in the field of multicultural education, as well as on his many students. Even though I loved most of my classes at UMass, Bob's captivated my attention the most. That first course gave me the language I had been searching for throughout my public school and Brooklyn College teaching years. *Cultural pluralism, antiracist education, liberatory education, diversity, equity, access*: all these terms became the analytic tools I would use to understand and define my ideas and my work. In Bob's classes, I was introduced to many of these concepts and theories. I learned about the history of US immigration and race relations, characterized by both inclusion and xenophobia, as well as the history of inequality in public education. In these classes, I became familiar with the names of Horace Kallen, W. E. B. DuBois, Horace Mann, Carter G. Woodson, Howard Zinn, and

Paulo Freire and was reintroduced to John Dewey, Jonathan Kozol, and Herb Kohl, among many others. That first semester, I read DuBois's *Souls of Black Folk* (1903), Dewey's *Democracy and Education* (1916), Woodson's *Miseducation of the Negro* (1933), and Freire's *Pedagogy of the Oppressed* (1970), and many other books and mountains of articles that were to shake up, and shape, my thinking.

Bob was a demanding teacher, and I was an enthusiastic student. In the four years I was a doctoral student, I took every course he taught. I learned not only about multicultural education but also about the context in which it had developed. In those classes, I first realized that nothing, including schooling, could be understood without taking into account its sociopolitical context. This has been one of the greatest discoveries in my life of learning. With this realization, I soon decided that with curriculum as my major area of interest, multicultural education would be one minor and bilingual education the other. These three areas of study and work are still my anchors.

Nothing could be understood w/ out taking in to account socio political context

Bob Sinclair was my major adviser and an excellent mentor, teaching me not only about the field of curriculum, but also what to expect as a graduate student and future teacher educator. Bob was a significant part of our lives during those first years in Massachusetts. He went beyond his responsibilities to me as a student by also reaching out to my family, such as when he and his wife Ann unexpectedly showed up at our house with a bottle of champagne the day after we adopted our daughter Marisa. If in subsequent years as colleagues, our relationship became strained because of the stresses of academia, I will nonetheless always be grateful for Bob's mentorship and his confidence in me in those early years.

adopted daughter Marisa

Sylvia Viera, whom Bob Sinclair had introduced me to on my first visit to UMass, also became a mentor. A gutsy fighter, she was the first Puerto Rican woman faculty member at the university. She had come from Puerto Rico, and though she hadn't been involved in the struggles for bilingual education in the States, her courses on the topic were rigorous and thought-provoking.

Both Sylvia, who was the director of the Bilingual Program, and Sarah Nieves, the other faculty member in the program, left unexpectedly after my first year at the School of Education. Those of us who had received federal Title VII (bilingual education) fellowships—ten of us in all—in effect had to step up to manage the program. We scrambled to figure out how to teach the courses and advise the undergraduate and masters' students. Calling ourselves La Colectiva, we taught, counseled other students, represented the program at meetings both in the university and beyond, and did the day-to-day chores associated with program management. We also had long and sometimes contentious meetings, discussing everything from the curriculum to how courses should be evaluated. Because we were left with no faculty, we also had a search to hire two faculty members. As the only Title VII Fellow with a history in both bilingual education and university teaching, I was encouraged by the dean and others to apply for one of the positions. I decided against it, however, because I knew that, just as in the case of Brooklyn College and given the demands of home, family, and academia, completing a doctoral degree while also serving as a faculty member would be almost impossible. Gloria de Guevara, another Fellow, accepted one of the faculty positions and remained in the School of Education for several years before taking a position in the central administration at the university, where she remained for many years.

Luis Fuentes, the other faculty member La Colectiva recruited that year, became another significant mentor to me. Luis was a tried-and-true veteran of the struggle for bilingual education and community control movements in New York City. He had served as community superintendent in the Lower East Side (Latinos christened the area "Loisaida"). Because newspaper and television news reports often referred to him as the "controversial Luis Fuentes," Luis used to joke that his children thought his first name was "Controversial." "Feisty" was another adjective often used to describe him. He did everything, from introducing bilingual education to District 1 schools to changing the cafeteria offerings to reflect the Latino, African American, and Chinese heritage of the children in the district's schools.

Besides becoming dear and close friends of ours, Luis and his wife, Dora, became central public figures and significant leaders in the Latino community in Amherst and throughout Western Massachusetts. Luis's wife, Dora, was also a gifted educator. A school district administrator in New York City before she and Luis moved to Amherst, she became the director of bilingual education in the Holyoke Public Schools and, later, the first Puerto Rican school principal in the history of that town. Luis almost singlehandedly recruited more Puerto Ricans, other Latinos, African Americans, Asians, and other students of diverse background to the university than anybody before him had managed to do. A fervent believer in access and equity, Luis sometimes erred on the side of an unrealistic optimism when recruiting doctoral students who might not be able to handle the intellectual rigors of doctoral studies. Some of the students he recruited, on the other hand, might never have thought they could complete a doctorate yet later became important leaders and thinkers in education. Luis became immersed in many community struggles, from Latino/a parents' demands for bilingual education services for their children, to a takeover protesting the local Five-College Radio's decision to eliminate *¿Qué Tal Amigos?*, the station's only Spanish-language offering. For me and many others, Luis was not only a mentor but also a cheerleader and an advocate. I was privileged to be his student and, after completing my doctorate, his close colleague, ally, and friend. After retiring to Puerto Rico in 1995, he died in 2014 at the age of eighty-five.

My DOCTORAL EDUCATION at UMass was, intellectually speaking, the most exhilarating time of my life. Through the courses I took, the books I read, and the people with whom I interacted—faculty, other students, guests, and speakers—my eyes were opened wide. I was able to give voice to a deepening consciousness about education, culture, and politics. I was like a sponge, soaking up everything in reach. I did all the required work and more in my courses. And with no pressure about grades, I was free to explore and experiment with the ideas that most intrigued me, whether it was to investigate the philosophy of John Dewey, read the story of Sylvia Ashton-Warner, or study the work of Maria Montessori.

It was especially Paulo Freire's ideas about education that captivated me from the start and that profoundly changed my outlook on education and life. After I read his *Pedagogy of the Oppressed*, it was inevitable that my philosophy about education would evolve. A number of his ideas grabbed hold of me from the start and have influenced my teaching, my philosophy of education, and my research and writing since. Given his experiences as a literacy worker—the role that led to, first, his being jailed and, later, exiled from Brazil—one of the key ideas he discussed in *Pedagogy* was that

*True learning is about reading the world.

it isn't sufficient for people to learn to "read the word," but that true learning is about "reading the world." That is, people need to understand the world in which they live so that they can change oppressive conditions. What particularly appealed to me about this idea is that it was built on the belief in people's agency, their ability to change the conditions in which they live. Paulo defined education as either liberatory or domesticating. Rather than positioning readers, workers, or anyone else as simply empty vessels waiting to be filled with knowledge (what he defined as "banking education"), Freire's ideas brought a sense of power to the powerless and those who work with them. Although his work was primarily with adults in Brazil, these ideas resonated powerfully with me in terms of the K–12 education of disempowered youths and communities in the United States, especially in urban areas.

Freire's focus on education as *conscientização* inspired me. The term is often translated from the Portuguese as "awareness" or "realization," but I think a better translation is "consciousness-raising"—also an important element of the feminist movement in those years. Rather than rote learning or banking education, the purpose of education, in Freire's view, was freedom. I found these ideas compelling not only in my doctoral work, but also in my community work and, later, in teaching future and practicing teachers. Actually meeting, listening to, and participating in numerous events with Paulo a few years later during his visits to UMass were among the most powerful experiences of my life. When I became a professor at UMass a year after completing my doctoral studies, I consistently used his work in my classes. Although there were considerable differences between teaching peasants in Brazil to read and teaching young people in American urban areas, his philosophy transcended geography, culture, and time. After reading one or another of his books, I would have my students write a letter to Paulo at the end of the semester. I collected some of these letters over the years and, in 2008, edited a book of those letters, including several from well-known Freirean scholars. The book, *Dear Paulo: Letters from Those Who Dare Teach*, was my way of thanking him.

I began to understand as well that the role of most schools around the world is to have young people serve as apprentices in what Michel Foucault called the "regimes of truth," that is, the underlying truths that help perpetuate the status quo, even (or perhaps especially) when the status quo is unjust. Specifically, regimes of truth are the discourses promoted by each society as its truth. They are produced, transmitted, and kept in place by systems of power such as schools, universities, the military, and the media. As a result, perspectives and realities different from those officially sanctioned tend to remain invisible. At the same time, Antonio Gramsci's theory of *hegemony*, that is, the process by which dominant groups create and maintain social control over others, had a powerful impact on me. Hegemony often results when those who are dominated come to believe that they are naturally inferior in culture, language, and experience. I had often seen this attitude among my own people. I myself had fallen victim to it as a child and young adult, believing, for instance, that we Puerto Ricans speak an inferior Spanish, that our culture and history had nothing of value to offer, and that we had been responsible for messing up the neighborhoods we had moved to, in contrast to the "good" immigrants (European) who had come before us. All of these theories influenced my thinking and my practice as a teacher educator, researcher, and writer.

Other courses besides those I took at the School of Education were memorable as well. One in particular stands out: taught by Samuel Bowles and Herbert Gintis, it centered on the political economy of schooling. Because of their radical views, Sam and Herb, already well-known economists, had not received tenure at Harvard University. But as two of the newly recruited radical economists, they put the UMass Department of Economics on the map as a destination for graduate students and scholars interested in Marxian economics. At the time, Sam and Herb were just on the brink of also making a big name for themselves in education with the publication of their groundbreaking book, *Schooling in Capitalist America* (1976). The book has become a staple of graduate coursework not only in schools of education but also in departments of sociology, anthropology, and, of course, economics. Our textbook for the course consisted of the page proofs of their manuscript, which was due to be released a few months after the class ended.

I loved going to that class. Besides being excellent professors, Sam and Herb made every session an engrossing experience. One of the key ideas we discussed was the notion that the quality of a person's education was based on his or her family's political and economic power. This idea, while not exactly new, so contradicted the prevailing wisdom—that public education was the great equalizer, that our society was a meritocracy, and that getting ahead required only hard work and determination—that it shook my idealism and tacit belief in the promise of public education.

In the long run, although these ideas were significant in my developing consciousness, they did not alter my firm conviction in the potential of public education. I was one of three doctoral students from the School of Education in Sam and Herb's class; our classmates were graduate students from the Department of Economics. Right away, I noticed a difference in our perspectives: the economics students seemed resigned to the idea that education was based on who had the most power and resources. Those of us from the School of Education, on the other hand, maintained a firm hope in the promise of public education. Had we accepted the inevitability of power and resources as the only guarantee of a decent education, we would have had to throw up our hands in despair. If we didn't believe in public education, what would be the use of our being educators?

Then, as now, I refused to accept the fatalistic view that public education was doomed to failure or that it couldn't accomplish the social justice goals supported by most progressive educational thinkers. Although I certainly understand—and often share—the disappointment and even despair over policies and practices in public education, I nonetheless believe that change is possible. Paulo Freire's philosophy, his undying hope and faith in the power of people to change their destiny—these provide a powerful antidote to the prevailing pessimism and cynicism.

SOMETHING ELSE HAPPENED on the first day I walked into Bob's Suzuki's class in September 1975. To my surprise, there sat Rosa Gastón, a fellow teacher from PS 25. As was the practice in those days among many African Americans and others of the African diaspora, she had changed her name to Jamila, an African name. Now living in Amherst, Jamila was, like me, a doctoral student. We became close friends, even closer than we had been at PS 25, because we began to collaborate on a project that would become very important in my life, the Che-Lumumba School. The school had been started in the early 1970s as a result of a graduate course on alternative education taught by Professor Gloria Joseph. The school was named after Che Guevara, an Argentinian leader of the Cuban revolution, and

Patrice Lumumba, an anticolonialist leader and the first democratically elected prime minister of the Congo (Lumumba was later reportedly assassinated by the CIA). I was intrigued by the idea of an alternative school that included a focus on topics generally silenced in books and history. So, when Jamila invited me to a meeting of the teachers and parents at the school, suggesting it might be a place for me to do research and to enroll Alicia, I readily accepted.

Angel and I immediately became involved in the Che-Lumumba School. By January 1976, we had enrolled Alicia, transferring her from Marks Meadow, our local public elementary school in Amherst. It was not an easy decision. Coming from New York City and its schools with crowded classes, concrete yards, and difficult conditions for both students and teachers, we found Marks Meadow an almost idyllic place. It had, in contrast, small classes, engaged teachers, a playground on a grassy field, and other conditions that made both teaching and learning easier than in New York.

The Che-Lumumba School consisted of four rooms on the fourth floor of the New Africa House, where the Department of Afro-American Studies on the UMass campus was located. It didn't look at all like a typical school. Rather than desks, there were conference-style tables with chairs where the children worked. There was only one chalkboard, few supplies and books, no playground, and no special services. But there were also no bells, no standardized tests, no structured curricula. Lunch was served in Yvonne's Place, a restaurant in the basement of the New Africa House. Yvonne John, the proprietor, was from Guyana and had a talent for cooking delicious and nutritious meals. She insisted on charging an embarrassingly low price for the kids' lunch, saying it was her "contribution to the cause." The children had recess on the hill outside the building. They were called back to class not with bells but with one of the teachers yelling out the window, "Time to come in, kids!" Alicia said it felt like home and the teachers felt like family.

The Che-Lumumba School was a decidedly radical place, though in the five years we were closely associated with the school, it changed, reflecting who was enrolled and who was in charge. For some of the parents and teachers, the school was an Afrocentric or a Latinocentric school; for others, it was a school with progressive politics, including feminist values;

*Che- Lumumba School

for still others, it was simply an opportunity for their child, who might be having trouble in the Amherst public schools, which in those years were quite traditional, were overwhelmingly White, and had little experience in teaching children of color. For Angel, the school was where he could live his long-held values of solidarity, equity, and love. For me, it was a place to put into practice the antiracist and critical multicultural educational philosophy I was developing. These differing perspectives made the Che-Lumumba School both an exciting and a contentious place. We discussed every decision, sometimes ad nauseam: Who should develop the curriculum? What should it include? Which holidays should we celebrate? Who should teach? Who should be the director? Should we charge tuition or not? And so on.

I remember one particular flare-up about whether we should include "This Land Is Your Land" in the children's repertoire of songs. Some people argued that the United States *wasn't* our land, that it was stolen from Native people. Others, myself included, contending that like it or not, it was *now* our land and we needed to teach the children to feel part of it, to be responsible for it, and to care for it.

On a more serious note, we had an all-day meeting sometime in the summer of 1978 to discuss whether to enroll White children. The debate was an especially prickly one, pitting friends against friends. Angel suggested meeting at our house, as we had by then moved to a lakeside cabin in Belchertown, a neighboring town. We thought it would be a good idea to have a place where the parents and children could cool off, both physically and emotionally. At one point during the meeting, Angel said, "Okay, everybody in the lake!" That helped cool tempers. Some, including White parents who had children of color in the school, argued *against* enrolling White children. Others, including parents of diverse backgrounds such as Angel and me, argued *for* enrolling White children whose families had progressive politics and wanted a different kind of education for their children. The latter argument ultimately prevailed, although it was a hard-fought one. As it turned out, we never had more than a couple of White children at the school.

Despite the disagreements, or perhaps because of them, we all became very close. The times help explain the intensity of the politics and why such strong bonds developed among the families and children. The early 1970s, when the school first opened, were clearly an extension of the 1960s. The politics included the Vietnam War, the extreme levels of government-military-industrial complex violence and exploitation and, in terms of public education, the absence of any reflection whatsoever on the history, or even the mention, of people of color in the regular school curriculum.

group did everything together

The Che-Lumumba School became our family in Amherst. We did everything together: We were the teachers, developing the curriculum and organizing fund-raisers. We held weekly meetings; organized numerous potlucks; and celebrated birthdays, weddings, naming ceremonies, and more. We attended demonstrations about the many hot political issues of the time, including US involvement in Central America, anti-apartheid protests, and the bicentennial counterdemonstration in Philadelphia. During that last demonstration, it rained so heavily we were completely soaked and shivered all the way home on the bus. Even though the bus driver claimed that the air-conditioning was not functioning properly, to this day my friend Maddie Márquez is certain he kept the air conditioner on to spite us because he didn't like our politics.

Angel was the go-to person for almost everything that needed to be done, even creating a number of games we sold through the *Guardian* newspaper. José Tolson, another parent and the partner of Susan Markman, the main teacher, created beautiful posters for use in fund-raising. I became the primary curriculum developer and the Spanish teacher. Our fund-raisers at the UMass Student Union Building were popular events, often bringing together our friends and colleagues, UMass students both undergraduate and graduate, students from the surrounding colleges, and people from the community at large. The most memorable events were concerts featuring folksinger Pete Seeger, jazz musician Gil Scott Heron, and the Chilean musical and vocal group Quilapayún.

The children had pen pals, but not your typical pen pals. Alicia, for example, wrote to Lolita Lebrón, who led an assault on the US House of Representatives in 1954 and demanded independence for Puerto Rico. Though no deaths resulted from the assault, the five participants in the attack were held in federal penitentiaries for twenty-five years and were finally granted clemency by President Jimmy Carter on a quiet Friday afternoon in 1979. Shortly after their release, we invited them to Amherst to visit the Che-Lumumba School. Lolita said that receiving letters from the children was one of her greatest joys during those difficult years of imprisonment.

I didn't always agree with everything the school stood for. I remember being uncomfortable the first time I saw the full name of the school, the Che-Lumumba School for Truth. This name has bothered me even more in the years since. What truth? Whose truth? These are questions worth exploring but we probably weren't ready to explore them during those years. We were convinced that we had right on our side, so it was hard for us to consider other perspectives. I doubt that some of us who were involved in the school would still support some of the ideas we professed at the time; viewpoints often change with age, experience, and a changing sociopolitical context. The 1970s were, after all, radically different from our world today. The school was, in many ways, emblematic of the times: a radical, counterculture experiment that challenged a traditional Eurocentric curriculum and proposed a different way of educating children by giving them information and insights they would never have gotten in conventional public schools. These are things I feel very good about. If sometimes we were dogmatic or inflexible, we nevertheless provided our children with an education that was affirming and nurturing, that encouraged them to think critically, and that planted seeds for a fertile future growth. I don't for a moment regret our involvement with the school, though I might well do it differently today.

We developed lasting friendships through the Che-Lumumba School. Although our philosophy and politics have evolved over the years, many of these friendships have persisted. We became especially close with numerous people: Maddie Márquez was the original director and at the time a doctoral student, and her husband, Roberto (Bob), was then teaching at Hampshire College. The first year we were associated with the school, Susan Markman, the twenty-one-year old head teacher, had agreed to teach for the unbelievable sum of one thousand dollars for the year. Her husband, José Tolson, worked in Student Services at UMass. Mauricio Hernandez was my student in a winter session course I taught as an adjunct professor at Hampshire College in 1977 while I was a doctoral student. Eshu Bumpus, then a student at Hampshire College, volunteered at the school and is now a storyteller of some renown. Theresa Jenoure, a violinist and artist from the Bronx, came to Amherst to study and, years later, became my doctoral student and close friend. Finally, there was Jamila, whom I mentioned earlier.

Maddie and I have become like sisters over the past forty years. She is, in Angel's words, my *consigliere*—as in *The Godfather*—and as her husband Bob puts it, my partner in crime. Maddie has been my best friend, confidante, supporter, and devil's advocate. We usually agree but sometimes disagree on everything from politics to school policy, from wall paint color to shoe style. But I always learn from her. She has been there with wise advice and moral support through the many times of stress and pain in my life. She has advice on everything and has often said that she should put up a shingle, "All Problems, Large or Small." She'd probably do very well.

Susan Markman and José Tolson became Alicia's godparents. A gifted teacher, Susan was wise beyond her years and was completely dedicated to the school, the children, and the community we formed. She went on to work as a resource teacher for the Amherst Public Schools, to which she brought the considerable talents of her work with children. Jamila Gastón and Mauricio Hernandez became our daughter Marisa's godparents.

Alicia attended the Che-Lumumba School until it effectively closed in 1980, at the end of her fifth grade. A few of the children and their families were moving, either because they had completed their studies at UMass or for new jobs. It seemed a propitious time to close the school. With never more than thirteen children at the school, keeping it open had been a tremendous amount of work, and only three or four students would have remained. We had a ceremony for the five graduates on the front porch of our home facing Lake Arcadia in Belchertown. It was a bittersweet moment, the end of an era for us.

━━━◦•◦━━━

Probably the decision that most changed our lives after we moved to Massachusetts—even more than my doctoral studies, even more than studying Paulo Freire, even more than anything else—was our decision in 1976 to adopt our daughter Marisa. Soon after we were married, Angel and I had resolved to have four children: two birth children and, thinking about the many children who needed parents, two adopted ones. In the five years after Alicia was born, I had two miscarriages. Both were so heartbreaking that after the second miscarriage, we chose to start the adoption process then rather than try again.

Going through the home study was frustrating. Very early in the process, the social worker said flatly, "You won't be eligible to adopt a White baby."

"We don't want to adopt a White baby," I assured him. "We want to adopt a Puerto Rican baby."

"Yes, that's fine," he insisted, "but it will have to be a *Black* Puerto Rican, not a *White* Puerto Rican."

We were astounded that they made this distinction. Perhaps we shouldn't have been. Race issues in the United States are complicated and often bizarre. Yet, because Puerto Ricans are a mixed-race people—and although we can't deny that racism exists in Puerto Rico and among Puerto Ricans in the United States—it is not at all uncommon for a Puerto Rican family to contain various shades from black to white.

"It doesn't matter what *color* the child is; we just want to adopt a Puerto Rican child," I reassured him.

But it was almost as if we had to swear not to hanker after a White child before we could be approved to adopt. We learned that the reason for this stipulation was that there were White couples willing to "settle" for a light-skinned Puerto Rican child and they preceded us on the waiting list! We knew what would happen with those children: they would be raised as White, probably never knowing they were Puerto Rican. Such is the reality of mixed-up US racial politics.

We were approved as adoptive parents shortly before moving to Massachusetts. Once there, we decided to try again for me to get pregnant, and we succeeded for a third time just a couple of months later. Sadly, I had another miscarriage, this time on New Year's Eve, 1976. I remember not only the physical pain but also the emotional pain of being separated from Angel and Alicia that night and of knowing, once and for all, that I would never give birth again. A nurse came by at midnight with a cup of eggnog to welcome the New Year, something I was not keen on celebrating.

A few months after my third miscarriage, we restarted the adoption process, now at the Children's Aid and Family Service office in Northampton. This time, there was no stipulation that we had to adopt a Black

Puerto Rican; the staff understood that we would be happy with any kind of Puerto Rican. In early fall of 1976, we received a call asking if we would be interested in adopting a Puerto Rican baby girl of five months. We were far from first on the list, but the birth mother, herself not Puerto Rican, had requested that the baby be adopted by a Puerto Rican family because the birth father, who never found out he was the father, was Puerto Rican. Naturally, we jumped at the chance.

We made all the preparations we could make in what I called "the shortest pregnancy ever," a period of two weeks. We involved Alicia in the entire process: shopping for clothes and other necessities, finding a crib, informing family and friends, organizing our "Welcome Home, Marisa" get-together, and preparing the room she and Alicia would share. A week after receiving the call, we made a visit to meet Marisa for the first time. Alicia, who had brought a Raggedy Ann doll she had chosen as a gift for the baby, was excited that finally she would have a little sister. Of course, we loved Marisa almost immediately. A week later, we picked her up and brought her to her new home for good.

We were to learn that adoption is clearly not for the fainthearted, a lesson reinforced for us many times over the years. The entire story of Marisa is best left for another book, one that I hope to write with her someday. Suffice it to say that we faced many challenges over the years, challenges I believe made us better parents but, at the same time, were heartbreaking reminders that parenting is tough work.

PART III

Research and Writing

CHAPTER 11

Life as a Professor

I GRADUATED FROM UMASS, a freshly minted PhD, in June 1979. Angel and Alicia were there, as was Mami, who had recently moved to Massachusetts from Brooklyn. Lydia and Jimmy also came up for the momentous occasion.

But before starting my academic career, in April 1979, I traveled to Cuba as a volunteer with the Venceremos Brigade, an organization founded in 1969 to send young people to Cuba to work side-by-side by Cuban workers in solidarity with the Cuban Revolution. Given all the changes taking place in Cuba, especially in health care and education, it was an exciting time and I didn't want to miss it. Although I was already thirty-five years old—the cutoff age for volunteers—I was curious to see the changes that were taking place, particularly in schools, after the Cuban Revolution of 1959. At the same time, I was disinclined to go because Marisa was still so young (she would turn three years old that month), but Angel convinced me to go, saying, "You'll never have this possibility again." Lydia, meanwhile, took Alicia and her son Jimmy to Disney World for a week to give Angel a break from taking care of both girls for the five weeks I would be away.

We went through Canada and returned via Mexico, as neither country had cut off relations with Cuba after its revolution. The volunteers were from all over the United States. We lived at a camp near Havana, living communally and working in construction, specifically, building houses. It was exhausting work, but we spent the final two weeks touring the island and visiting factories, schools, and museums. I was especially intrigued with the changes in education. Some of Paulo Freire's ideas were

Travelled to Cuba to volunteer

being used in public schools as well as in a massive adult literacy campaign throughout the nation. It was a fascinating trip, one I don't regret having made, even though it was against US policy and the ongoing embargo (finally to be ended in 2015).

———◆———

Wanted to be a teacher & academi

I BECAME AN ASSISTANT professor at the University of Massachusetts in Amherst in 1980, a year after completing my doctoral work. Before that, for a year I had worked at a job that convinced me I could never be happy as a bureaucrat and needed instead to be a teacher educator and researcher. In spite of what I had written in my journal years earlier about not wanting an academic life with "phonies" and "pseudo-intellectuals," given my penchant for writing since childhood and my love of teaching and learning, I was destined to become an academic. But after defending my dissertation in June 1979, there were no faculty positions available in the area when I began my postdoctoral life. I thus reluctantly began working in a newly created position as the Lau coordinator (so named after the mandate that resulted from the US Supreme Court decision in the *Lau v. Nichols* case) in the Bureau of Equal Education at the Massachusetts Department of Education, Springfield region. My job consisted of working with school districts, administrators, parent groups, and teachers in Western Massachusetts to make sure they were in compliance with the Lau mandate. The result of a 1974 federal lawsuit, the mandate stipulated that all children for whom English was an additional language needed to be provided with services to learn English while learning their academic content. Though I missed teaching terribly, I was glad to have this job: I worked with good people, some of whom became friends, and I learned a lot, especially about education law and the struggles over bilingual education. These became some of the topics I would explore with my students as a teacher educator in the coming years.

Started in job through bureau & Equal Ed

As luck would have it, my mentor and by now close family friend, Luis Fuentes, had written a large federal grant in collaboration with Ade Becker at the Bilingual Education Service Center at Brown University. Luis had me in mind for the position at UMass. After fourteen months of working at the Department of Education, I was rescued and hired as an assistant professor at the University of Massachusetts. Thus began my twenty-six-year career as a faculty member at the University of Massachusetts.

———•◦•———

NEAR THE BEGINNING OF my life as an assistant professor at UMass, the school hosted Paulo Freire as a visiting professor for a number of month-long visits every year in January. He was invited by Mario Fantini, dean of the School of Education, and Peter Park, a professor in the Department of Sociology. His visits were noteworthy not merely for our faculty and students, but also for community members from the entire New England region. Each year, I made sure to be on the hosting committee, which was made up of faculty members and graduate students. We organized seminars, talks in classes, public lectures, and other events with groups as diverse as Casa Latina (a social service agency in Northampton, a small city close to Amherst) to a dinner party with community members in Boston.

We kept Paulo busy from morning till night, something that I now regret, knowing firsthand the toll such a schedule can take, regardless of how rewarding each event can be. Still, the demand on Paulo's time was so great we had no choice but to schedule him heavily. As with everything else, he was gracious to a fault about this overbooking, though one day he said shyly, "Remember, my friends, I also need time to read and think." That was as close as he ever came to demanding anything from us. With Paulo, I instinctively felt I was in the presence of greatness. Yet, he was, in spite of his fame and influence, one of the humblest people I had ever met. His first wife, Elsa, who accompanied him on most of those visits, was, if it's possible, even more humble.

My experiences with Paulo had a greater impact on my intellectual growth than anything else had during those years. I read everything he wrote. With each reading, I absorbed more of his ideas. Sitting in on the seminars, classes, and community talks he gave, I saw the link between education and politics more clearly each time. Being with Paulo, I felt I was seeing history in the making. We were fortunate also to host other critical pedagogues during Paulo's visits, including Ira Shor and Maxine Greene, both of whom became my friends and colleagues.

I also got to know Paulo on a more personal level. To accompany him to various events, I would sometimes pick him up, or pick up both Elsa and him, at the apartment the university had provided them. Paulo was not one to give formal talks with the usual accompaniments of lecture notes, slides, and other aids. His was a decidedly nonacademic style. He never had a prepared script, rarely stood up, preferring to stay seated, and might seem, to those who didn't know him, unprepared for the task. Nothing, though, could be further from the truth. After he was introduced, he would continue to sit on stage and wait for what seemed an uncomfortably long time to most of us in the audience. Finally, someone from the audience would stand up and pose a question: "Paulo," he or she would, for example, ask, "how can we in the United States use your ideas in our own literacy work?" Or some such query. He would then give a long, thoughtful, and brilliant response as if he had been waiting for months for just this question. Even at dinners and other less formal events, I was astonished at the gems of wisdom he dropped so casually.

Paulo often asked his host at an event to join him on stage, or if it was in a classroom, to sit by his side, as he didn't like to be by himself. For him, everything was about dialogue and community, about connecting with other human beings. A number of times, he asked me to sit with him, saying sheepishly, "If I have a problem with the English, you can help me." Though Portuguese was his native language, Paulo also spoke Spanish fluently: he had lived in a number of Latin American countries during his exile from Brazil. I never really had to do much, because Paulo also spoke English quite well. He just wanted someone to sit next to him, someone he could touch. He was very Latin in that regard. I remember the first time I saw him: it was during his first visit to UMass at a reception in his honor at the Faculty Club. He was in the center of the room, one arm draped around Dean Fantini, who was shorter than Paulo, and the other arm around Dick Clark, our assistant dean and considerably taller. It was a lovely image but also unusual, in the United States, to see a man embracing another man, let alone two! I was immediately impressed.

The highlight of Paulo's visits for me was when I hosted a dinner party at my home for him and Elsa, around 1982. I had invited a small group of colleagues and friends, including Luis and Dora Fuentes, Maddie and Roberto Márquez, Anaida Colón-Muñíz and Mac Morante, Ruth

Rodriguez-Fay, Cathy Walsh, and Juan Aulestia. I prepared a typical Puerto Rican meal: arroz con pollo, my signature Puerto Rican beans, tostones, and a salad. Alicia, about eleven at the time, made dessert. Relishing the food, Paulo said it reminded him of home. Our daughter Marisa, about six at the time, sat on his lap throughout dinner. Paulo loved children: it was enchanting to see this great intellectual of a man, this internationally renowned scholar, with a child on his lap, as she played with his hands and his beard and occasionally gave him a kiss.

I believe it was after his third visit that Elsa died unexpectedly. Beside himself with grief, Paulo canceled everything and we didn't see him again for a few years. When he eventually returned, he had remarried. His new wife, Nita, brought him back to life, helping him regain the hope and possibility that always characterized him. I was grateful he had been given another opportunity to love. Paulo died in 1997, the year that Angel and I were on our second sabbatical in Spain. It was striking to me that the news of his death made the front page of a major Spanish newspaper; in the *New York Times*, it was included only in the obituary section. What I do know is that he had an immense influence on scholars, activists, teachers, linguists, educators, and many others around the globe, including me.

———◆———

IN MY FIRST HALF DOZEN years or so at UMass, I felt like an apprentice, learning what it meant to be an academic, starting to do research and writing, presenting at conferences, mentoring students, reviewing manuscripts, and so on. Though I had worked at Brooklyn College for three years as an instructor, my experience there was not the typical one of an academic. It had been more about political struggle and activism. An experience I will never regret, it did not position me well for the academy. As a new faculty member at UMass, I was making my way, learning the ropes, sometimes intimidated by it all. In the beginning, my old fears of not fitting in and feeling like a fraud were constant companions. *¡Sensación de poderío!* (Feel powerful!) I would repeat Angel's old adage to myself. Sometimes it helped.

I vividly remember the first time I presented my research at the American Educational Research Association, the premier professional research organization in education. A massive affair, it brings together annually

AERA

up to fifteen thousand education professionals, mostly from the United States but some from other nations as well. In 1980, when I first presented, AERA was an overwhelmingly White male organization, far more than it is now. I could see only a few women as I looked around, and even fewer identifiable people of color. Most of the panels had little to do with the topics that interested me. What really turned me off, though, was how the discussant on my panel dismissed my work. In presenting my dissertation research, I talked about the important role that parents and other community members can play in curriculum development for bilingual classrooms. The discussant pooh-poohed this idea. It was foolish to think, he glibly said, that "those parents" (immigrant, poorly schooled, and non-English-speaking) would know anything about curriculum. I was to find that this kind of dismissal and lack of respect, though not common, can be characteristic of academics who want to show how smart or important they are.

AERA

My first experience at AERA was so negative that I swore I'd never return. And for nine years, I didn't. In 1989, however, my friend María Torres-Guzmán, then an assistant professor at Teachers College, Columbia University, sent me a lovely engraved invitation to an AERA event where she was to be honored as a Distinguished Young Scholar by the AERA Committee on the Role and Status of Minorities in Educational Research (since renamed the Committee on Scholars of Color). I was thrilled for her and, putting aside my misgivings about AERA, decided to attend. Awards were also given to a senior scholar and a midlevel scholar. It was an emotional affair where, finally, scholars of color were given some recognition for their largely unheralded work. As I looked around, I couldn't believe the number of people of color, as well as supportive Whites, in attendance. It was then and there that I thought, *Perhaps there is a place for people like me at AERA*. I have attended and presented at nearly every AERA conference since.

In the years since I returned to AERA, I have been honored with a number of awards, including the Enrique Trueba Lifetime Achievement Award, the Division G (Context of Education) Senior Scholar in Education, the Distinguished Career Award from the Committee of Scholars in Education (the committee that had honored María almost two decades earlier), the Division K (Teacher Education) Legacy Award, and the Social

Justice in Education Award. More importantly, in the years since I first attended AERA, the membership has changed substantially, with more Latinos, African Americans, Asians, Native people, and international scholars and with more topics related to social justice in education. Moreover, by the early 1990s, an annual party organized by the growing Latino/a community at AERA became one of the most popular events at the conference. Held in the suite of the then executive director, Bill Russell, the first few of these parties were organized by María Torres-Guzmán, Luis Moll, Estéban Díaz, Richard Ruiz, and others who were among the first Latino/a members of AERA. I remember sneaking food and drinks up to the suite, something strictly forbidden by hotels, but we couldn't afford the hotel's prices. After a few years, the party outgrew the executive director's suite and had to be moved out of the hotel to another venue in the host city. By the early 2000s, hundreds of conference-goers, both Latinos and non-Latinos alike, attended. The Latino party, for me, changed AERA from a staid and stiff conference to one that demonstrated that academics could indeed dance and have some fun.

Though the presence of Latinos at the AERA conference was growing, there were just a handful of Puerto Ricans, as far as I knew. Sometime in the mid-1990s, I suggested to María and to Ursula Casanova, who had been attending the conference for years, that we start a Puerto Rican women's luncheon at the conference. I remember a couple of people chuckling: the three of us seemed to be the only Puerto Rican women in attendance! By 2014, the Puerto Rican women's luncheon drew over two dozen of us from the States and Puerto Rico. Professor Sandra Quiñones Rosado, who joined as a doctoral student and is now an assistant professor at Duquesne University, offered to take over organizing it each year. Now all I have to do, I'm glad to say, is just sit back and revel at what María, Ursula, and I started some two decades ago. To see these competent, brilliant, and beautiful scholars carrying on, and improving upon, the work that a few of us began when there were next to no Puerto Rican women in AERA is inspiring. More to the point, their work will no doubt change the educational trajectory of many Puerto Rican, Latino/a, and other youths who have been poorly served by our public education system.

During my first years at UMass as an assistant professor, I also developed a relationship with other scholars in multicultural education. James

(Jim) Banks was particularly helpful and became a great supporter of my work early on. Sometime in the early 1980s, he called me, saying I had been recommended by a professional colleague of mine at the Centro (the Center for Puerto Rican Studies at Hunter College in New York) as someone who could help him with the revision of his chapter on Puerto Ricans in his groundbreaking book, *Teaching Strategies for Ethnic Studies*. I jumped at the chance, of course, and spent most of my January break working on it. I wrote seventeen pages on a ten-page chapter, adding numerous resources as well. When he received the thick package, he sent me a letter (this was before the Internet) telling me he had never before received such an extensive and impressive review. That started our long professional relationship, which has continued to the present day.

My personal life, meanwhile, was busy as well. Angel and I were now raising our two daughters. Marisa had started attending a child-care center in one of the UMass-sponsored centers. Angel began to work first as a child-care provider and a part-time instructor of Spanish at both Hampshire and Greenfield Community Colleges and later as a full-time bilingual teacher in the Holyoke Public Schools. His favorite job during those years was as a teacher in the infant center at UMass. He was a natural, singing and playing hand games, all in Spanish, with the babies, none of whom were Latino/a. Propping them up on pillows to listen to international music, he organized circle time with them. He has always had a special way with young children. (He used to say, "Give me any child from birth to five years old, and I'm happy.") This was not only true with other people's children, but also with our own daughters and grandchildren. Angel could spend hours and hours looking for stones in the woods or shells on the beach, making up fantastical tales, creating extraordinary structures with blocks and other materials. I, on the other hand, have most enjoyed children five years and older. I love to talk with them about their ideas and try to figure out what they're thinking. In that sense, we were a perfect complementary match as parents.

In 1976, we had moved to a small house in Belchertown. Although Amherst was the center of our social and academic lives with a much more diverse population, as a university town it was also quite a bit more expensive. We couldn't afford to live there. Our small Belchertown house—a cabin, really—had three small bedrooms, one bathroom, and a staircase to the second floor. The staircase was so narrow that Angel, six feet three inches tall, had to turn his head sideways to get upstairs. Once upstairs, he could not walk straight, or his head would hit the ceiling. The house had been built as a summer cabin, with knotty pine siding throughout the first floor and a splendid view of Lake Arcadia, a lovely lake where Alicia and, later, Marisa learned to swim in the summers and to skate in the winters. It was only because Mami paid the down payment for us—$2,500—that we were able to buy the house, which cost a modest $24,500.

A year after we moved there, our friends from Brooklyn College, Tony and Milga Nadal, visited. When we opened the drapes of the living room window the morning after they arrived, Tony saw the view. "Shit, Sonia!" he said. "This is Dick-and-Jane country!"

We loved our house—my mother called it "una casita humilde," a humble little house—but it was all we needed. Being one of the very few families of color in town, however, was hard. After Alicia graduated from the Che-Lumumba School, she attended Belchertown public schools starting in sixth grade. Throughout her years in elementary, junior high, and high school there, she was one of only three Puerto Ricans; the other two were sisters. Not only was the student body almost completely White, so was the teaching staff. In our eleven years in Belchertown, we knew of only two African American teachers in the entire school system, both at the elementary level. Alicia had been accustomed to a more relaxed school day, a personal relationship with all her teachers, and a far more progressive philosophy. To say that the curriculum was different from the curriculum at the Che-Lumumba School would be a gross understatement. Alicia gradually accommodated, but it wasn't easy at first. She was, nonetheless, privileged to have some excellent teachers—Robert Hansbury and Paula Christian left an especially indelible imprint on her—and she graduated with honors from Belchertown High School several years later.

The situation was different for Marisa. Although we adopted her when she was an infant, she nevertheless struggled with abandonment and rejection, issues that were common to other adopted children and compounded

Daughter went to primarily white school only 2 other P. Ricans & 2 African Amer. teacher by what I suspect was undiagnosed ADHD. While her most difficult problems didn't occur until she reached adolescence, some of her challenges began to emerge earlier.

Living in a town with so few people of color was difficult and not what we wanted for her. She was always the only child of color in her classes, but I made sure to have her assigned to the two teachers of color in town, one in second grade and the other in fifth.

By this time, I had been a faculty member at UMass for about seven years and we could now afford to live in Amherst. We decided to move after we went to a school chorus event when Marisa was in fifth grade. When we looked up on stage, we saw one little brown face among the seventy-five or so children in the chorus, and that was Marisa. I turned to Angel. "We need to move!" I said.

Marisa started school in Amherst in sixth grade. She attended the junior high and high school as well, until she dropped out in her junior year. She received special education services by the time she was in junior high school, but it wasn't enough. I often wonder whether the Amherst schools could have done more for Marisa; I believe they could have. But I also know that the school was not to blame for all her problems. Though she has brought us great joy, she also made me question, for the first time, my dogged belief that nurture beats nature every time. I know now that it's more complicated than one or the other.

———◆———

WE BOUGHT LAND IN North Amherst, then looked for the perfect design for a house. In December 1987, Angel, Marisa, and I moved to our dream home, a post-and-beam house we helped design. Alicia, just completing her first semester at Wellesley College, helped us move in and joined us during school breaks and summer vacations. A three-bedroom, two-bathroom home in North Amherst just five minutes from my office, it was the smallest home on our street but was grander than I could ever have imagined when I was a child.

Angel was gloomy about leaving our little house with the view of the lake. But I loved living in Amherst, closer to our friends and my job, with better schools for Marisa and, later, for Jazmyne, the granddaughter we raised. In a short time, Angel became an expert gardener, creating one of the most beautiful backyards in the neighborhood. That helped him get over the loss of Lake Arcadia. We had spent eleven years at our wonderful Belchertown home.

On a professional level, my life was flourishing. On the personal level, those were difficult years for a number of reasons. Mami had not been doing well after Papi's death in 1973. She was struggling with Freddy (who was still at home), with her own delayed grief, and with trying to take care of everything by herself without Papi's presence.

Mami was well into her late sixties, alone and mentally fragile after Papi's death. As wrenching a decision as we knew it would be, Angel, Lydia, and I all urged her to commit Freddy to a state hospital. There were simply no other options at that time. It was clear she could no longer care for Freddy and, after a while, even for herself. Her deteriorating mental state by this time was confirmed when a neighbor of hers called me in Massachusetts to say that Mami was walking the streets alone in the middle of the night in what had now become an unsafe neighborhood. Mami finally agreed to put Freddy in another state mental facility. This time, however, the hospital was in Brooklyn, just three blocks from her home. She visited every day, bringing him a hot lunch. He was there for almost two years, but Mami was even more saddened by the conditions at the hospital. Though brand-new and boasting a state-of-the-art facility, it was just a newer version of the same kind of warehouse as other mental hospitals. All that changed with the passage of deinstitutionalization laws, first in Massachusetts and later at the federal level.

In 1979, as I was completing my doctoral studies, we finally persuaded Mami to come live with us in Massachusetts. She agreed only if we could find a suitable place for Freddy. At the time, I was working for the Massachusetts Department of Education. Emory Hall, one of my colleagues who worked in special education, told me about the Massachusetts deinstitutionalization law, which mandated the closing of mental hospitals and required instead community settings for people with mental disabilities. Emory gave me the name of someone who might help us find a place for Freddy. Within a few weeks, his friend found a community placement for Freddy, something for which I will always be grateful both to him and

[handwritten margin note: Found a community home for Freddy built by Dept of Mental Health]

to Emory. Shortly thereafter, we moved Mami and Freddy to Massachusetts, she to our home and Freddy to a state-sponsored community setting.
I became his legal guardian and remain so today.

When Mami saw how well he was treated and the services he received
in the first apartment in which he lived with three other residents and
full-time help, Mami was finally at peace. As of this writing, Freddy is
sixty-nine years old and living in a small town in a state-sponsored community setting, a beautiful, new, clean, and spacious home built by the
Department of Mental Health specifically for people with mental disabilities. With a lovely private room, just three other residents, and kind staff
members twenty-four hours a day, Freddy is loved and well cared for. He
goes to a community center each day and participates in many activities.
After both Papi and then Mami died, and when he was already living in
Massachusetts, Freddy lost most of the few words he had, saying only my
name occasionally. Now he doesn't even say that. Though he doesn't speak,
he seems to be at peace and content to see me when I visit. It is a far cry
from the kinds of facilities to which people like Freddy were doomed in
the past.

Nevertheless, I often think about what might have been if deinstitutionalization and special education had come three decades earlier than
they did in the 1970s. Would Freddy be able to speak today? Would he
have had a more consequential life? My parents spent years trying to get
help for Freddy, everything from legitimate doctors to quacks, from heal-
ers to soothsayers. Nothing helped.

Mami moved several times after relocating to Massachusetts. At first,
she lived with us in Belchertown for several months, but when the house
next door went on the market, she bought it with the money she had
made from selling her house in Brooklyn. She liked living there, but it was
an untenable situation because of its layout: a tiny house with a kitchen
downstairs, it had a steep staircase to the bedroom and bathroom upstairs.
The layout made it difficult for her to get up and down. Her housekeeping
skills, never stellar to begin with, suffered a lot: her house was unkempt
and, worse, unsanitary. Angel often went over to clean out her refrigerator,
which Angel said sported some amazing "sculptures" of food gone bad.
When she fell down the stairs and broke her arm, we made the decision to

move her. After that, she lived in a small apartment in congregate housing for the elderly in Amherst, which she loved. After repeated falls, there was a brief stint at a rest home before she returned to the congregate housing and, finally, to a nursing home after a doctor insisted she could no longer live without constant care.

I looked into a number of nursing homes and selected the one that felt most homey, with a friendly and attentive staff. Of course, I felt terribly guilty. I had always resisted the idea of a nursing home. But with our two demanding jobs and difficult years with Marisa, we really had no choice. Imagine my surprise, then, when I went to visit her a couple of days after we had moved her in and she said simply, "I like it here." I was relieved and happy. It was clear, too, that the staff were crazy about her. She had become a talkative and friendly woman in her old age, probably because she no longer had the tremendous responsibilities she had been strapped with for so many years. She was also thankful that Freddy was well taken care of and that we took her to see him regularly.

Three months after being in the nursing home, Mami suffered a massive stroke. Hospitalized for a week or so, she was then moved to a rehabilitation hospital. Before her stroke, Angel and I had made reservations for a week's vacation at a cabin on the ocean in Maine. We considered canceling the trip, but the doctor assured us that Mami wasn't getting worse and the situation would probably hold for at least another week. Despite some foreboding about the trip, we decided to go, visiting Mami, then in a coma, at the hospital to say good-bye. On the third day in Maine, as we were driving into town, the girls in back of the car, I quietly reminded Angel that it was the sixteenth anniversary of Papi's death that day. Angel patted my hand, assuring me nothing would happen. I looked at the clock on the dashboard and noticed it read 4:50 pm. As I turned away from Angel to look out the window, I thought, "Mami died today," and tears came to my eyes. When we returned to our cabin, the owner ran up to us with his house phone, saying, "There's a Doctor Loescher on the line for you." I knew what he would say. Dr. Loescher confirmed that Mami had died at ten minutes to five, at just the time I had looked at the clock.

We drove back to Amherst, all of us in tears, ready to make preparations for a wake in both Amherst and New York, with a burial at St. Raymond's

Cemetery in the plot next to Papi's. Mami died on August 22, 1989, sixteen years to the day after Papi died.

***

BUT I GET AHEAD OF MYSELF. From 1980 to 1983, while I was an assistant professor, I was also a trainer for the Bilingual Education Service Center at Brown University. This meant I traveled throughout the New England region, providing training and technical assistance in bilingual education for parents and teachers. It was a difficult balancing act teaching two or three courses each semester, the usual requirement for a faculty member, while also driving all over the region to meet with parents, teachers, and administrators in the six-state region. Luis Fuentes had also set up a quasi-official satellite program at UMass Boston, two hours away, so once a week, I also drove to Boston to teach a course. Besides service and teaching, my time was consumed with raising two children while also caring for my mother—the typical situation of the "sandwich generation." Consequently, research and publishing took a back seat. There was simply no time to do it all. This was disappointing to me, as I had looked forward to a typical academic position. Even so, I was lucky to have gotten the job I had. Besides, I loved working with parents and teachers; it was some of the most fulfilling work I ever did. I just wished that it wasn't so all-consuming.

After three years of this crazy schedule, the School of Education opened up a tenure-track position in bilingual and multicultural education. Luis had helped push for the position and was anxious for me to have it. Bob Suzuki, by then vice president for academic affairs at California State University, Northridge, wrote a powerful letter of recommendation. This meant a great deal to me. There were, however, ups and downs in the process, exemplifying the messy politics of academia. Although, for example, a White man had received an affirmative action waiver and had been hired that year, I received no such waiver as a Puerto Rican and a woman (two of the protected classes under affirmative action)! Such are the ways of higher education. Nevertheless, I was hired for the position and in 1983 finally started my journey on a tenure track. Though by this time I had been a faculty member for three years, Associate Dean Ron Fredrickson suggested that rather than count those years as credit for tenure, I take a full five years to apply for tenure because I had very little scholarship to my name. I was at first insulted by the suggestion (*Who does he think he is? I'm as good as anyone else going up for tenure!*), I reluctantly agreed. It was a good decision: as it turned out, Ron was right. With the added years, I was able to put my publishing and scholarly record on firmer footing, making for a stronger tenure case.

In the meantime, my career was forging ahead with the typical academic pursuits. I presented my work at regional, national, and international conferences; I had a few publications to my name; and I devoted a great deal of time to teaching my courses, which, soon after I began, were mostly in multicultural education. I loved those classes, although I must admit there came a time every semester when I found it hard to go on. The topics associated with multicultural education and diversity are challenging, often contentious, and always personal as well as political. Countless students, particularly White ones, ended up in my office over the years, crying, feeling guilty, angry, or defensive. Angry students of color, outraged by the ignorance or blatant racism of their White peers, also came to me to vent their frustrations. Each time, usually by the middle of the semester, I would return home after one of these classes and tell Angel, "I can't do this anymore! It's just too hard!" He would smile, shake his head, and say something like, "Don't worry; it'll get better." He was right, of course. By the last day of the semester, I was always elated. I would get home and carry on about how magnificent the classes had been, how great the students, how amazing the progress . . . Again, Angel would just smile.

I think I made a difference for many of the students in those classes. At the very least, I honed my teaching skills and learned how to approach difficult topics. While at Brooklyn College, I had already learned that I couldn't hit people over the head with what I thought was correct thinking; my own thinking, after all, has evolved over the years—I hope it will always do so—and I believe that's the case for everyone. What I could do was present as much research and information as I could, especially research and other information that hardly ever made its way into the mainstream media. I learned to curb my defensiveness, leaving it at home or tucked away in the recesses of my mind. This isn't to say I never became angry at some of the ignorance, bias, or simply sloppy thinking I encountered among some students. I sometimes did feel angry. Usually, though, I kept the feeling to myself, knowing that anger would accomplish nothing in terms of my students' education. Instead, I always attempted to have a dialogue with students, asking them to share their perspectives. I used readings, videos (movies, in the early years), other media, and guest speakers. The material often had a dramatic impact on students, particularly White students who had never thought about the perspectives or experiences of those different from themselves.

I've also tried to maintain a calm voice and exterior. I've always joked that I'm helped by my low blood pressure and slow pulse, so a calm exterior comes pretty naturally to me. I've had more than one former student, now professors in their own right, ask, "How do you *do* that?" Kristen French, a former doctoral student and now an associate professor at Western Washington University, says that in those difficult moments when she's ready to get angry or impatient, she asks herself, "WWSD?" (What would Sonia do?). I chuckle each time I hear her say it.

By this time in the early 1980s, I was also receiving my share of invitations to serve on community boards and journal editorial boards, to present at conferences, and, occasionally, to present a keynote address. In those years, the requests were mostly local or within Massachusetts. A few stand out. Once, early in my tenure at UMass, I gave a sermon at our local Unitarian Church, a first (and only) for me! A 1987 keynote address at the Traprock Peace Center in Deerfield, a town near Amherst, foreshadowed a major turning point in my career. The title of the talk, "Affirming Diversity," would become the title of the first book I wrote five years later—the book that changed the trajectory of my career.

That keynote address probably marked the day when my ideas on multicultural education finally jelled. It was certainly the first time I had articulated them so clearly: that multicultural education is not only about classroom practice but also about theory and history, and not only about celebrations and so-called "minority" (a term I neither like nor use) heroes, but also about the institutional and structural barriers that need to be torn down to make educational equity possible. I listed what I thought were the salient characteristics of multicultural education. The list included terms like *antiracist, important for all students,* and *social justice. Antiracist* was at the top of the list because I wanted to get across the idea that without this

Multicultural education is:
(1) antiracist
(2) important for all children
(3) social justice

focus, multicultural education was at best a salve and at worst a cover-up for the inequities that exist in schools and society. When I looked over the list years later, I was glad to see that the characteristics of multicultural education I wrote about in my book *Affirming Diversity*, though not exactly the same, were quite similar; they still are. I owe a debt of gratitude to Bob Suzuki for advancing my thinking on these things many years earlier.

As described above, my research and writing, however, were not going as well as my classes and presentations during my first years as an assistant professor. I've often said that if I were to go up for tenure today with the record I had established by then, I would never make it. Yes, I had a handful of book chapters and an equal number of journal articles to my name, but that would be a puny output nowadays to be granted tenure at a Research 1 institution such as the University of Massachusetts. I had gotten a late start, of course, because of the nature of my first job at UMass, which stressed technical assistance and not research. And although I had terrific mentors, for the most part they could not have prepared me for the rigors of academic life as they now exist. The only consolation was that many of those who stood in judgment over me had even fewer publications than I did by the time they had gone up for tenure years earlier. Over the years, the context had changed greatly: when I started at UMass, the expectations had been far less rigorous than they were by the time I was considered for tenure. They are even more arduous now.

When I finally went up for tenure, I learned that of the seven committee members on the School of Education Personnel Committee, one had voted against my tenure. I found this out in a roundabout way. It seems that when some of my colleagues got wind of the vote, a small group— I heard that Judith Solsken, Patrick Sullivan, and Irving Seidman were among them, but there may have been others—went to the dean, adamant that he support my tenure. He assured them he would. As one person told me afterward, "We would *never* have permitted them to deny you tenure!" I was touched, and still am, by this show of solidarity. I would not have asked for it, but I appreciate that my colleagues thought to support me. I received tenure in 1988. Only after that did my career take off.

1 person had voted against her tenure

At around this same time, I returned to AERA after a nine-year hiatus. Jim Banks had invited me to have coffee to again thank me for my help with by then a couple of editions of his classic book, *Teaching Strategies for Ethnic Studies*.

He quickly got to the point. "Sonia," he said, "you've been acknowledged many times for your help with other people's books."

This was true. Besides Jim, other friends in multicultural education, including Christine Bennett and my longtime friend Patty Ramsey, had acknowledged me in their books.

"It's time you wrote your own book," he said.

"Really? Well, it's not that I haven't thought about it. But," I said, smiling, "if I write a book on multicultural education, it'll compete with yours."

"The more, the merrier!" he said enthusiastically. "We need all the competition we can get. This is about creating and building the field. I know that whatever you write will be high quality."

Jim has always been supportive of my work, even before I was known widely outside Massachusetts or New York and before I thought I was ready for such an undertaking. Because his was such a prominent voice in the field, his encouragement meant a great deal to me. It started me thinking about writing my first book, the one that would change my life.

CHAPTER 12

Affirming Diversity and Beyond

IN 1988, JUST ABOUT THE TIME I received tenure, an education editor from Longman Publishers came to my office. Editors often roam the halls of academia not only to sell their wares, but also occasionally to ask professors about their ideas for potential books. Nobody before had ever come to see me about writing a book, but this particular editor said that he came "because one of your colleagues says you have some interesting ideas that could make for a good book." That professor was Masha Rudman, a colleague, a friend, an extraordinary teacher, and a well-known children's literature scholar. I'm glad Masha saw something in me that I hadn't yet seen. I've always been grateful to her for this. The editor gave me his card and said he'd send me the guidelines for a prospectus. And that's how it all started.

Editor asked her to write a book

I was by now in my mid-forties, but still, I was taken aback, thinking, *Me? A book?* It wasn't that I wasn't a capable writer, but even though it had been my lifelong dream, it seemed out of my league. Nevertheless, as soon as I received the prospectus guidelines, I got to work.

I started, of course, with the principles of multicultural education I had been thinking about for some time, wanting those principles to develop organically from the discussion of the sociopolitical context of public education. I also decided to include case studies of students of various backgrounds, ages, and experiences. Knowing that the case-study approach hadn't been done before in a book on multicultural education, I was especially enticed by this idea. I wrote a description, added a tentative table of contents, and sent off the prospectus.

wanted to do principles multicul. education and have case studies

A couple of months later, Naomi Silverman, another editor at Longman, came to see me in Amherst. She had spoken to the education editor who had received my prospectus. He had been doubtful about the prospectus, and riffling through the pages, he had told her, "There are no lesson plans. I don't think it'll work."

"Let me take a look at it," Naomi had offered.

Thank goodness she did. Naomi understood from the beginning that I had no intention of writing a book with prepackaged lesson plans. That would be as far removed from my idea of multicultural education as you could possibly get. During our lunch at Judie's Restaurant in Amherst that day, she suggested a textbook different from others, what she called "a critical, unauthoritarian textbook." Encouraged by her enthusiasm, I rewrote the prospectus and in a few days sent it to her. And that is how the idea for *Affirming Diversity: The Sociopolitical Context of Education* was born. The book made my career.

Naomi, as I was to find out, is one of the most gifted editors in the world of education publishing. She has an intuitive sense about good ideas and can help authors shape books that have an impact on the field. In addition, and very importantly for me, she is a politically progressive thinker who has managed to get many cutting-edge books published.

Naomi and I became fast friends after that first lunch and have remained close through her moves to other publishers. In 1999, she invited me to become editor for a series of books on language, literacy, and culture. I was ecstatic about the opportunity as it seemed like the next logical step for me. I became editor for the Language, Culture, and Teaching series, which now includes over twenty books, some of which have won important awards.

As I was preparing to write *Affirming Diversity*, I asked other friends for counsel. I remember a dinner in San Francisco one evening during an AERA conference. My friends Patty Ramsey and Christine Bennett were eager to hear about my book. I had received some cautionary advice from others about using case studies—the approach could easily degenerate into stereotypes, they said, among other potential problems. Patty and Chris, however, were enthusiastic supporters of the idea from the start. Whatever doubts I may have had about using case studies disappeared after we talked that night. The case studies in *Affirming Diversity* have, in fact, become the signature element in the book.

⬥◦⬥

IN LATE SPRING 1989, Alicia completed her second year at Wellesley College, and in August, shortly after Mami died, Alicia flew to France to spend her junior year abroad. In December of that same year, Angel, Marisa, and I moved to Madrid, Spain for my first sabbatical. We were quite a sight when we got off the plane: there we were with numerous suitcases and two huge boxes containing our Apple 2e computer and a printer, so different from today, when a personal computer fits into an undersized envelope. Angel's brother José Ramón (aka Món) helped us find a small apartment in Carabanchel, a working-class Madrid neighborhood that, some people warned us, was "dangerous" and "full of Gypsies" (Roma people). We loved that neighborhood: it was lively, with friendly people and dozens of small stores and fresh-food markets, and it was close to the center of the city, with a metro just downstairs from our flat. We enrolled Marisa in a private school in Pozuelo, a suburb of Madrid. At thirteen, she was able to take public transportation to the school, leaving Angel and me free to devote most of the day to our writing—he to his poetry and short stories, I to my book.

Living in Madrid had nothing to do with writing *Affirming Diversity*. Rather, we decided to live in Spain so that we could spend time with Angel's family and also get away for a while from the States and my academic responsibilities. At the time, almost no one in Spain had even heard of multicultural education. When family members or friends in Madrid asked me what I was working on and I told them it was a book on multicultural education, they generally responded in one of two ways. Either they asked, "What's that?" or, if they had heard of it, they said, "Oh, we don't have those problems here." This statement always gave me pause, considering the centuries-long mistreatment of Roma people, the expulsion of the Jews and Arabs in 1492, the Inquisition, and the Crusades, not to mention the poor treatment of the large influx, just beginning at the time, of immigrants from Africa, Latin America, and Eastern Europe. Ironically, about three years after my book was published, Professor Miguel

Spain too had to confront ideas of racism

Anxo Santos Regó, provost of the Universidad de Santiago de Compostela in Spain, approached me at an AERA conference, saying he was familiar with my work and wanted to invite me to Spain. Imagine that! By then, it was 1995 and immigration from the former Soviet Union, Latin America, and sub-Saharan Africa was in full swing. Spain had no recourse but to confront issues of diversity, inequality, and racism.

We loved living in Madrid that winter and spring of 1990, seeing family, and having a respite from the anxiety and worry with Marisa's difficult adolescence. She was doing well in school and getting accustomed to living in Madrid. Angel and I got into a comfortable routine: I usually stayed home mornings to write. He would often take a walk, pick up the newspaper, and sit at a café and read. At around one o'clock in the afternoon, we took time for an *aperitivo* before lunch, going to one or more of the many local bars for wine and tapas, and after lunch and a nap at home, we would often take long walks in the city. We had not lived in Madrid since our courtship twenty-four years before and relished every moment of getting reacquainted with what was now a far different city and country than in 1966. Alicia, living in Aix-en-Provence for her junior year abroad, visited us during vacations. Lydia and Joe, her longtime companion at the time, joined us for a week that spring, and with them, we visited Toledo, Aranjuez—site of our four-day honeymoon in 1967—and other small cities near Madrid.

Other than time with family, I spent every possible moment either reading in preparation for writing or actually writing. Here I came full circle, finally writing my first book, my great ambition since the age of ten. It was an exciting time: each day as I sat at my computer in our little extra-bedroom-turned-study with a space heater to warm my feet, I faced an empty screen. But soon, my fingers were flying over the keyboard, typing sometimes for hours, with an endless stream of words hurling out of my head. It all seemed to be coming together: everything I had learned from my own education and my teaching experience, all the books and articles I had read, and the ideas, great and small, I had thought about. A couple of years later, at the first book party after *Affirming Diversity* was published, someone asked, "How long did it take you to write this book?" My answer? "I could say it took two years, and that would be accurate, but the real answer is, 'My whole life,' and that would be the truest answer."

I had written several articles and given countless talks, but this was different; writing a book felt like exposing myself in ways I never had before. Angel read every word I wrote and, like now, always gave me helpful suggestions. Lydia, my fan each step of the way, also read and commented on my drafts. Even Alicia, just twenty years old at the time, read some of my chapters and gave me feedback. And since this was before the Internet, I frequently wrote long letters to Naomi, sent via snail mail, updating her on my progress. With my permission, Naomi shared several chapters with her husband, the well-known educator and author Joel Spring, whose work had inspired me from doctoral student days. I was euphoric to receive his critique: "This is not only an important book in multicultural education, but it is also reconceptualizing the field." Maybe, I thought, I *do* have some important ideas to share.

When we returned from sabbatical, it took me another year to complete the book. With great trepidation, I sent the first draft to Naomi. What if the publisher didn't like it? What if I became a laughingstock or, worse, what if the book was forgettable and no one even gave a damn? I also remember a moment of panic when Naomi told me she had seen a recent book that was somewhat like mine. "Oh, no!" I said. "Now my book will be meaningless!" Naomi laughed, assuring me that only *I* could write my book, and that it would be wonderful. I was somewhat reassured but still nervous.

Most of the blind reviews of the manuscript were overwhelmingly positive, while one review offered snarky but ultimately helpful feedback for improvement. The comment I most remember from one reviewer was, "James Banks, move over!" It made me laugh, but also made me even more thankful for the encouragement Jim had given me a few years earlier to write my book.

I received the first two copies of the book in the mail on December 7, 1991, coincidentally the fiftieth anniversary of the attack on Pearl Harbor. I took one copy with me to New York City, where I was to speak on a panel at a conference honoring Paulo Freire on his seventieth birthday. Once there, I gave the first copy to Paulo. I figured he would probably never read it—he received so many books from his admirers—but for me, it was important because even though Paulo had never explicitly said or written about multicultural education, his ideas had an enormous influence on how I have always conceptualized it.

It is no exaggeration to say that my most productive years as a scholar and writer came after I wrote *Affirming Diversity*. Although I had been an academic at Brooklyn College for three years and at UMass for twelve, it was this book that catapulted my career. Somehow, the book captured my thinking, my practice, and my values in a way that no talk, no journal article, and no book chapter ever could.

Soon after its publication, numerous reviews of *Affirming Diversity*—all positive—were published. The book was also being reviewed in serious journals—highly unusual for a textbook. And I still recall the first time someone referred to the book in public: I was a keynote speaker at the University of Vermont in Burlington. After my talk, I went into a workshop being presented by David Shiman, a professor at UVM. As I sat in the room, he said something like, "And as Nieto says . . ." My book was being cited—and I was in the room! I know I blushed as people looked over at me.

Several months after the publication of the book, I was thrilled that Gladys Capella, a doctoral student at the Harvard School of Education and a member of the Editorial Board of the *Harvard Educational Review*, invited me to write an article for the journal. Because it is one of the premier education journals in the country, and given the reach of *HER*, my article, "Lessons from Students on Creating a Chance to Dream" (1994), also helped define my academic career. The article has been reprinted in seven HER books and, in 2000, was selected as one of twelve "classic articles" from the *Harvard Educational Review* from 1931 to 2000. That was the first of several articles I would write for *HER* in the coming years.

The publication of the book also led to requests to write dozens of book chapters and journal articles, as well as nine subsequent books that I wrote and more than twenty that I edited for the Language, Culture, and Teaching series. I also began receiving many invitations to speak. As the number of invitations to be a keynote speaker or "distinguished lecturer" skyrocketed, within a few years I had visited almost every state in the nation and several other countries. After a while, I no longer became nervous before speaking. Today, at this point in my life, I've spoken to groups as large as three thousand. Giving so many talks means that I've been fortunate to meet thousands of teachers, teacher educators, and other scholars, and I can honestly say that every time I have gone to a different venue, I have learned something new. My travels have also reinforced my awe and gratitude for what teachers at all levels do every day.

The book has done tremendously well, becoming the best-selling or second-best-selling textbook in the field every year since it was published, and it has been used throughout the United States in dozens of universities and professional development settings. It has also been translated into Japanese and used, in its English version, in Canada, South Africa, and other places. Some of my other books have been translated into Chinese and Spanish as well. Without *Affirming Diversity*, I doubt I would have gotten the many awards and other public recognition I've been fortunate to receive, including honorary doctorates, a fellowship in urban education from the Annenberg Institute for School Reform, a residence at the Bellagio Center in Italy, and visiting professorships from Maine to South Africa. I am still incredulous and humbled by all this recognition.

Win awards for Affirming Diversity

But more than just my own career, I am gratified that *Affirming Diversity* has also made an impact on the field. Since its first edition, I have heard from hundreds of teachers and other educators—through mail, email, on the phone, or in person—that the book has made a difference in their ideas, in their teaching practices, and even in how they see the world. It has inspired some Latinos and Latinas who had never before read a book by another Latina, as well as many others, to pursue higher education or even a doctoral degree because they could now find a place for themselves in the academy. *Affirming Diversity* and many other books on multicultural education have challenged the Eurocentric stranglehold on curricula in the academy and have helped college students of color and others who have felt marginalized feel more validated. Teaching courses in multicultural education has become, if not always trouble free, at least an expected part of teacher education programs. I'm glad to have played a small part in this change.

Grateful it has made such an impact on the field.

It is remarkable the difference one book can make. It can make or break a career, and that certainly is the case with me. I wonder what might have happened if Masha Rudman had not suggested my name to the education editor who showed up at my door that day in 1988, or if Naomi Silverman had not taken a look at my first tentative attempt at a book prospectus. My career path might have been dramatically different. And to think it all started with a prospectus with "no lesson plans."

———◆———

EVEN THOUGH MY PROFESSIONAL life was flourishing after the publication of *Affirming Diversity*, life at home was more complicated. In 1992, Marisa was sixteen and going through a very difficult adolescence, heartbreaking and painful for all of us. On March 10, 1993, a month short of her seventeenth birthday, Marisa gave birth to a baby girl, Jazmyne. I was with Marisa in the hospital and was the first person to hold Jazmyne, a foretelling of what was to come.

At first we had hoped that Marisa could raise her daughter and that Angel and I would, of course, help, but just a few days after Jazmyne was born, it became clear that this was not going to happen. Family friends Diane and Roberto Torres agreed to raise Jazmyne until Marisa was able to do so. Despite Diane and Roberto's loving job as foster parents, we were happy when Marisa decided to move back home with Jazmyne a year and a half later. But for various reasons, Marisa was not ready to raise Jazmyne, and Angel and I decided to take over. It was February 1995, shortly before Jazmyne turned two.

So there we were, Angel at fifty-four and I at fifty-one, becoming parents again. Many people, even friends and family, thought we were crazy to do it. But it's a cultural thing: children stay with family, not with strangers. My friend Maddie Márquez was one of the few who celebrated our decision. "It's a *splendid* idea," she said. Having her support in this venture has meant a great deal to me over the years. Our friend Susan Markman also thought it was the right thing to do, and she gave us support over the years, often taking care of Jazmyne, particularly when our granddaughter was a preschooler.

As soon as Jazmyne started saying her first words, she called Angel "Abú" (she couldn't pronounce *Abuelo*) and me "Alala," because she also couldn't say *Abuela*. *Abu* means "father" in Arabic, and of course, that's what he's been. It has become Angel's favorite name for himself ever, and his identity. Whenever he meets someone who can't pronounce *Angel* in

Spanish (something that happens frequently), he just asks them to call him Abú.

We made the decision to raise Jazmyne willingly and with great love, but it turned our lives upside down. *How could we go through this all over again*, I thought? With demanding jobs and no longer as young as we were when we were raising Alicia and Marisa, we were, frankly, terrified of the strain of parenthood, more demanding at our age. Within a few years, the University of Massachusetts would be among the first universities in the country to adopt a parental leave policy, but this was years before that policy began.

Angel and I decided he would take a one-year leave of absence from his teaching job. Naturally, it meant he wouldn't be making his salary that year or getting credit for his pension, but we thought it would be worthwhile. Angel was a talented and caring teacher, one who was loved by his students and their families alike. But his arthritis had been bothering him for over a decade already; he had missed some days at work because of it. One day, a colleague had to bring him home, Angel doubled over in pain, a sign that the situation was worsening. More importantly, Angel had stayed home with both Alicia and Marisa, and unlike most men, he was a natural at it. Since my career was taking off big-time after the publication of *Affirming Diversity*, we also thought it made sense for him rather than me to stay home.

So began Angel's major responsibility as Jazmyne's full-time caregiver. They spent their days going on walks in search of flowers and stones, building fanciful structures with blocks, cardboard, and rocks; gardening; making up imaginative stories; cooking; and, in general, exploring life in the neighborhood and beyond. When she was a toddler, Jazmyne took to falling asleep on Angel. He was her favorite bed—she called it sleeping "encima de Abú"— and still recalls it fondly. Angel became the wonderful dad Jazmyne deserved, the only one she would ever know. That first year, he not only took care of Jazmyne full time but also started cooking every night, doing the food shopping, cleaning the house—chores we had previously shared—and thus becoming the house-husband most women only dream of. It was what made my career possible, so when people would ask, "How do you do it all?" referring to my teaching, advising, writing, speaking, traveling, and so forth, I would simply respond, "Angel."

A year after Jazmyne came to live with us, when Angel asked for another leave of absence so we could go to Spain for my second sabbatical, he was turned down. Because he hadn't been in the Holyoke Public Schools long enough, he lost his pension. It was a big loss for our family, especially for Angel and his students, but we felt it was the right decision for us. Jazmyne benefited from having a full-time parent at home, and I from having a full-time spouse. Even Angel, although he lost more than any of us, also gained by becoming Jazmyne's Abú.

<hr />

In 1991, a year after Angel, Marisa, and I returned from our semester in Spain, Alicia graduated from Wellesley College. She had majored in French (the language I had loved so in high school) and anthropology (what Angel had studied at Brooklyn College). To keep up with her French, she decided she wanted to live in Paris after graduation. She came home to work for a few months to earn enough money to afford the trip. On November 4, 1991, her birthday, I asked if she wanted to go with me to hear Jonathan Kozol speak about his new book, *Savage Inequalities*, before we went to dinner to celebrate her birthday. "Sure," she said, and we took off for the university. It was to be a historic decision on her part.

Alicia never had any intention of becoming a teacher; it was too hard, she said, and she couldn't imagine spending the hours preparing classes, reading, writing, and worrying about her students, as she saw Angel and me doing. But after hearing Kozol speak that night, as we were leaving the auditorium, she declared, "That's it. I have to become a teacher. It's the most important thing I can do . . . Maybe I won't go to Paris."

Thrilled to hear her say this, I nevertheless said, "Go to Paris; the problems will still be here when you return." I knew the opportunity might well be lost if she didn't do it then, before a career, marriage, and children.

And that's how Alicia decided to become a teacher. She lived and worked in Paris for two years, first as a nanny and later at the US Fulbright Office. When she returned, she secured a job in an after-school program while looking for full-time employment as a teacher. But she had never taken any education courses and had no teaching certification, so a job in a public school was out of the question. Her first full-time teaching job was at an elite private girls' school in Manhattan, where the administration required French teachers to have native fluency, which Alicia had developed. Shortly after arriving, she was given two mentors and a budget. In the seven years she was there, she became the faculty sponsor for the school's diversity club, organized several events, and attended the annual People of Color conference of the National Association for Independent Schools with other faculty and students. Public schools cannot give anywhere near this level of support to novice teachers, so Alicia was more fortunate than most. It was the best possible initiation she could have had to teaching.

My second sabbatical, for which Angel had quit his job, was in 1997, a couple of years into Alicia's teaching. Again we were in Spain, Angel, Jazmyne, and I living in Angel's brother's apartment in Cádiz. Món had just moved to Málaga, where his company had transferred him. He turned the apartment over to us for the seven months of my sabbatical, scot-free, which was fortunate for us since we were living on just half of my salary and nothing more. It wasn't a fancy building, but the setting was spectacular: an eighth-floor, fully furnished, three-bedroom apartment overlooking the Atlantic Ocean. Across the street from the beach, it offered a view with stunning sunsets. We spent many days having lunch or dinner or—Jazmyne's favorite mealtime, *aperitivos*—on the spacious balcony. We invited Alicia to join us at the end of her academic year, thinking she needed a little break and could also help with Jazmyne, who turned four that March.

Alicia joined us on June 15. Upon her arrival, she, Jazmyne, and I immediately headed across the street to the beach. Within a few minutes, a young man called out, "¡Jazmyne! ¿Qué tal estás?" My granddaughter looked different from most people in Cádiz, with brown skin and curly, closely cropped hair. He recognized her from a local dance studio where his mother, Carmen, was the director and Jazmyne was taking flamenco dance lessons. But I know the real reason he came over is because he saw Alicia, a beautiful young woman who piqued his interest. I introduced them, and as they started talking, he suggested she might want to go out with some young people while she was in Cádiz. He said he might phone her "un día de estos," one of these days. He called two hours later, and they spent every day together for the next week until she, Angel, Jazmyne, and I left on a ferry to the Canary Islands.

The young man's name is Celso, and he is now my son-in-law. As it turns out, Alicia's story repeated my own story, at least somewhat. Within a year, Celso moved to New York to be with Alicia. They married several months later. I helped arrange their wedding in Amherst. Almost a plane-load came from Spain, including Celso's parents, his four siblings, a grand-mother, an aunt, and several friends. The reception was held at a beautiful mountaintop hall in Holyoke. Jazmyne, six years old and beautiful in a long organza dress with French braids and flowers in her hair, was the flower girl. We have a video of her pirouetting around Alicia and Celso as they danced to their song, Elvis Presley's "Love Me Tender." Within three years, they had two children, Celsito and Clarita, followed by Lucía a year later. To this day, Jazmyne reminds them that had it not been for her, they might never have met or had the three beautiful children they have today. "You owe it all to me," she says.

⚬—◦—⚬

They became Jazmyne's parents, raised her

AS A YOUNG CHILD, Jazmyne learned how to answer the inevitable ques-tions that came up: How come you're living with your grandparents? Where's your mother? Are you adopted? Why don't you look like your grandparents?

We became Jazmyne's parents, but living without her mother was hard and took its toll. Jazmyne was a handful, especially for aging parents. Still, she was a delightful child, with a particularly outgoing nature. I recall when the mother of a child at her day care center asked me if I was the mother of "the girl with the *big* personality," and I said yes, I was indeed. A big personality is what she has always had: a lively little girl, Jazmyne was frequently the center of attention. She won everybody over, still does. One indication of the effect she has on people is that in 1997, when she was four and we lived in Cádiz, she was voted "Señorita Simpatía" (Miss Con-geniality) on the ferry we took to the Canary Islands.

unhappy @ school

Jazmyne did fairly well until middle school, but adolescence was diffi-cult. Always popular with her teachers and classmates, she was nevertheless unhappy at school, and this concerned us a great deal. The age-old ques-tions came up for me again: What are the limits of public education? Can schools meet the needs of all students?

Jazmyne gave us a run for our money during her adolescent years. I'm glad to say those days are past. We no longer worry about her as we did for years. As I write this, she is twenty-two years old and, to our great happiness, has graduated from community college. She is planning to go to a four-year college and is working as a server at a restaurant, something she has been doing throughout her time as a college student. She's a beautiful, strong, and enchanting young woman who brings a lot of joy to our lives. At this point, when people ask me how many children I have, I always answer "three." After all, we've earned the right to take credit for raising her.

Marisa, meanwhile, is now singlehandedly raising six children. She is working as a medical assistant and doing the best she can under difficult circumstances. I am astounded that she can do it all. Her children—Monique, Tatiana, Aliya, Mariya, Kalil, and Angela (yes, named after Angel)—are great kids and a source of delight. I hope, at some point in the future, to write a book about Marisa's story, one that I believe would be helpful for other adoptive parents. But I'm waiting for the time that she can write it with me, and we're not at that point yet.

[handwritten margin note: Marisa (adopted daughter) had 6 more kids]

As HARD AS IT IS for me to believe, *Affirming Diversity* was published over two decades ago. Though my commitment to diversity, equity, and social justice has remained steadfast, my work shifted somewhat as the context of education also shifted. It started when the so-called education reform movement hit the scene, beginning slowly with the 1983 report *A Nation at Risk*, which gloomily described "a rising tide of mediocrity" in our nation's schools (National Commission on Excellence in Education, 1983). Warning about the nation's growing inability to keep up with global competition, the report was followed by numerous other reports and calls for more accountability. Ironically, the idea of accountability was reserved only for students who have benefited the least from our public education system, particularly those who have historically been the victims of an inferior education, and for teachers, who often do the best they can with few resources and little support.

Unlike previous education reform movements, which had focused their efforts on smaller class sizes, equitable funding, improved professional development, and more opportunities for children living in poverty, this new movement has had a nasty and mean-spirited edge to it. It ushered in such changes as an epic increase in standardized and high-stakes testing, vouchers, charter schools, and other privatization schemes, all of which would fundamentally change the nature of public education in the years since. The movement reached a fever pitch after the passage of No Child Left Behind in 2002. Testing has become the order of the day in the nation's schools. I've heard of some schools where fifteen, twenty, or even thirty days of testing is not unusual.

The tests have unfortunately not led to a giant leap in the quality of education for the children they are purported to help, but rather have led to dispirited teachers, unhappy children, and an ever-narrowing curriculum. Especially in urban areas where the quality of education is often notoriously bad to begin with, students are treated to little more than a "drill and kill" curriculum. Teachers, students, and even principals are feted when scores go up, punished to a purgatory status of "underperforming" when scores go down. The testing frenzy is being felt even in schools that have adequate resources and excellent teachers. My granddaughter Clarita, now a sixth-grade student in a good school, tells me she and her classmates have dubbed the high-stakes tests in Massachusetts (the MCAS, or Massachusetts Comprehensive Assessment Systems) "Murdering Children at School."

Charters too are proliferating, with some entire cities taken over by these quasi-private organizations. Ostensibly also part of the public school system, charter schools nevertheless drain resources from public schools. Thus, schools already suffering from depleted resources are left with fewer than ever. For these reasons, I am no fan of charters, although I certainly understand the frustration of parents and community members fed up with the poor quality of the education their children receive in many urban public schools. There are, of course, some charter schools that are doing a good job of educating the children most in need of a high-quality education. Unfortunately, however, charters have usually done no better than public schools.

Accompanying the privatization of public education has been a decided turning away from some of the more progressive policies of the 1960s and 1970s, including busing for racial and cultural integration, magnet schools, and bilingual and multicultural education. Our public schools, as a result, are now more segregated than they were at the time of the historic *Brown v. Board of Education* court case in 1954. They are also less likely to provide needed services to children learning English or to offer engaging and demanding curricula. The arts and even recess have been eliminated in many schools, making these schools even less joyful places. These developments have affected me greatly as a teacher educator, a parent, and a grandparent. The tremendous hope I have always had for education for social justice has faded, although it will never die.

THE FIRST EDITION OF *Affirming Diversity* barely mentioned the reform movement, but in subsequent years, the situation only worsened. As a result, in later editions and in my other, later books, I have reflected more critically on how the so-called reforms sweeping the nation have affected public education. That was the case for my second book, *The Light in Their Eyes*.

In 1996, my old friend Jim Banks asked me to write a book for his Multicultural Education Series. Delighted, I told him about a couple of ideas I had been contemplating for some time, one a book on Puerto Rican students and the other on creating multicultural learning communities.

"Write the book on multicultural learning communities for my series," he advised. And that became the project for my second sabbatical. The resulting book, *The Light in Their Eyes: Creating Multicultural Learning Communities*, was published in 1999 under the expert guidance of Brian Ellerbeck, my editor, and Carole Saltz, the director of Teachers College Press. Both Brian and Carole are gifted editors and have become good friends.

Just as with *Affirming Diversity*, I spent my days, this time in Cádiz, reading and writing *The Light in Their Eyes* while Jazmyne attended a lovely preschool around the corner from our apartment. The book, which included excerpts from the journals of previous students, was very well received. I didn't abandon the other idea, however. While I was working on *The Light in Their Eyes*, I was organizing an edited book titled *Puerto Rican Students in US Schools*, which was released in 2000, with my friend Naomi Silverman as senior editor. In contrast to previous books on the topic, which had been edited or whose chapters had been written primarily by non–Puerto Ricans, *Puerto Rican Students in US Schools* was almost completely written by Puerto Ricans. In this way, it acknowledged and celebrated some of the growing cadre of Puerto Rican scholars. Also, I felt it was about time that we Puerto Ricans researched and wrote about our own communities.

Because teacher education has been my life's work, in subsequent years it also became a primary subject of my research and writing. As a result, I shifted slightly the focus on whom I was writing for and about. In the past decade and a half, my work has emphasized teachers and prospective teachers, those teaching the growing number of students of diverse backgrounds in our society and beyond, as well as those who would be the next generation of teacher educators. My recent research and books have been primarily concerned with what teachers can do to connect with their students. Rather than see teachers as objects, I wanted them to become the subjects of my books. I've done this by inviting them to write essays, as in *Why We Teach* and its recent sequel, *Why We Teach Now*, and to collaborate in the actual writing with me, as I did in *What Keeps Teachers Going?*, a book that resulted from a year-long inquiry group I organized with a group of Boston high school teachers in 1999. In addition, instead of using pseudonyms for the teachers with whom I've collaborated, I've invited them to use their real names, which, in every case but one, they have willingly done. Additionally, I've shared credits, royalties, or stipends with them. Never very lucrative, these tokens of my appreciation have, I hope, nonetheless demonstrated my great respect and admiration for them and what they do every day.

DESPITE MY ARDENT COMMITMENT to public education, it has not worked for everyone, even for my own children. As a result, my ideas about life, family, and education have shifted over the many years I have been an educator, and they are evolving still. For example, many years ago, when Angel and I placed Alicia at the Che-Lumumba School, we did so because it was a place that reflected our values of education as liberatory and multicultural, something even the good public schools in our town were incapable of providing at the time. The passion we parents and teachers felt, and the energy it took to maintain the school, are evocative of the energy needed in alternative schools today.

Another example was when we lived in Spain in 1990. Before we left for Spain, Marisa, at the time thirteen, had been having a hard time keeping up in public school. Rather than enroll her in the local public school in Madrid, where she would be expected to do challenging academic work in Spanish—a language she spoke but didn't master academically—we made the conscious decision to look for a school where she could thrive. We were fortunate to find in a neighboring town an English-medium school especially geared to children who didn't quite fit into traditional public schools. International in scope, the school enrolled some well-to-do Spanish children, along with others from Colombia, the Dominican Republic, Japan, Korea, and the United States, among other nations. It was a sacrifice to pay the tuition. What's more, the school violated one of my greatest values, namely, support for bilingualism and bilingual education. It was uncomfortable for me to see the teachers enforce an English-only policy. At the same time, Angel and I were pleased to see that during lunch, recess, and other free times, the students spoke only Spanish to one another. Marisa became more fluent in Spanish at that English-only school than she had been in Amherst.

As it turned out, the school gave Marisa the only successful experience she had in school as an adolescent; it was the right choice for her and for us. It gave Marisa a respite from her feelings of failure in school, and us from what had been her growing rebelliousness.

A similar experience with Jazmyne's education opened my eyes and my mind. In 1997, when we returned to Spain for my second sabbatical, we had three-year-old Jazmyne in tow. Lucky to find a small, charming preschool just around the corner from our apartment, we enrolled Jazmyne immediately. She loved it from the moment she stepped into the little front yard, bathed as it was in sunlight and warmth and the sound of children playing. As is the custom in most Spanish preschools, the children wore pinafores, which was fine with us as they protected Jazmyne's good clothing. But some of the school's other practices boggled my mind: sitting at tables, the children were frequently asked to keep their hands folded, with eyes on the teacher. They had some formal lessons, more formal than I had seen at any preschool in the States. They dutifully completed worksheets at their tables. When I saw what went by the name of the "English class," I was dismayed to find mistakes in the words and phrases the children were learning. All of these things contradicted how I defined good education. In fact, these were the kinds of practices I cautioned my students, preservice and practicing teachers, about.

Much to my surprise, I ended up loving that school. Jazmyne skipped to school joyfully every morning, swinging her bag, anxious to join her new friends and teachers. The teacher and her assistants clearly loved the children, who were greeted at the door each morning with kisses and hugs. They were given free rein to run around the small interior yard, and when inside, they often called out, even if seated at their tables. I was especially surprised to see Jazmyne, who at home ate competently on her own, allowing one of the teachers to feed her! In US preschools, everything is about promoting the independence of young children; I know that the practices in this preschool would be viewed as absolutely contrary to that goal. But then I realized it wasn't about whether or not she could feed herself. Instead, it was about the values promoted by the school. Feeding Jazmyne was an act of love, not a way to infantilize her. I was already in my fifties and had been a teacher educator for twenty years, and I was pretty sure concerning my ideas about education. But that school reinforced a valuable lesson: teaching is always about relationships, about believing in one's students, and about honoring who they are. It is only then that they are free to learn, to feel competent and successful.

These experiences showed me how much I had—and still have—to learn. They have been uncomfortable reminders of the pitfalls of holding on to ideas that might not always work. Another thing I have learned is this: dogma is rarely useful; instead, flexibility and openness are better ways to approach life.

———

Alicia stayed at the first school where she taught in Manhattan for seven years. Then, because of their growing family, she and Celso moved to a larger apartment in Queens. There, she found a job at another private school, where she taught both French and Spanish.

One night, in late spring of 2003, during her third year at the school, Alicia and I were speaking on the phone as we did several times a week. I missed Alicia and her family terribly and was telling her how I wished they were living near us, as were Marisa and her three children, Monique, Tatiana, and Aliya, who lived in Springfield at the time.

"Well," she said, "we may be there sooner than you think . . . We just found out I'm pregnant again, and we've decided we need to be near family if we're going to survive."

I was ecstatic with this news, both about a new baby and about the possibility of their moving to Massachusetts. But, Alicia said, they'd have to wait at least a year because she would be eight months pregnant by September and nobody would hire a new teacher at that point. But she was wrong. Patty Bode, not only my research assistant at the university but also an art teacher at the Amherst Regional Middle School (ARMS), sprang into action. It was June, and Patty knew that one of the Spanish teachers at ARMS was moving to the high school. Patty immediately ran to the principal's office, declaring that she had the perfect candidate to replace the Spanish teacher: a native speaker (also fluent in French) with ten years' experience and an exemplary record. A quick interview was arranged, and Mary Cavalier, then principal, hired Alicia on the spot. Within a month, Alicia, Celso, Celsito (then three), and Clarita (one year old) moved to Massachusetts. Eight months pregnant, Alicia started teaching at ARMS that September. She gave birth to her daughter Lucía a few weeks later. Even though they barely knew Alicia, her colleagues at ARMS gave her a lovely baby shower. The principal made sure Alicia received all her sick days, and any other personal days she could take, as a made-up "maternity leave" of about six weeks. Alicia says she has never encountered a more caring and dedicated teaching staff than at ARMS. After ten years, she is still there.

Two years after moving to Massachusetts, Alicia and Celso bought their first home in Amherst, one that Patty thought would be ideal for them and that was, coincidentally, across the street from her own. Just as Alicia and Celso moved closer to us, Marisa and her growing family moved to New York, where she has since had three more children. We see them on holidays and a few other times a year, occasions when the cousins, who love one another, have a chance to be together. We're hoping that one day, Marisa and her children will make it back to Massachusetts and we'll all be together again.

Alicia, who never thought she'd be a teacher, is now in her twentieth year in the profession, first teaching French, then Spanish, and now ESL. She has become a gifted teacher and is one of my heroes. Known as a

Alicia received same award mum did years ago.

community-oriented teacher who goes the extra mile for her immigrant students and their families, she is highly regarded by her colleagues and loved by her students. Recently, in 2015, she was awarded the Civil Rights Academic Achievement Award from the Martin Luther King Breakfast Committee, a local organization, as well as the state Human and Civil Rights Award from the Massachusetts Teachers Association (MTA). Coincidentally, I had received these same awards, the latter in 1989 and the former in 2001.

THE PAST TWENTY PLUS years since *Affirming Diversity* was first published feel like a flurry of activity: preparing courses, mentoring great students, collaborating with colleagues, attending numerous conferences, and engaging in research, writing, and the other trappings of academia. I was also active outside the university, becoming an adviser or trustee to many organizations, most of which focus on social justice in education, and I have been an editorial adviser for numerous journals. More recently, I was elected as the first Puerto Rican woman to the National Academy of Education, a singular honor that includes fewer than two hundred education professionals and, at this point, only two other Puerto Ricans. I have traveled around the world to speak and consult. I became comfortable with all of it, no longer feeling like an outsider or a fraud, and I made sure to tell my graduate students, many of whom were also students of color or had grown up in poverty, that they too belong and have something to contribute.

In spite of the professional recognition and acclaim I've been fortunate to receive, the past two decades have not always been easy. Because of his chronic arthritis, Angel's health has deteriorated, resulting in three separate back surgeries and a great deal of pain. He now walks with a walker most of the time, and we see an unending group of specialists to handle his pain. Given his condition, I decided we needed to move from our dream home, the post-and-beam house in North Amherst we had helped design, to a much smaller, one-story house that would be more accessible for Angel. Neither Angel, who had a spectacular garden at that house, nor Jazmyne, who had known only that home for most of her life, was happy about the move. Alicia went with me to look at houses, and when we saw a house around the corner from hers, she begged us to buy it.

We now have the great good fortune of living around the corner, just three houses away, from Alicia and her family. We can see the back of their house from the back of ours. The kids frequently bike over or walk over through the backyards. Alicia comes every day to talk, have coffee, check on us, and, in sum, make us very happy indeed. And Patty, my former student and close friend, lives across the street.

Affirming Diversity is now in its sixth edition, a new one every four years, with another to be published soon. But even though I'm tremendously proud of the book and grateful for what it has done for my career, preparing new editions can be onerous work. In some ways, it's easier to write an entirely new book. Patty was helping me enormously by the time the book was in its fourth edition, not only with updating research and citations, but also with suggestions for making it a more attractive book. As an art teacher, Patty has an artistic eye second to none. For the first time, the fourth edition included artwork by her students, something that has continued in subsequent editions.

When it came time to think about starting to work on the fifth edition (to be published in 2008), I was not looking forward to it. At the same time, I didn't want to let it go quite yet.

I decided, then, to think about a coauthor who could help me with it. The choice was obvious: I asked Patty, who had by then completed her doctoral studies and was director of art education at Tufts University in affiliation with the School of the Museum of Fine Arts, Boston. The subsequent editions have all been well received.

Affirming Diversity has also been strengthened by an instructor's manual, something I never thought I would agree to. But after being convinced that courses on diversity are often assigned to faculty who either know little about multicultural education or happen to be people of color (with the assumption that their ethnicity or race alone makes them competent to teach these courses), I agreed to an instructor's manual but only if I could select the person to write it. I asked Kristen French, an American Indian scholar, then one of my doctoral students and now an associate professor of multicultural education at Western Washington University in Bellingham, Washington, to do so. Kristen did an extraordinary job, writing a "critical, non-authoritarian" manual to match the character of the book. Patty and Kristen have helped maintain and add to the quality of *Affirming Diversity* and bring it into the twenty-first century.

In 2014, twenty-two years after the first edition of *Affirming Diversity* was published, Craig Kridel, director of the Museum of Education at the University of South Carolina, Columbia, wrote to inform me that the 1992 edition had been selected for the Education Readers' Guide web exhibition, which led to a commercial reference publication "featuring those distinguished education books that have helped define the field." The exhibition was a continuation of the museum's earlier Books of the Century project, which identified one hundred works that helped guide the field of education during the twentieth century (although the list ended with books published up to 1985). Craig wrote, "We feel that we can now identify those works that have helped define the field during the latter years of the 20th century, and we believe that *Affirming Diversity* is among these publications."

I thought back to my first attempt at writing a book when I was ten. I would never have believed then that my first real book would make this notable list of one hundred education books of the twentieth century. It was beyond my wildest dreams as I was writing it in 1990 in our little apartment in Madrid.

———◆◆◆———

I SPENT MY FINAL YEARS AT the University of Massachusetts in the Language, Literacy, and Culture Concentration, a wonderful way to end my time at UMass. Besides me, the LLC faculty at its inception included Jerri Willet, Judith Solsken, Masha Rudman, and Theresa Austin. Most of these faculty have now retired. Those final years in the School of Education were rewarding and invigorating. We developed a state-of-the-art program, and we did so collaboratively, with more collegiality than I had ever experienced before or that is typical of academia. We defined the program together, and from time to time, we also taught, did research, presented at conferences, and wrote together. By the time I was ready to leave UMass, I felt that my colleagues and I had created a legacy we could be proud of.

Even though I loved my life at UMass, I always felt too busy, with a pace so frenetic that it was hard to keep up with everything. Teaching;

being chair of LLC for several years and mired in administrative work (the thing I liked least); writing books and countless articles and book chapters; mentoring dozens of students each semester and having to disappoint others who wanted to work with me; presenting at hundreds of conferences; and in general trying to keep up with all the latest research—the bustle of activity was exciting, but also draining. Sometime in my midfifties, I began to fantasize about retiring early and dedicating myself to those "extras," the things I loved doing but with none of the administrative or bureaucratic work: no boring meetings, no grading papers, no more "restructuring" or new mandates. I was inspired by Lydia, who retired at fifty-four to pursue her real love, writing and the arts. But every year, there were new adventures and challenges, wonderful new students whom I didn't want to miss mentoring. Somehow my midfifties led to my late fifties, and still I hadn't retired.

One day, in late 2005, a couple of days after having had my yearly mammogram, I received a call from my doctor's office.

"The doctor would like to see you, Sonia," the receptionist said. "There were some irregularities with the mammogram." Sure, I said, and arranged to meet with my doctor in a week. It never occurred to me until I was driving to her office a few days later that something might be seriously wrong. *Oh*, I thought, *I wonder if it's cancer?* Why I never thought of this beforehand I don't know. Perhaps I just didn't want to contemplate the possibility.

The doctor confirmed that they saw something "troubling" in the mammogram and wanted me to have another one, this time at Baystate Hospital in Springfield, the most comprehensive hospital in Western Massachusetts. Confirming that I had breast cancer, the oncologist suggested we set up an appointment to see him. By the time I went to this next appointment, it had finally dawned on me that I might be receiving very bad news. As the oncologist described the cancer and discussed the prognosis, I could hardly look at him. But it turned out to be the best scenario I could have hoped for: stage 1 DCIS (ductal carcinoma in situ). It was a small tumor, slow growing, and easily removed with a lumpectomy. The lumpectomy, though, didn't leave "clean margins," so I would need a mastectomy. Still, I was fortunate: with the proper treatment, I would be cancer-free within months.

[margin, handwritten] battle w/ breast cancer

Angel cried when I told him. We decided to let our family know within a few days. When I told them, Alicia, Marisa, and Lydia cried as well. But a few days later, as we sat at the dining room table and I told Jazmyne, she remained quiet and then asked if she could go play with Caitlin, her friend across the street. It was clearly difficult for her to face this reality. Only recently, at age twenty-two, did Jazmyne tell me that as soon as she left the house, she ran not to Caitlyn's house but instead to the woods, where she sobbed. As for me, I didn't cry until months later, when all danger had passed.

It was January 2006. Since the tumor was slow growing, there was no rush to set up the surgery immediately. I arranged for it to take place on April 25, Papi's birthday. This would give me time to complete most of the semester. Though Papi had died twenty-seven years earlier, his birthday has always been symbolic for me. Patty taught the final two sessions of my courses and took over most of my end-of-semester tasks. For three months after my surgery, I slept downstairs in a small cot in my study. Alicia and Patty organized friends and colleagues to bring dinner to my house so I could focus on recuperating and Angel on taking care of me. For weeks, we had so much food we didn't know what to do with it. But seeing those friends and colleagues arrive every afternoon was the best cure. They would come in and sit with me to visit for a while. It was a difficult time, but it was also an exceptionally affirming one; I felt loved and cared for by everyone. Alicia was a constant presence; Lydia came and stayed for a week to help out. Angel, who had retired years before but kept busy with a great deal of community service, decided to quit everything to devote himself to my care.

The most important thing about getting cancer, however, was that it pushed me again to consider seriously the possibility of an early retirement, though it turned out not to be as "early" as I had hoped. The experience made me realize that life is short, that putting off such a decision is foolish, and that I deserved a bit of a rest from a very hectic life as a scholar and teacher educator. I informed the dean and my colleagues of my decision. The staff member of the Human Resources Department at the university was very helpful. Within days and after consulting with Angel, I decided I would retire the following semester, shortly after turning sixty-two in September. At that final class in December 2006, my students gave me a standing ovation, something that took my breath away.

Jubilación

I LOVE THAT THE SPANISH word for retirement is *jubilación*. It sounds so much better than *retirement*, a word that conjures a withdrawal from life. *Jubilación*, on the other hand, implies joy and energy. It's an apt metaphor for what my life has been like for the past nine years. My retirement has not been your typical retirement; I'm much too busy to feel retired. But it has been jubilant and fulfilling.

Dean Christine McCormick, new to the School of Education that final semester I was at UMass, offered to commemorate my departure with a retirement party and a symposium. The date was set for a Saturday the following spring. Patty and other students, former and current, as well as several colleagues, helped organize it. It was a joyous day, more than I could have hoped for. Starting with several workshops, all presented by current graduate students, the day continued with a brunch with Bailey Jackson, our former dean, as keynote speaker. José Gonzalez, a music teacher, former student, and well-known musician and his group played exuberant Puerto Rican music for the occasion, and Alice Goodwin-Brown, a teacher from Crocker Farm School where Alicia's three children were in attendance, brought her students, who enthusiastically belted out a number of songs. It was just what I wanted: an occasion filled with music, children, and teachers.

In the evening, a more formal dinner at the UMass Campus Center also served as a fund-raiser for what was to be the Nieto Scholarship Fund, later renamed the Nieto/Rudman Scholarship Fund, honoring both my dear colleague Masha Rudman and me (Masha retired several years after me). It was a memorable evening with well over one hundred close friends, colleagues, and family in attendance. Angel, Jazmyne, Alicia, and

251

Celso were at the family table, as were Lydia and her son, James. Tony and Milga Nadal, from my Brooklyn College days more than thirty years earlier, and other colleagues and former students from far and near also attended. After a lovely dinner, the associate dean, several current and former students, and some friends and colleagues spoke. Patty Ramsey, my monthly lunchtime companion for the past twenty-five years and friend from my UMass doctoral student days, read a hilariously funny poem, and Angel, as reserved as ever, insisted I sit next to him while he read a touching and funny poem written for the occasion. Lydia told poignant and funny stories about our childhood and about how, despite how different we are, we continue to be so close. Alicia presented a PowerPoint of photos of me from childhood on, and of the family, and Maddie did the closest thing to a lampoon.

It took me a full semester to clear out of my office. So many books, student records, and papers, manuscripts, posters, awards, all defining a lifetime of work: it was hard to know what to do with it all. I decided to sell many of the books to students for a modest sum and turn the money over to the Language, Literacy, and Culture concentration to help defray the cost of the community meeting dinners we organized several times a year. I brought home what books and other materials would fit in my study and basement, and I filled two huge garbage containers with what was left. After twenty-six years, I was finally ready to leave my office, 210 Furcolo Hall, the only office I had ever occupied at UMass.

THE YEARS SINCE RETIREMENT have been as busy, although in a different way, from the frenzied days before retirement. Although I no longer serve on doctoral committees, advise graduate students, attend department meetings, or even teach, my days have been filled with preparing talks and writing books, journal articles, forewords, and endorsements for other people's books, as well as letters of recommendation for former students and sundry other tasks. I have traveled extensively, from nearby cities and states to Finland, Norway, Spain, and South Africa, to speak at conferences or serve as a visiting scholar. I have loved it all.

Most mornings, when I am not traveling, I am home in South Amherst in my new study that, though lovely, is not as spacious as the one we had in our home of twenty-four years in North Amherst. We've had to give away countless books since moving here, and the great majority of my awards and plaques are stored in boxes in the basement. But we love our study, which also serves as our den. Designed by our friend, the architect and professor Joseph Krupczynski, it features a desk that's built into the wall as a triangle, both sides facing our large backyard, with Angel on one side and me on the other. As I write my articles and books and book reviews, he writes his poetry and short stories.

And now, instead of 210 Furcolo Hall, my office is, I joke, at Rao's Coffee Shop in Amherst. It is there, or in a number of other local coffee shops, that I can be found on many afternoons, either writing or meeting with former students and colleagues or strangers who want to speak with me about the present state of public education, or with students eager to consult me about a paper they're writing for a class or a journal or to interview me about my work and professional life. I have served as mentor to several new young scholars at UMass and elsewhere, a commitment that brings me great satisfaction, particularly as I see the next generation of professors—many of whom are people of color—take their rightful place in the academy.

———◆———

SINCE *JUBILACIÓN*, I'VE BEEN given the opportunity to ponder the questions I've had for years about my life's work: What does it mean to be a public educator, an academic, a teacher, a scholar, and a mentor? And even more important to me, what does it mean to be a daughter, wife, and mother? To me, these roles have always been intertwined. In all these areas of my life, I've come to the conclusion that something I learned over fifty years ago in an education course at St. John's University—to "start where the kids are at"—is a fundamentally important truth for all educators. That is, education *can* work for students but only if it builds on the strengths they and their families bring with them. I have tried to connect this simple truth to my body of work in multicultural education.

In the final analysis, I am left with the realization that my life, like that of most people, has been a complicated tapestry: full of bursts of color as well as shadows and, unseen to most, loose threads and even knots on the reverse side. It has also been full of contradictions and unresolved dilemmas, both in my personal life as a mother and in my professional life as a teacher and public educator.

When I was a child, I wondered if and how I could ever fit in, because there seemed to be no place for me. My culture, language, and social class seemed to be viewed as barriers to being accepted and getting ahead. Now I realize that those markers of identity have instead been assets allowing me to have a beautiful life and career. However, our nation too often still continues to see diversity as little more than a problem to be solved, and certainly the same is true of schools. There is a long road ahead until true equity for students of all backgrounds is a taken-for-granted reality. Nevertheless, I hope that my work has helped push the field of education in a more socially just direction.

I haven't changed the world, but like everyone else, I have tried to leave my mark on it.

References

Banfield, B. (1968). *Africa in the curriculum*. New York: Blyden Press.

Banks, J. A. (1975). *Teaching strategies for ethnic studies*. Boston: Allyn & Bacon.

Bowles, S. and Gintis, H. (1976). *Schooling in capitalist America: Educational reform and the contradictions of economic life*. New York: Basic Books.

Cortés, L. (2000). I remember. In S. Nieto (Ed.), *Puerto Rican students in U.S. schools* (p. 3). Mahwah, NJ: Lawrence Erlbaum Associates.

Dewey, J. (1916). *Democracy and education*. New York: Free Press.

DuBois, W. E. B. (1903). *The souls of Black folk*. Chicago: A. C. McGlurg & Co.

Engel, P. (2013). *It's not love, it's just Paris*. New York: Grove Press.

Espada, M. (1993). Borofels. In *City of coughing and dead radiators* (pp. 30–31). New York: W.W. Norton.

Fassler, J. (2013). All immigrants are artists. *The Atlantic*. Retrieved from www.theatlantic.com/entertainment/archive/2013/08/all-immigrants-are-artists/279087/.

Foucault, M. (1980). *Two lectures, power and knowledge: Selected writings and other interviews*. New York: Pantheon.

Freire, P. (1970). *Pedagogy of the oppressed*. New York: Seabury Press.

Gramsci, A. (1971). *Selections from prison notebooks*. London: New Left Books.

Kaufman, B. (1965). *Up the down staircase*. Englewood Cliffs, NJ: Prentice-Hall.

Kohl, H. (1966). *36 Children*. New York: New American Library.

Kozol, J. (1968). *Death at an early age*. New York: Bantam Books.

Margolis, R. J. (1968). *The losers: A report on Puerto Ricans and the public schools*. New York: Aspira.

Márquez, R. (1995). Sojourners, settlers, castaways, and creators: A recollection of Puerto Rico past and Puerto Ricans present. *Massachusetts Review, 36* (1), 94–118.

Márquez, R. (2010). One boricua's Baldwin. In *A world among these islands: Essays on literature, race, and national identity in Antillean America* (p. 157, n. 12). Amherst: University of Massachusetts Press.

Mastropasqua, K. (2013). Puerto Ricans in the United States: Research Roundup. In *Journalist's Resource*. Cambridge, MA: Shorenstein Center, Harvard Kennedy School. Retrieved from http://journalistsresource.org/studies/government/immigration/puerto-ricans-in-the-united-states-research-roundup#.

McCourt, F. (1999). *Angela's ashes: A memoir*. New York: Scribner.

National Commission on Excellence in Education (1983). *A nation at risk: The imperative for education reform.* Washington, DC: US Government Printing Office.

Nieto, S. (1992). *Affirming diversity: The sociopolitical context of multicultural education.* New York: Longman Publishers.

Nieto, S. (1994). Lessons from students on creating a chance to dream. *Harvard Educational Review, 64* (4), 392–426.

Nieto, S. (1999). *The light in their eyes: Creating multicultural learning communities.* New York: Teachers College Press.

Nieto, S. (Ed.) (2000). *Puerto Rican students in U.S. schools.* Mahwah, NJ: Lawrence Erlbaum Associates.

Nieto, S. (2005). Public education in the twentieth century and beyond: High hopes, broken promises, and an uncertain future. *Harvard Educational Review, 75* (1), 57–78.

Nieto, S. (2008). (Ed.). *Dear Paulo: Letters from those who dare teach.* Boulder, CO: Paradigm Publishers.

Nieto, S. (2013). *Finding joy in teaching students of diverse backgrounds: Culturally responsive and socially practices in U.S. classrooms.* Portsmouth, NH: Heinemann Publishers.

Oakes, J. (1985). *Keeping track: How schools structure inequality.* New Haven: Yale University Press.

Pantoja, A. (2002). *Memoir of a visionary: Antonia Pantoja.* Houston, TX: Arte Público Press.

Pietri, P. (1971). Puerto Rican obituary. In Young Lords Party and Michael Abramson, *Palante: Young Lords Party.* New York: McGraw-Hill.

Pimentel, F. (2005). The decline of the Puerto Rican fulltime faculty at the City University of New York (CUNY) from 1981–2002. Policy Paper from the New York Latino Research and Resources Network (NYLARNet). Albany: State University of New York.

Pritchett, W. (2002). *Brownsville, Brooklyn: Blacks, Jews, and the Changing Face of the Ghetto.* Chicago: University of Chicago Press.

Rand, C. (1958). *The Puerto Ricans.* New York: Oxford University Press.

Sotomayor, S. (2013). *My beloved world.* New York: Knopf.

Spring, J. (2007). *The American school: From the Pilgrims to No Child Left Behind.* New York: McGraw-Hill.

Wielk, C. A. (1969). *The Ocean Hill–Brownsville School Project: A profile.* New York: Queens College, City University of New York, Institute for Community Studies.

Woodson, C. G. (1933). *The miseducation of the Negro.* Washington, DC: Associated Publishers.

Acknowledgments

While every book may have just one parent, it inevitably has many godparents. I want to thank all those who took the time to read, comment, advise, consult, critique, and in other ways help to bring this memoir to fruition. I begin, of course, with Angel, my life partner and constant companion, the person who has brought more joy to my life than I ever imagined. Alicia, Marisa, and Jazmyne, our daughters are, each in her own way, an inspiration to me. They have taught me the meaning of love, resilience, patience, and redemption. I thought of them and especially of their children, my beautiful grandchildren, as I wrote.

Lydia eagerly read everything I wrote and helped jog my memory, especially about our childhood. As we grow older, she continues to be my confidant and ally. Patty Bode was one of the first people to suggest I write a memoir. I am thankful that she thought my story would be worthy of a book. Others followed and I am grateful to them as well. As soon as she heard I was thinking of writing a memoir, Mary Cowhey, a former student, gifted teacher, and writer, gave me a book on memoir writing that convinced me I could write my own. Gail Hall, who teaches classes on memoir writing, gave me beautiful and encouraging feedback on the manuscript, as did my friend Pat Romney, who also has taught classes on memoir writing.

My other first readers were Angel, Alicia, Roberto and Maddie Márquez, Susan Markman, and Mary Ginley, whose feedback was not only helpful but also empowering. I want to especially single out Roberto, who is among the most attentive and thoughtful readers I've ever had. His editorial recommendations have made the book clearer and, I hope, more engaging for my readers.

A great benefit of writing this memoir is that it has given me the opportunity to thank some of the many people who have had an impact on my life. These include Hernán LaFontaine, my principal at PS 25 who first gave me the idea that I could be a leader; Bob Suzuki, the professor of the first course I took as a doctoral student, a course that changed the trajectory of my life; Joanne Ansell, my best friend in junior high school who eased my transition to a different neighborhood and social class; my friend Ed Peduzzi from St. John's University who, so many years ago, encouraged me to apply to study in Spain with him; Milga and Tony Nadal, friends and colleagues in the struggle at Brooklyn College, who taught me that struggle against unjust power is just; Masha Rudman, whose suggesting of my name to an editor led to my writing *Affirming Diversity*; and Naomi Silverman, who saw promise in the prospectus I prepared for Longman Publishers even though "it didn't include lessons plans." To my great delight, I've reconnected with all of them, even some whom I hadn't seen or spoken with for many years. Most important, I have told them firsthand what they've meant to me. Luis Fuentes, who died as I was writing this memoir, did not get to read how important he was in my life. I hope that I have honored his memory nevertheless.

There are also friends and family members who helped me remember key events and people or who recommended other resources or changes: Lydia, of course, as well as my cousins Herminio (aka Tito) Cortés and Sari Cortés; Hernán LaFontaine; Elizabeth Capifali and her daughter Camille Solá; Herminio Vargas, my colleague at both PS 25 and Brooklyn College; Susan Markman, a lead teacher at the Che-Lumumba School; and Maryann Dickar, who was a teacher at Erasmus Hall decades after I attended and filled me in on recent developments.

Besides those who were involved in some way as I wrote the memoir, I am also grateful to my wonderful colleagues who were in the Language, Literacy, and Culture Concentration at UMass for my final years there: Jerri Willett, Judith Solsken, Masha Rudman, Cathy Luna, Theresa Austin, Meg Gebhard, and Pat Paugh. They, and our fabulous students, made going to work every day exquisitely fulfilling. My former doctoral students—too numerous to mention but too difficult to forget—have also filled my life with purpose and happiness. One of the most difficult parts of living in a college town is that cherished friends and colleagues pick up and leave after their studies or after their tenure. I especially miss Carmen May and Anaida Colón-Muñíz and her husband, Mac Morante. Fortunately for me and my family, although Maddie and Bob Márquez tried to get away for a few years in the 1980s, they returned to Amherst and have continued to enrich our lives with their friendship.

One of my cousins, Jaime Cortés, became so fascinated by the stories surrounding his great-grandfather (my grandfather) Francisco Cortés that he did extensive research in both Puerto Rico and New York to document our paternal family genealogy and stories. I am grateful to Jaime for his help in uncovering the odyssey and collective past of the Cortés clan.

At Harvard Education Press, I am forever grateful to Editor-in-Chief Caroline Chauncey, who one day happened to ask me, "By the way, what are you working on these days?" When I mentioned I was contemplating writing a memoir, she jumped in her car to drive to Amherst a few days later to speak with me about it. Her singular support, careful but tough editing, and constant enthusiasm for the project kept me going when I was running out of steam. I am so impressed with Patricia E. Boyd, the best copyeditor I've ever worked with—and there have been many—who, although we've never met in person, seemed to intuitively know my mind and made many helpful editing suggestions. I am grateful as well to the entire team at Harvard Education Press—Laura Cutone, Sumita Mukherji—who saw this project to its successful production.

I am indebted to all these godparents. I hope this memoir will live up to their expectations and that it will also provide some level of confirmation to those who still believe in the promise of public education.

About the Author

Dr. Sonia Nieto has devoted her professional life to questions of diversity, equity, and social justice in education. A native of Brooklyn, New York, she began her teaching career in 1966 in an intermediate school in Brooklyn, moving two years later to P.S. 25 in the Bronx, the first fully bilingual school in the Northeast. She later taught in the Puerto Rican Studies Department at Brooklyn College before moving on to the University of Massachusetts, where she taught preservice and practice teachers for twenty-five years before retiring in 2006.

Her research focuses on multicultural education, teacher education, and the education of students of culturally and linguistically diverse backgrounds. She has written or edited eleven books as well as dozens of journal articles and book chapters on these topics. She has received numerous awards for her scholarly work, teaching, activism, and advocacy, including six honorary doctorates. She has been a visiting scholar at various universities in the United States, as well as in Puerto Rico and Spain, and in 2012 she served as the Wits-Claude Distinguished Scholar at the University of Witwatersrand in Johannesburg, South Africa. In addition, she was elected as a Laureate of Kappa Delta Pi (2011) and a member of the National Academy of Education (2015).

She is married to Angel Nieto, a poet, children's book author, and former middle and high school teacher. Together, they have raised two daughters, Alicia and Marisa, and their granddaughter, Jazmyne. They are the proud grandparents of twelve grandchildren.

Index

siblings. *see* Cortés, Freddy; Cortés, Lydia
student teaching, 112–114
teacher at JHS 178, 130–151
teacher at PS 25 Bilingual School, 154–169
teacher of ESL for adults, 154
teaching aspirations, 2–3
trips to Puerto Rico, 33–36, 178–179
trips to Spain, 229–230, 237–238
trip to Cuba, 209–210
What Keeps Teachers Going? (Nieto), 242
Why We Teach (Nieto), 242
Why We Teach Now (Nieto), 242
writing aspirations, 2
Nieves, Josephine, 174, 190
NYU (New York University), 117–127, 161

Ocean Hill-Brownsville. *see* JHS 178

Papi. *see* Cortés, Federico
parents. *see also* community control of schools;
    Cortés, Esther; Cortés, Federico; genera-
    tional differences
    involvement in children's education, 155,
        157
    support of children's education, 40–41, 42
Pedagogy of the Oppressed (Freire), 196–197
Peduzzi, Ed, 117, 119–120, 123
Perez, Richie, 174, 181
la perla del Caribe. *see* Puerto Rico
poverty
    biases of middle class against those in,
        36–37
    education as escape from, 3, 7, 39–40,
        173
    limited opportunities caused by, 4–5, 40,
        44, 135, 157, 166
    in Puerto Rico, 14, 16, 17, 34, 35, 54
PS 25 Bilingual School, 154–169
PS 45 elementary school, 52–53
PS 55 elementary school, 42–52
public education. *see also* education (of SN);
    multicultural education
    activism regarding. *see* activism
    basic skills as prerequisites for, 38, 40
    bilingual education, 154–169, 171–190
    community control of schools, 133,
        148–149, 156, 161–162, 172–174

desegregation and, 133, 147–148
failure of, for students with limited opportu-
    nities, 4–5, 9–10, 39–40, 147–148
history of, 39–40
lack of information about other cultures in,
    53–54, 55, 79–81, 99, 100–101
location of schools, related to quality, 69–70
reform movements, 239–241
role as "great equalizer," 39–40
US rituals of, 40–41, 45–46
Puerto Rican Catskills, 33
Puerto Ricans
    biases against, by Americans, 55–56, 80–81,
        98–99, 101
    biases of, against Africans, 18–20
    biases of local Puerto Ricans against those
        living in US, 36
    failure of public education for, 4–5, 7
    increasing support for, in higher education,
        172–173, 175, 196, 215
    indigenous Taíno people, 14, 19
    proportion of, in schools, 41, 44, 53, 67,
        95
    reasons for migrating to US, 6–7, 13–16
Puerto Rican Students in US Schools (Nieto),
    241–242
Puerto Rico. *see also* culture, Puerto Rican
    history of, 13–16
    lack of information about, in school, 53–54,
        79–81, 99, 100–101
    relationship to US, 15–16
    SN learning about, 161, 176–177
    SN's trips to, 33–36, 178–179
    social classes in, 34–35

race and ethnicity. *see* activism; Africans and
    African Americans; culture; Jews; Puerto
    Ricans
Rudman, Masha, 227, 251
Ryerson Street. *see* Fort Greene neighborhood

Sacconino, Willie, 17, 180
Sánchez, María Engracia, 174, 175, 177,
    180–184
school. *see* education
Schooling in Capitalist America (Bowles; Gintis),
    198–199